GNED500 Global Citizenship: From Social Analysis to Social Action

Third Custom Edition for Centennial College
Authored by Centennial College, School of Advancement

CENTENNIAL COLLEGE

Excerpts taken from:
Writing: A Journey, Canadian Edition
by Lester Faigley and Melanie Rubens

Building Cultural Intelligence (CQ): Nine Megaskills
by Richard D. Bucher

The Media of Mass Communication, Fifth Canadian Edition
by John Vivian and Peter J. Maurin

What Every Student Should Know About Avoiding Plagiarism
by Linda Stern

Impact! A Guide to Business Communication, Seventh Edition
by Margot Northey and Joan McKibbin

Politics, Power, and the Common Good: An Introduction to Political Science, Second Edition
by Eric Mintz, David Close, and Osvaldo Croci

Understanding the Global Experience: Becoming a Responsible World Citizen
edited by Thomas Arcaro and Rosemary Haskell

Learning Solutions

New York   Boston   San Francisco
London   Toronto   Sydney   Tokyo   Singapore   Madrid
Mexico City   Munich   Paris   Cape Town   Hong Kong   Montreal

Cover Art: Courtesy of Shutterstock Images and PhotoDisc/Getty Images

Taken from:

Writing: A Journey, Canadian Edition
by Lester Faigley and Melanie Rubens
Copyright © 2011 by Pearson Education Canada, Inc.
Published by Pearson Canada, Inc
Toronto, Ontario

Building Cultural Intelligence (CQ): Nine Megaskills
by Richard D. Bucher
Copyright © 2008 by Pearson Education, Inc.
Published by Prentice Hall
Upper Saddle River, New Jersey 07458

What Every Student Should Know About...Avoiding Plagiarism
by Linda Stern
Copyright © 2007 by Pearson Education, Inc.
Published by Longman
New York, NY 10010

Impact: A Guide to Business Communication, Seventh Edition
by Margot Northey and Joan McKibbin
Copyright © 2008, 2005, 2002, 1998, 1993, 1990, 1986
by Pearson Education Canada, Inc.
Published by Pearson Canada, Inc
Toronto, Ontario

The Media of Mass Communication, Fifth Canadian Edition
by John Vivian and Peter J. Maurin
Copyright © 2008 Pearson Education Canada, Inc
Published by Pearson Canada, Inc
Toronto, Ontario

Understanding the Global Experience: Becoming a Responsible World Citizen
by Thomas Arcaro and Rosemary Haskell
Copyright © 2010 Pearson Education, Inc
Published by Allyn & Bacon
Boston, MA 02116

Politics, Power and the Common Good: An Introduction to Political Science, Second Edition
by Eric Mintz, David Close, and Osvaldo Croci
Copyright © 2009, 2006 Pearson Education Canada, Inc
Published by Pearson Canada, Inc
Toronto, Ontario

Pearson Learning Solutions, 501 Boylston Street, Suite 900, Boston, MA 02116
A Pearson Education Company
www.pearsoned.com

Printed in Canada

1 2 3 4 5 6 7 8 9 10 XXXX 15 14 13 12 11 10

000200010270607843

MHB/CO

ISBN 10: 0-558-93180-4
ISBN 13: 978-0-558-93180-3

Acknowledgements

Publishing a new course textbook can be a long and arduous task. Not so for this third edition of Global Citizenship: from social analysis to social action. It is my pleasure to express gratitude to our faculty and management staff for their dedication and commitment to the creation of this text. They made it all seem so easy.

This new text was developed following a comprehensive review of our GNED 500 course which is a critical component in Centennial College's Signature Learning Experience. It is an honour for me to acknowledge the comprehensive review team, Kisha McPhearson, Agnes Kieltyka, John Bisonette, Gina Marshall, Paula Green, and Meera Mather for their exceptional contribution to the review process and course revision. A special thanks to Moreen Jones-Weeks and Khalid Ali for their feedback on course concept. I must also thank the countless other faculty who contributed to earlier versions of this course. We leveraged your passion, creativity, thoughtfulness and intelligence. Your groundbreaking work was a foundation upon which we built.

It is also a pleasure to thank those who made this text possible through their tireless efforts of writing and editing. I am grateful to Agnes Kieltyka for project coordination and writing, Renee Sgroi for writing and editing several chapters of the book, Khalid Ali, Kisha McPhearson, Sarah Duffy, Doug Kerr, Gina Marshall, Stanley Doyle-Wood, Holly Baines, Julia Satov, Zabeidia Nazim for writing, and to other faculty and students for their work as peer reviewers. My special thanks to Sarah Duffy and Tabish Surani for content support, Anwaar Syed for proofing the manuscript and to Jared Purdy, Alice Kieltyka, and our marketing department for photography. Finally, I would like to express my gratitude to Meera Mather, Chair of General Education and Liberal Studies, for overseeing the entire project.

Dr. Carol Roffey
Dean, School of Advancement
Centennial College

Table of Contents

CHAPTER 1

Citizenship in a Global World

Courtesy of Shutterstock.

CHAPTER OBJECTIVES:

- Defining and reflecting upon global citizenship

- Applicability of the GNED500 course to personal and professional life

- The Signature Learning Experience (SLE) and Centennial College

Renee M. Sgroi and Agnes Kieltyka

Introduction

In this introductory chapter you will become more familiar with the mission and vision of Centennial College and its commitment to global citizenship, **social justice**, and equity. You will also learn about the GNED500 course, 'Global Citizenship: From Social Analysis to Social Action,' and how the knowledge you acquire can benefit you both personally and professionally. Most importantly, we hope that GNED500 will be the starting point of a life-long journey of growth that allows you to act on your responsibilities as a citizen of this world.

> **Social Justice**: A concept based upon the belief that each individual and group within a given society has a right to civil liberties, equal opportunity, fairness, and participation in the educational, economic, institutional, social and moral freedoms and responsibilities valued by the community (Degan & Disman, University of Toronto, Date Unknown).

"Creating harmony amidst diversity is a fundamental issue of the twenty-first century. While celebrating the unique characteristics of different peoples and cultures, we have to create solidarity on the level of our common humanity, our common life. Without such solidarity, there will be no future for the human race. Diversity should not beget conflict in the world, but richness."
~Buddhist Philosopher Daisaku Ikeda

Centennial College and Global Citizenship

The past few years have seen a number of changes worldwide. From a growing respect for the environment, to an emerging awareness of our roles as citizens of the world, the start of the 21st century has been marked by an increasing sense of global interconnectedness.

Centennial College acknowledged this global current and responded, a few years ago, with the introduction of the Signature Learning Experience (SLE) which recognizes the importance for understanding Global Citizenship and Equity (GC&E). One outcome of the SLE was the introduction of a new course, GNED 500, to address the College's commitment to learning in a globalized world.

> *"Distance does not decide who is your brother and who is not."*
> ~ Bono, singer and musician, activist

The purpose of the GNED 500 course is to ensure that all our students graduate with an understanding of five core concepts that affect who we are, how we see the world, and how we participate in and engage with the world we live in. Those concepts are: identity and values; equality and equity; social analysis; social action; and reflective practice. Working through each of these core concepts, students can engage in seeing the world through a global perspective.

> *"Responsible world citizens learn not only about what was and what is, but additionally they embrace their potential to make an impact on what will be: that is, to be informed agents of positive change."*
> (Thomas Arcaro and Rosemary Haskell (Eds.) in <u>Understanding the Global Experience</u>, p. xvi) (2010)

Global Citizenship

What does it mean to think about the world from a global perspective?

Global Citizenship recognizes that the world is interconnected in terms of communication, transportation, economics, environment, cultures, religions, and so on. This interconnectedness means that ideas, images, and cultural forms can circulate around the world quickly, making infinite possibilities for global connections. Beyond this kind of interconnectedness, Global Citizenship also recognizes that people are **diverse**, and that the voices, ideas, concepts, and images we share come from particular religious, cultural, ethnic, racial, economic, and historic contexts. Despite our differences, we are able to communicate at great distances. We bring different knowledge and viewpoints to the discussion and to the ways in which we interpret the world. In this way, Global Citizenship promotes the need to recognize and respect our differences in order to create positive spaces in which to share our thoughts and ideas.

> **Diversity:** A concept based upon the idea that each individual is unique and encompasses respect for our individual differences. These can be along the dimensions of race, ethnicity, gender, sexual orientation, religious beliefs, socio-economic status, age, physical abilities, political beliefs, or other ideologies.

Global Citizenship requires you to question and challenge commonly held assumptions and beliefs. It requires that you think, read, write, and act appropriately in your interactions with the world. At times, being responsible as a Global Citizen may be complex and difficult. It might make you uncomfortable, it may force you to wrestle with ideas, and it may even compel you to shift your way of thinking. These are some of the experiences that you may encounter as you think about your responsibilities as a Global Citizen.

As a citizen of a nation you work towards the betterment of your nation, its people, its economy, and its environment. Global Citizenship asks you to do the same, but instead of thinking about one nation, you must consider the best interests of the entire world and all of the people within it. This does not mean that we should forget about the needs of people in our local communities, province, and country; rather, it means gradually working towards positive betterment for all. As a responsible Global Citizen, you carefully consider your actions and behaviors, ensuring that they are respectful and **inclusive**.

> **Inclusion:** A concept based on the belief that all people in society are valued and able to fully participate in economic, social and cultural aspects of society.

> **Equity:** A concept based on fairness and the equality of outcomes. It recognizes that particular groups in society do not have the same opportunities and thus, aspects of the system should be changed to achieve equality.

A Global Citizen is one who takes active responsibility in ensuring that all the citizens of this world share **equitable** opportunities and benefits. What does this mean? How can one person do all of this? The responsibilities of Global Citizenship should not overwhelm or discourage you; instead they should motivate you to contribute your part in whatever capacity you can. If each one of us who shares citizenship on this earth made a contribution, we would be much closer to social justice.

Courtesy of Shutterstock.

Stop and Reflect

What does citizenship mean to you?

_____
_____
_____
_____
_____
_____

How do you think national citizenship differs from global citizenship?

_____
_____
_____
_____
_____
_____
_____
_____
_____
_____
_____

Courtesy of Shutterstock.

EVENTS THAT CONTRIBUTED TO SOCIAL CHANGE

Event: Viola Desmond takes a stand against racial segregation in Nova Scotia

WHEN: 1946
WHERE: New Glasgow, Canada
WHAT: A case that raised the awareness of segregation policies in Canada

Compiled by Sarah Duffy

Viola Desmond was a Black-Canadian, born and raised in Halifax, Nova Scotia. In 1946, she owned a hairdressing business and was working to expand her business across the province. As part of this effort, she travelled to another city in Nova Scotia, New Glasgow. While in New Glasgow she encountered car troubles and decided to see a movie while her car was repaired. She bought a ticket to the movie theatre and took a seat on the main floor. She was unaware that the theatre had segregated seating and that the main floor was reserved for white customers. The theatre staff demanded that she move to the balcony to watch the movie. Desmond refused. The theatre staff called the police, who charged Desmond and placed her in jail overnight. She was charged with tax evasion for defrauding the Nova Scotia government of the difference in the tax between a ground floor and balcony seat. Desomnd decided to fight the charges. Her case received public support and raised awareness about the reality of segregation in Canadian society.

Black History Canada – Viola Desmond. (Date Unknown). Retrieved from http://blackhistorycanada.ca/profiles.php?themeid=20&id=13.

"Each person must live their life as a model for others."
~ Rosa Parks, civil rights activist

Global Citizenship: A Definition

The term 'citizenship' has both legal and social meanings. In a legal sense, it is that set of rights and responsibilities granted to a people in recognition of their attachment to a particular country. In a social sense, it refers to the participation of people in their community as they fulfill and debate their rights and responsibilities. Citizenship is when you belong to a community and understand your rights and responsibilities as a member of that community. Global Citizenship is an increasing awareness that our lives are connected to the lives of people across the world, that we are members of a global community with rights and responsibilities to do our part to ensure sustainability of resources, social justice and equity, for all are achieved locally and globally. (Centennial College, COLT, Global Citizenship and Equity Portfolio Student Handbook, 2009, p. 2)

Courtesy of Shutterstock.

Why should you learn more about Global Citizenship?

Gaining an understanding of Global Citizenship and Equity are especially important as our world continues to get smaller, with increased efficiency of global travel and communication. Our interactions, both personal and professional, are no longer exclusive to one country. We interact with the world daily. For example: you phone a company located in Toronto, but your call is routed to a customer service representative in India, who orders a replacement part for you from the United States that was originally made in Mexico. The part is shipped to Canada and installed by a technician living in Markham. This is a simple transaction that we would often not think twice about, but it touches individuals from many different parts of the world. As you can see, employers today need individuals who understand and are capable of working with diverse groups of people from around the world.

Global Citizenship and Employability

Building the knowledge to think critically and to act globally is very relevant in Canada, a country with one of the highest immigration rates and one of the most diverse populations in the world. According to information collected in the 2006 Statistics Canada Census, the ethnocultural diversity of Canada's population has increased from 25 ethnic origins in 1901 to over 200 ethnic origins in 2006 (Statistics Canada, 2008). It is projected that this ethnocultural diversity will only continue to grow as global immigration to Canada continues.

> *"The only real nation is humanity"*
> ~ Paul Farmer, anthropologist, physician, and global health activist

The face of Canada is changing, which means that our labor market is also changing. Organizations are striving to become more inclusive, equitable, and diverse. According to *Canadian Immigrant Magazine*, a publication created to support newcomers to Canada, companies that want to "remain competitive must learn to tap into the talents of immigrants, visible minorities and other under-represented groups like aboriginals, the disabled, gays and lesbians, and women" (Jetelina & Siad, 2008). Skills training is not only linked to a specific profession. Employers invest significant financial resources to train their employees in equity, diversity, and inclusion. Centennial College has recognized this trend in the work force and has responded by providing its students with a course in Global Citizenship to give Centennial graduates a leading edge in the labor market.

A Case for Global Citizenship in the Workplace

Harva works as a travel agent located in the heart of Toronto. She enjoys her job and makes an effort to provide exceptional customer service, especially since she is working to build her client base. Recently, Harva booked a trip for an elderly couple, Mr. and Mrs. Faulkner, looking to explore new destinations. She was confident that the trip would be a fantastic experience for the couple and that their satisfaction would bring in several referrals. Two weeks later, as Harva sits at her desk, Mrs. Faulkner walks into the agency. Harva is pleased to see her client so soon; it was only yesterday that the plane had landed. She is certain that Mrs. Faulkner enjoyed her trip so much that she could not wait a day longer to come in and share her destination stories and experiences with the person who was responsible for making it happen! Harva's joy soon fades as she sees Mrs. Faulkner's body language which signals that something is wrong. It is only a matter of seconds before Mrs. Faulkner is raising her voice and spilling out complaints at Harva. Harva soon learns that the Faulkner's trip was a disaster. The couple experienced numerous inconveniences and unpleasant encounters during the course of their trip as they were unaware of the cultural and religious customs of the country they were visiting, including appropriate modes of dress. Harva feels guilty, as it was her responsibility to provide them with information she took for granted that they knew. She should have given them more information so that they were better prepared for their visit.

Questions for Discussion:
1) In this case, do you think that Harva fulfilled her obligations as a travel agent? Why or why not?
2) What could the Faulkners have done differently to make this trip a better experience?
3) What type of training could have prepared Harva for this situation?

Did You Know? Multiculturalism in Canada

"The 2006 Census showed that nearly three-quarters (75.0%) of the immigrants that arrived between 2001 and 2006 belonged to a visible minority group. If current immigration trends continue, Canada's visible minority population will continue to grow much more quickly than the non-visible minority population. According to Statistics Canada's population projections, members of visible minority groups could account for roughly one-fifth of the total population by 2017." (Statistics Canada, 2010)

Stop and Reflect

Courtesy of Shutterstock.

From your perspective, why do you think it is important for companies to invest money in training employees to gain a better understanding of diversity?

AGENTS OF SOCIAL CHANGE: GLOBAL CITIZENS IN ACTION

Activist: Muhammad Yunus

Born: June 28, 1940
Works to advance economic and social opportunities for the poor, Nobel Peace Prize recipient
Bangladesh

Compiled by Sarah Duffy

Muhammad Yunus was born on June 28, 1940 and is a Bangladeshi banker, economist and Nobel Peace Prize recipient.

In 1976, during visits to the poorest households in the Bangladeshi village of Jobra, Yunus discovered that very small loans could have a significant impact on the livelihood of a poor person. Jobra women who made bamboo furniture had to take out loans to buy bamboo and ended up paying their profits to the moneylenders. Yunus made a loan of $27 of his own money to the women in the village. The women were able to repay the loan and make a profit. Since traditional banks were not interested in this type of loan, given the high risk associated with repayment, Yunus realised that an institution was required to provide these loans and he believed that the individuals receiving the loans would repay the money if they were given the opportunity.

In 1983, after working as an economics professor and developing the concepts of microcredit and microfinance, Yunus established Grameen Bank. His objective, which was based on the belief that credit is a fundamental human right, was to help poor people escape from poverty by providing small loans, called microloans. Grameen Bank has led a movement toward reducing poverty through microlending and replicas of the Grameen Bank model now operate in over 100 countries around the world.

In addition to founding the Grameen Bank, Yunus has held a number of roles including acting as a member of the International Advisory Group for the Fourth World Conference on Women, a post to which he was appointed by the UN secretary general. He has also served on the Global Commission of Women's Health, the Advisory Council for Sustainable Economic Development and the UN Expert Group on Women and Finance. In 2006, Yunus received the Nobel Peace Prize for his work and contributions.

The Nobel Peace Prize, 2006 – Biography, Muhammad Yunnus (Date Unknown). Retrieved from http://nobelprize.org/nobel_prizes/peace/laureates/2006/yunus-bio.html#.

Muhammad Yunus. (Date Unknown). Retrieved from http://en.wikipedia.org/wiki/Muhammad_Yunus

GNED500: The Experience

GNED 500 is a course that provides students with an opportunity to think about their world from a global perspective. The following are some of the questions that you will encounter and explore in this textbook and in the GNED500 course: How does a person exist in this global society? How do you come to define your identity? What are the values you hold? How do you deal with inequalities and stereotypes in a world were equity doesn't always exist? How can you make a positive change in the world? And why would you even want to?

Courtesy of Shutterstock.

As you journey through this course, you will develop your own individualized perspectives and perhaps responses to some of these questions. Our goal is to guide you along this journey and enhance your understanding to better prepare you to live and work in a global world.

The structure of GNED500 is formed with the following components: Identity and Values, Media Literacy, Social Analysis, Social Action, and Global Citizenship and Equity. *Figure 1* outlines the framework for GNED500. In this course, you will have the opportunity to explore, analyze, and reflect upon issues and concepts within each unit moving from an individual to collective understanding of Global Citizenship and Equity.

At the beginning of the course you will develop the skills required to analyze social issues. This will lead you to examine and reflect upon your identity and values and their complexities. In addition, you will explore the influences of society and the media on how you view and interpret the world. Using the knowledge acquired throughout the course, you will better understand how you can make a positive change in the wold, which is referred to as 'Social Action.' The concept of Global Citizenship and Equity that is introduced in this chapter will be revisited at the end of the course when you will be asked to explore your responsibilities as an individual who is connected to the world.

GNED500 will also allow you to develop and strengthen the following skills: research, critical thinking, reflection, and teamwork. These skills will help you to be successful both personally and professionally in the 21st century.

> *"We all have an obligation as citizens of this earth to leave the world a healthier, cleaner, and better place for our children and future generations"*
> ~ Blythe Danner, actress and social activist

GNED500 Course Framework

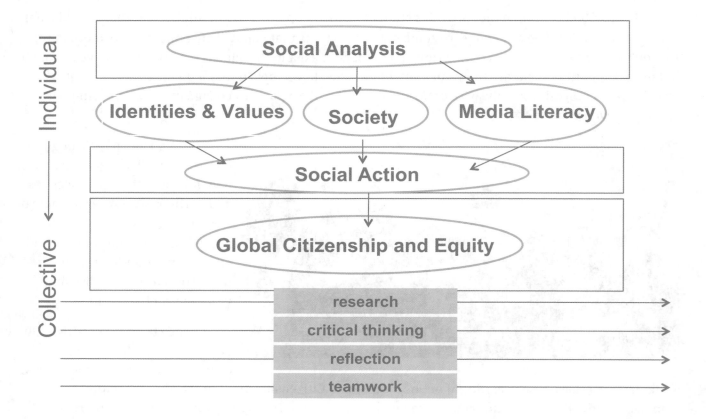

Figure 1: Framework outlining the structure of the GNED500 course and the skills that students will develop.

Getting Engaged: Activities

List three goals that you would like to accomplish this semester in GNED500:

1. _____
_____
2. _____
_____
3. _____
_____

What do you hope to learn from this course? _____
_____
_____
_____
_____
_____
_____

Making a Difference: A Question for Debate

Do you think that you can make a difference in the world on your own, or do you feel that you need to work with a group or community? Select a position and debate with the class:

Position A: One person can make a difference in the world.

Position B: One person needs to become a part of a community group in order to make a difference.

In your opinion...

After completing the debate, what is your position?
_____
_____
_____
_____
_____

Case Study: Putting Your Competence of Global Citizenship to Work

You are an employee at a manufacturing plant. You have recently been appointed to lead a team on the production of a new product that management believes will be successful in the market. This is your opportunity to prove yourself and get that promotion you have worked so hard for over the last seven years with the company. As you learn more about the new product, you realize that the company will be disposing harmful waste materials. You are aware of Canadian laws about waste disposal, but you know that these laws do not apply in the country where the product will be manufactured. Proper disposal of the waste will be costly, and the company would not be willing to invest in the manufacturing process; it is just not in the budget. What would you do? How would you respond to this new information?

Response to Case Study: _____

_____

_____

_____

_____

_____

_____

_____

_____

_____

_____

_____

Discuss with a partner or in a small group. What are their responses?

_____

_____

_____

_____

_____

_____

_____

_____

_____

_____

_____

Pre-Reflection on Global Citizenship

Take a moment to reflect on the question:

What does global citizenship mean to you?

_____
_____
_____
_____
_____
_____
_____
_____
_____
_____
_____
_____
_____
_____
_____
_____
_____
_____
_____
_____
_____
_____
_____
_____
_____
_____
_____
_____
_____
_____
_____
_____
_____
_____
_____
_____
_____
_____
_____
_____

Assignments

Pre-Reflection Assignment: Refer to pg. 13 in the text.

Chapter Summary

Definitions:

Diversity: A concept based upon the idea that each individual is unique and encompassing respect for our individual differences. These can be along the dimensions of race, ethnicity, gender, sexual orientation, religious beliefs, socio-economic status, age, physical abilities, political beliefs, or other ideologies.

Equity: A concept based on fairness and the equality of outcomes. It recognizes that particular groups in society do not have the same opportunities and thus, aspects of the system should be changed to achieve equality.

Inclusion: A concept based on the belief that all people in society are valued and able to fully participate in economic, social and cultural aspects of society.

Social Justice: A concept based upon the belief that each individual and group within a given society has a right to civil liberties, equal opportunity, fairness, and participation in the educational, economic, institutional, social and moral freedoms and responsibilities valued by the community (Degan & Disman, University of Toronto).

Main Concepts:

- Overview of GNED500 course and Centennial College's SLE
- Understanding of Global Citizenship
- Establishing your personal definition of Global Citizenship
- Differentiating between Global Citizenship and national citizenship
- Establishing the need for equity and diversity training in the workplace
- Thinking about your contributions to making positive changes in the world

Additional Resources

Centennial College and the SLE
http://www.centennialcollege.ca/AboutUs/SignatureLearningExperience/elements

Global Citizenship and Equity Portfolio Student Handbook (COLT)
http://www.centennialcollege.ca/adx/aspx/adxGetMedia.aspx?DocID=7503

Human Race Book http://centennialcollege.ning.com

References

Arcaro, T. & Haskell, R. (2010). *Understanding the Global Experience: Becoming a Responsible World Citizen.* Toronto: Pearson Publishers, pp. xvi-25.

Black History Canada. (Date Unknown) *Viola Desmond.* Retrieved on October 2, 2010 from http://blackhistorycanada.ca/profiles.php?themeid=20&id=13.

COLT (Ed.). (2009) *Global Citizenship and Equity Portfolio Student Handbook.* Toronto: Centennial College, p. 2.

Daisaku, Ikeda. (Date Unknown) Words of Wisdom: Global Citizenship. Retrieved on August 10, 2010 from http://www.ikedaquotes.org/global-citizenship.html

Danner, B. Citizenship Quotes. Retrieved August 12, 2010 from http://www.betterworld.net/quotes/citizenship-quotes.htm

Degan, R., & Disman, M. (Date Unknown) *Cultural Competency Handbook.* Department of Public Health Sciences, Toronto: University of Toronto.

Farmer, In Arcaro, T. & Haskell, R. (2010). *Understanding the Global Experience: Becoming a Responsible World Citizen.* Toronto: Pearson Publishers, p. 8.

GNED500 Comprehensive Review (2010) *Figure 1: GNED500 Course Framework.* School of Advancement. Toronto: Centennial College.

Hewson, P. (Bono) Quotation. In Archer, T. & Haskell, R. (2010). *Understanding the Global Experience: Becoming a Responsible World Citizen.* Toronto: Pearson Publishers, p. 6.

Jetelina, M. & Siad, S. (2008). *Changing the Face of Canadian Business.* Immigrant Canada. Retrieved June 28, 2010 from http://www.canadianimmigrant.ca/careers/article/765.

Nobel Peace Prize. (Date Unknown) *Biography, Muhammad Yunus*. Retreived on October 2, 2010 from
http://nobelprize.org/nobel_prizes/peace/laureates/2006/yunus-bio.html#.

Parks, Rosa. (Date Unknown) Citizenship Quotes. Retrieved October 5, 2010 from
http://www.brainyquote.com/quotes/authors/r/rosa_parks.html

Statistics Canada. (2008). *2006 Census: Ethnic origin, visible minorities, place of work and mode of
transportation, Statistics Canada The Daily, Wednesday April 2, 2008.* Retrieved June 29, 2010 from
http://www.statcan.gc.ca/daily-quotidien/080402/dq080402a-eng.htm

Statistics Canada. (2010). *Canada's Ethnocultural Mosaic, 2006 Census: National picture, Analysis Series,
2006 Census, Statistics Canada, Catalogue no. 97-562-XIE2006001.* Retrieved June 29, 2010 from
http://www12.statcan.ca/census-recensement/2006/as-sa/97-562/p5-eng.cfm.

Wikipedia. (Date Unknown) *Muhammad Yunus.* Retrieved on October 2, 2010 from http://
en.wikipedia.org/wiki/Muhammad_Yunus

Notes

CHAPTER 2

Portfolio Learning

Courtesy of Shutterstock.

Gina Marshall, Stanley Doyle-Wood, Holly Baines, Julia Satov, and Zabedia Nazim

CHAPTER OBJECTIVES:

- Defining portfolios as a tool for learning, self-assessment and self development

- Applying portfolio learning to the GNED500 course and coursework

- Situating reflective practice and critical thinking as central to portfolio learning and growth in the area of global citizenship

- Defining the benefits of portfolio learning

- Developing a portfolio

Introduction

In GNED500 you will be engaged in portfolio learning. This means that you will collect the activities and assignments you complete during the course, and you will reflect upon your growth and learning in the area of global citizenship and equity as a result. This chapter will provide you with an understanding of what portfolios are, and how they can help you not only to demonstrate your learning, but also allow you to understand how your learning has had an impact on your development as a global citizen.

What is a Portfolio?

Simply stated, a **portfolio** is a purposeful collection of student work that shows effort, progress and learning in a particular area over time (Paulson, Paulson, & Meyer, 1991). The items included in your portfolio (commonly called **artifacts**) together illustrate your skills and achievements. This is a straightforward understanding of portfolios; most of us are aware of portfolios that are used to demonstrate skills to potential employers when seeking a job or creative portfolios used by artists to show off their talents and works of art.

> **Portfolio:** A purposeful collection of student work that exhibits the student's efforts, progress, and achievements in one or more areas (Paulson, Paulson & Meyer, 1991)

However, a portfolio is more than just a collection or showcase of skills used to impress others. Portfolios also allow you to observe the process of your learning, to understand the way you learn, and to reflect on the artifacts in your collection, in order to discover the meaning this knowledge brings to your life.

> **Artifact:** An item that is included in the portfolio that demonstrates a particular area of learning, discovery, skill or accomplishment. Artifacts can be course work or assignments but can also come from activities in your personal life or community.

Portfolios can assist not only in determining your achievements and strengths, but they help you to become aware of who you are, what your beliefs and values are, and how those shape the way you interact with others in a global world. A portfolio opens the door to the meaning behind your actions and what drives them, with a view to further positive growth. In GNED500, portfolio learning will enable you to see how far you have come with respect to global citizenship and equity, and you will begin to see where portfolio learning will take you.

Portfolio Learning and Global Citizenship

Courtesy of Shutterstock.

In GNED500, **portfolio learning** is about using a process of thinking and reflecting that will develop and strengthen your awareness of the social and political issues that exist in our world.

> **Portfolio Learning:** An ongoing process of personal and professional growth that demands continuous self-reflection and critical thinking through a system of collecting and reflecting upon items that represent student work, efforts, progress and achievements.

With an aim to help you to see the injustices that exist in the world, portfolio learning provides you with an in- depth knowledge of who you are, how you engage with the world, how you contribute to it, and how you can work towards its betterment. Working towards social justice and an improved world begins with the self. Since portfolio learning will help you to know yourself, engaging in this work is an integral part of your journey towards becoming a global citizen. This journey requires you to engage in *reflective practice* and *critical thinking*.

Reflective Practice: A Journey Towards Self Awareness

> **Reflective Practice:** The process of thinking about your experiences in a way that asks you to examine your own knowledge so that you might improve upon your practices and behaviors. Reflective practice demands that we question our own knowledge, behaviors and practices. Reflective practice is the basis for individual growth and a necessary component of professional and personal development.

When engaging in portfolio learning, you are also engaging in **reflective practice**. Selecting artifacts from your GNED500 coursework to include in your portfolio requires that you reflect upon these items, and consciously think about what you learned and how it impacts your life and the part you play as a citizen in our global world.

When you reflect upon the knowledge you are gaining in GNED500 through portfolio learning, you are not simply learning facts and figures about global citizenship, you will be moving towards greater emotional and psychological growth that benefits you and your relationships and interactions with others. For example, reflecting upon our interactions with others allows us to think about what has worked in terms of fostering positive, respectful relationships, or alternatively, what may have caused us to alienate or treat others unjustly.

Portfolio learning and reflective practice, therefore, set us on a journey to self-awareness. They provide us with an opportunity to engage in questions of what underlying assumptions, beliefs and values inform our actions, our ideas of who we are and why we think in a certain way about a given social or political issue. Reflective practice is a tool for us to question ourselves and guide us towards change.

Courtesy of Shutterstock.

> *"No one is born fully-formed: it is through self-experience in the world that we become what we are."*
> ~Paulo Freire (1998)

REFLECTING ON THE SELF

Identify an item (eg animal, object, mineral, material, sound, texture, visual image etc) which you feel most represents who you are, who you feel yourself to be, and reflect upon this in a short written-note form.

Ask a good friend, colleague or family member to also pick an item that they feel most represents who you are and who they feel you to be.

Then ask them to explain their choice. Lastly, reflect on the differences and similarities with respect to how you see yourself and how this other person sees you.

_____
_____
_____
_____
_____
_____
_____
_____
_____
_____
_____
_____
_____
_____
_____
_____
_____
_____
_____

Critical Thinking: A Journey Towards Action

With a focus on learning about ourselves and our place in the world, reflective practice provides an opportunity to draw upon our own experiences in society, where in our everyday world, we may experience daily encounters and practices that do not support social justice, equity and inclusion. When we start to consciously see and recognize the inequalities within these encounters and practices we are beginning to think

> *"The self is not something ready-made, but something in continuous formation through choice of action."*
> ~ John Dewey (1916)

Courtesy of Shutterstock.

critically. As you engage in the reflective practice of portfolio learning, you may begin to find ways to resist these injustices, and to transform yourself and take action to change the world. This type of critical thinking is the starting point for identifying and challenging unjust practices in our local communities and the world.

Critical thinking is a process that asks the question: "how is it we know what we know?" It involves continuously questioning what we read, hear, see, feel, experience, and believe. Critical thinking should start from the assumption that there are multiple knowledges and ways of knowing. Therefore, what we know is shaped by our values, beliefs, experiences, identities as well as the historical and geographical context in which we live. Critical thinking demands that we question and evaluate information in a way that takes into account these factors. It requires the use of reflective practice and problem-solving skills to find inclusive and equitable solutions.

What Does a Portfolio Look Like? How Do I Make One?

> **Critical Thinking:** A process of reflective thinking that questions and examines the assumptions and values that underlie what we do, believe, feel, read, see and hear with the goal of making a judgment, decision or solving a problem. Critical thinking is essential in bringing about social change and justice.

A portfolio can take many formats – a folder, electronic file or website, a 3 ring binder, accordion folder, etc. Whatever the format, there must be clearly identified sections, making your artifacts easily accessible. Your artifacts should be organized according to a theme of your choosing, for example, skill areas, knowledge areas, types of activities, etc. The format you choose for your portfolio will depend on what your portfolio will be used for. Students from some programs may be required to develop a portfolio for professional reasons. Others may require a portfolio that is used to illustrate learning only. Either way, what is important is that the portfolio is an organized collection that allows you to witness the process of your learning.

In the case of GNED500, the focus is not on the format of the portfolio; rather, it is on the learning and growth that the portfolio provides. Choose a portfolio format that suits your needs as an individual, student, or professional.

Remember that portfolios used for professional or job search purposes are taken outside of the safe space of your GNED500 classroom. When compiling a professional/job search portfolio, carefully select your artifacts, keeping in mind that your audience might make judgements on your personal experiences, values and beliefs.

> *"The portfolio is a laboratory where students construct meaning from their accumulated experience."*
> ~ Pearl and Leon Paulson (1991)

Stop and Reflect

You want to include an artifact that would showcase your professional skills. Name an artifact that you would include.

_____
_____

Explain why you chose this artifact. What does this artifact say about you as a professional and as an individual?

_____
_____
_____
_____
_____
_____
_____
_____

How does this artifact reflect your knowledge and skills of global citizenship and equity?

_____
_____
_____
_____
_____
_____

Does this artifact demonstrate something that a potential employer would appreciate knowing?

_____
_____
_____
_____
_____

The following flowchart will provide you with the basic steps for developing a portfolio, no matter what format you choose.

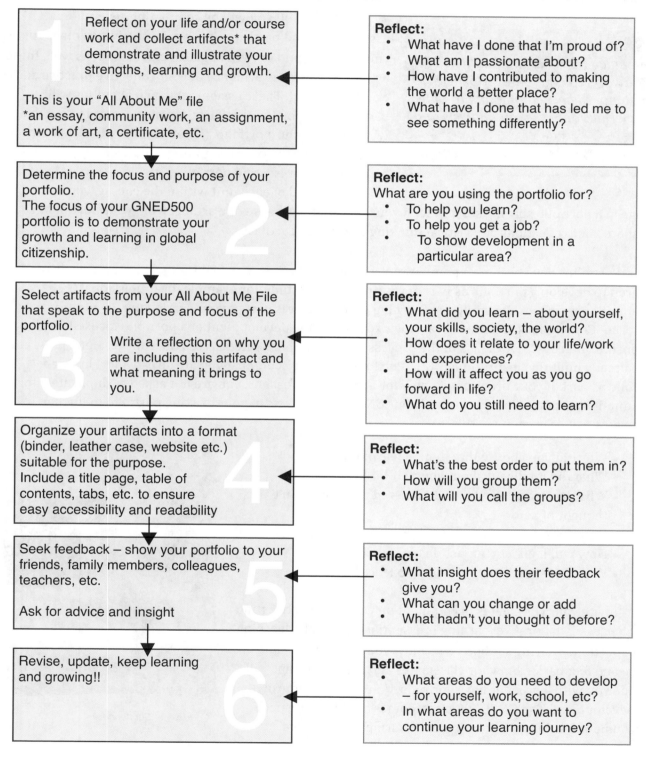

1 Reflect on your life and/or course work and collect artifacts* that demonstrate and illustrate your strengths, learning and growth.

This is your "All About Me" file
*an essay, community work, an assignment, a work of art, a certificate, etc.

Reflect:
- What have I done that I'm proud of?
- What am I passionate about?
- How have I contributed to making the world a better place?
- What have I done that has led me to see something differently?

2 Determine the focus and purpose of your portfolio.
The focus of your GNED500 portfolio is to demonstrate your growth and learning in global citizenship.

Reflect:
What are you using the portfolio for?
- To help you learn?
- To help you get a job?
- To show development in a particular area?

3 Select artifacts from your All About Me File that speak to the purpose and focus of the portfolio.
Write a reflection on why you are including this artifact and what meaning it brings to you.

Reflect:
- What did you learn – about yourself, your skills, society, the world?
- How does it relate to your life/work and experiences?
- How will it affect you as you go forward in life?
- What do you still need to learn?

4 Organize your artifacts into a format (binder, leather case, website etc.) suitable for the purpose.
Include a title page, table of contents, tabs, etc. to ensure easy accessibility and readability

Reflect:
- What's the best order to put them in?
- How will you group them?
- What will you call the groups?

5 Seek feedback – show your portfolio to your friends, family members, colleagues, teachers, etc.

Ask for advice and insight

Reflect:
- What insight does their feedback give you?
- What can you change or add
- What hadn't you thought of before?

6 Revise, update, keep learning and growing!!

Reflect:
- What areas do you need to develop – for yourself, work, school, etc?
- In what areas do you want to continue your learning journey?

Portfolio Sharing in GNED500

> *"Reflective practice and portfolio learning embraces the "ability to be self aware, to analyze experiences, to evaluate their meaning and to plan further action based on analysis and reflection."*
> ~ De La Harper and Radloff (1997)

In GNED500 you will be completing several assignments and participating in many activities that support your learning and growth in global citizenship. As well, these activities will act as evidence of your reflective practice and critical thinking. These assignments and activities will become your portfolio artifacts, forming the collection that will make up your portfolio. (If you are already developing a portfolio as part of your program of study, simply add these artifacts to your existing portfolio.)

At the end of each unit within the course, you will engage in a portfolio sharing session with your classmates. Choose one artifact from your portfolio. You will share your reflections and critical thinking around that artifact.

Portfolios have become a popular tool and are not exclusive to GNED500. You may already be required to develop a portfolio as part of your program of study, for example for professional/accreditation purposes or simply as a learning strategy that is part of your curriculum. In addition, in support of Centennial's Signature Learning Experience, the development of a portfolio focused on global citizenship and equity ("GCE") is in the process of being implemented across the college. Many programs have already built this institutional "GCE Portfolio" into curriculum. If you are already developing a portfolio as part of your program of study for any of these reasons, you are not asked to duplicate efforts or maintain two portfolios. Simply add your GNED500 artifacts to your existing portfolio to further demonstrate your learning in this area.

- Why did you choose that item of learning?
- What did it tell you about yourself?
- What have you learned or discovered that you hadn't thought of before?
- How does it relate to your life, your own experiences?
- How will it affect your actions in the future?
- What do you still feel you need to learn?

Courtesy of Shutterstock.

Invite your classmates to comment on your perspectives and experiences. Collaborative learning is essential to portfolio learning. These portfolio sharing sessions will allow you to obtain insight, advice and feedback from your classmates and instructor that will provide you with a broader basis for reflection and further growth and development. The GNED500 classroom is a safe and respectful environment for this collaboration and sharing to take place.

Benefits of Portfolios

- We can use the portfolio as a reflective instrument which gives us insight into how we see ourselves, how we see others and how others see us – *we benefit by becoming a witness to our transformation!*
- Learning about yourself through the reflective practice component of portfolio learning and development can also help you make better personal and career choices, and choices that guide you to become a global citizen
- It is a self-development tool that assists you in setting goals and guides you to achieve those goals
- The use of portfolios is increasingly becoming a popular tool when seeking employment that illustrates your skills to potential employers. The GNED500 portfolio artifacts will demonstrate skills such as: the ability to think critically, seek just alternatives, and incorporate equitable considerations in everyday situations. These are the skills sought by employers.

> *The benefit of your portfolio never stops; it only puts you on a journey of learning, re-learning and transforming – only to critically reflect on it and begin the journey again.*

Most importantly, we benefit from the portfolio by seeing the ways in which we are part of the bigger, global picture and that geographical, cultural, sexual, religious, racial and physical differences do not separate us from our responsibility to each other.

> *"Learning takes place through interaction, existing in the transaction between student and student, student and text, student and teacher"*
> ~ Murphy (1994)

Photo by Jared Purdy

Getting Engaged: Activities

YOUR TURN!

Is there an artifact that you are unsure about including in your portfolio?
What questions would you ask yourself when deciding whether or not to include this artifact?

_____
_____
_____
_____
_____

What are the possible conclusions you could come to based on the questions you ask yourself?

_____
_____
_____
_____
_____
_____
_____

THINK ABOUT IT!

You want to include an artifact that reflects "success."
What artifact would you include and why?

_____
_____
_____
_____
_____

Think about how social justice, global citizenship, and equity issues are reflected in your definition
of success and the artifact you have selected to reflect this.

_____
_____
_____
_____
_____
_____
_____

CREATING YOUR PORTFOLIO

What is the purpose of your GNED500 Portfolio?

_____

_____

_____

_____

_____

What course content will you include in your portfolio? Why?

List of Items	Rationale

What other materials will you include in your portfolio? Why?

List of Items	Rationale

PORTFOLIO LEARNING

What is the purpose of portfolio development? Why are you asked to develop a portfolio for GNED 500?

_____

_____

_____

_____

_____

_____

_____

How could you use a portfolio to demonstrate your skills and experience in an interview situation?

_____

_____

_____

_____

_____

_____

_____

_____

_____

_____

_____

_____

_____

_____

After you complete GNED 500, how will you use your portfolio in your other courses at Centennial College?

_____

_____

_____

_____

_____

_____

_____

_____

_____

_____

ON PORTFOLIO LEARNING

What it is like to learn in this way?

_____
_____
_____
_____
_____
_____

Does this form of learning work for you? Why or why not?

_____
_____
_____
_____
_____
_____

What kind of learning has emerged?

_____
_____
_____
_____
_____

Consider the process of reflection itself and its importance for other areas of learning as it relates to your studies and your life.

_____
_____
_____
_____
_____
_____
_____
_____
_____
_____

Assignments

Portfolio Sharing: Refer to pg. 236 in the text.

Portfolio Sharing Peer Assessment: Refer to pg. 238 in the text.

Post Reflection: Refer to pg. 253 in the text.

Post Reflection Rubric: Refer to pg. 254 in the text.

Chapter Summary

Definitions:

Artifact: An item that is included in the portfolio that demonstrates a particular area of learning, discovery, skill or accomplishment. Artifacts can be course work or assignments but can also come from activities in your personal life or community.

Critical Thinking: A process of reflective thinking that questions and examines the assumptions and values that underlie what we do, believe, feel, read, see and hear with the goal of making a judgment, decision or solving a problem. Critical thinking is essential in bringing about social change and justice.

Portfolio: A purposeful collection of student work that exhibits the student's efforts, progress, and achievements in one or more areas (Paulson, Paulson & Meyer, 1991).

Portfolio Learning: An ongoing process of personal and professional growth that demands continuous self-reflection and critical thinking through a system of collecting and reflecting upon items that represent student work, efforts, progress and achievements.

Reflective Practice: The process of thinking about your experiences in a way that asks you to examine your own knowledge so that you might improve improve upon your practices and behaviors. Reflective practice demands that we question our own knowledge, behaviors and practices. Reflective practice is the basis for individual growth and a necessary component of professional and personal development.

Main Concepts:

- Overview of portfolio learning and sharing sessions in GNED500
- Introduction to portfolios and portfolio learning
- Beginning the process of reflective practice and moving toward self-awareness
- Differentiating between a showcase portfolio used for employment (end result) and portfolio learning (the process, the learning)
- Establishing the need to think critically in order to enact personal and societal change toward equity and inclusion
- Continuing to think about how you can contribute to making positive changes in the world

Additional Resources

The learning portfolio: Reflective practice for improving student learning 2nd ed. by John Zubizarreta (Centennial College Libraries)

References

De La Harper & Radloff (1997) In Sugerman, D., Doherty, K.L., Garvey, D.E., & Gass, M.A. (2000) *Reflective Learning: Theory and Practice.* Kendal/Hunt Pub Co. Dubuque, Iowa, p.1

Murphy, S. (1994) Portfolios and curriculum reform: Patterns and practice. *Assessing Writing 1:2* , 175-206.

Dewey, J. (1916) *Democracy and Education: An Introduction to the Philosophy of Education.* New York: Macmillan Publishers, pg. Unknown.

Freire, P. (P. L. Wong, Trans.) (1998) *Politics and education.* Los Angeles: UCLA Latin American Center Publications, pg. Unknown.

Paulson, P. & Paulson, F.L. (1991) *Portfolios: Stories of knowing.* In Dreyer, P.H. (Ed.) (1991) *Knowing the power of stories.* Claremont Reading Conference 55th Yearbook. Claremont, CA: Center for Developmental Studies of the Claremont Graduate School. ERIC Document Reproduction Service: ED377209

Paulson, F. L., Paulson, P. R., & Meyer, C. (1991) What makes a portfolio a portfolio? *Educational Leadership, 48*(5), 60-63.

Notes

CHAPTER 3

Undertaking Social Analysis: The Roots of Change

Courtesy of Shutterstock.

CHAPTER OBJECTIVES:

- Define social problem

- Explore social structures that exist in society

- Understand the need for social analysis

- Compare and contrast social analysis frameworks

- Analyze social issues to understand how social analysis leads to social action

Khalid Ali and Renee M. Sgroi

Introduction

Most of you would agree that many social problems exist today. They are local and global. These social problems can range from issues of poverty, hunger, homelessness, violence to crime, discrimination, war, sex work and prostitution rings, climate change, drug and alcohol abuse, child abuse, child labor, human trafficking, gangs, famine, racism, ethnic cleansing, AIDS, unemployment and so on.

> How do you feel about these problems? How does it make you feel to know that people are suffering on a daily basis?
> _____
> _____
> _____
> _____
> _____
> _____

Often, we assume that social problems stem from people's unwillingness to change their lives. For instance, if a person is poor, many will think that this is because of an inherent individual circumstance or characteristic such as laziness, being "unintelligent," "dumb," "unwilling to work," lack of ambition, education, experience or skill. On the other hand, the perception exists that you can get out of poverty by "working hard," "finding a job," "drinking less," or by "being dedicated." Yet, as we shall see, social problems develop because of larger, structural issues that affect many people. Blaming an individual for his or her **location** in society does not help those who are suffering from illness, disability, hunger or unemployment. Nor does it help us to combat the larger, underlying causes that contribute to social problems. Understanding why these social problems exist, who is affected and what can we do to solve them are important questions in conducting social analysis.

> **Location:** The term refers to how we identify ourselves in terms of socio-economic class, culture, gender, sexuality, religion, and so forth.

Social analysis is a method of investigating the reasons **social problems** begin in the first place. Why do we have homelessness? Why do we have hunger? Or wars? Or environmental degradation? Social analysis provides us with the tools to explore how these problems develop, and in turn, social action allows us to raise consciousness or awareness, to create and implement strategies to effect social change. Social analysis is therefore about asking questions, critically analyzing all the available evidence from all perspectives, including the interests of those who are most affected by the social problems. At the same time, it is about looking for answers. In this chapter, you will read about and develop analytical tools that will help you to examine the root causes of social problems so that you can later create possibilities for the social actions needed to solve them.

Photo by Alice Kieltyka

What is a Social Problem?

To conduct social analysis we must first be able to identify what is a social problem. "Social" generally refers to the society that we are living in. In other words, social relates to the collective group of people who live and co-exist within a particular geographical or political boundary. Social can also be described as a shared or communal experience compared to an individual or private one. Another way to describe this is to recognize how an event, action, discussion, or image becomes "social" when it is shared by two or more people. Therefore, whenever we are discussing or analyzing social problems, we are referring to problems that we have in common, i.e., that are of a "social" nature.

> **Social Problem:** A social condition (such as poverty) or a pattern of behavior (such as violence against women) that people believe [requires] public concern and collective action to bring about change (Centennial College, 2009, p.7).

Secondly, we must ask: what is a "problem"? *Who* identifies a social problem as such? This is an important question because it addresses the ways in which the "problem" gets defined, ignored, or dealt with. The term "problem" is linked to issues of power. Those with power will define social problems differently compared to those without power, or to those who have limited access to power, or even to those who are impacted by the social problem itself. For instance, a few years ago, the provincial government in Ontario decided that the numbers of homeless youth working as "squeegee kids" on the streets of Toronto, was an important social problem. Squeegee kids hung out on the streets looking to clean cars at street intersections in return for small change.

What were the factors that led the government to decide that this was a social problem? Whose interests were served by the removal of squeegee kids from the streets of Toronto? What were the reasons provided for their removal? And for those drivers who encountered squeegee kids on the streets, how significant a social problem were they? What about the interests of the squeegee kids themselves?

Why were they on the streets in the first place? Why did they choose to clean people's windshields? And how did they view the government's decision to forcibly remove them from the streets?

Stop and Reflect

How many people do you think have to agree that a problem is a problem before social action is taken to solve it?

_____

_____

_____

_____

_____

Who are these people?

_____

_____

_____

_____

_____

Consider what would be different if those who suffered from "problems" in society defined for themselves the root causes of their "problems". Compare this to a definition provided by the rich or powerful and influential members of society, or to be provided by those who are not affected by the problems. What would be the difference?

_____

_____

_____

_____

_____

_____

_____

_____

_____

Can we compare and contrast each other's definitions, the root causes, the solutions and the perspectives?

_____

_____

_____

_____

_____

THINKING ABOUT SOCIAL PROBLEMS

In ch. 4, you will read about the influence of the media on our perceptions and our construction of knowledge. How do you think the media shape our ideas around social problems?

_____

_____

_____

_____

_____

_____

What other large groups or institutions might affect how we interpret the issues? (Think here about politicians, religious groups, advocates, educational institutions, or other organizations.)

_____

_____

_____

_____

_____

_____

_____

_____

_____

_____

_____

Putting this all together, we can begin to define a social problem as a "social condition (such as poverty) or a pattern of behavior (such as violence against women) that people believe warrants public concern and collective action to bring about change" (Kendall, Nygaard, & Thompson, 2008, p.2). Social problems are in essence public and collective and not private and individual. A social problem can be identified when it becomes of a concern to society. In addition, the authors also explain that social problems become such, "when they are seen as harmful by many of the people who wield power, wealth, and influence in a group or society" (p.2). What problems would we agree are social in nature? What problems affect us all? Can "individual" problems become social problems too? What if many individuals suffer from the same problem? How long do you think it would take for it to be recognized as a *social* problem?

What would *you* define as a social problem? Share your answers with a partner or in a small group. Did you identify the same issues? Discuss.

_____

_____

_____

_____

_____

_____

_____

Why Should a Social Problem be of Concern to Us as Individuals?

Having agreed that defining social problems involves thinking about whose interests are at stake, who is affected, who wields power and who does not, we must now explore why we should be concerned with social problems at all. From a global citizenship perspective, we are living in an increasingly interconnected world, where technology, access to travel, integration of world economies, and global policies and regulations impact all facets of our lives. For instance, Russia's drought in 2010, and its inability to sell wheat on the global market led to a worldwide increase of wheat prices. This event made wheat an unaffordable commodity for many countries. In Mozambique, for example, there was a food riot that led to the deaths of seven people. What social problems do you think the people of Mozambique experienced as a result of the increase in wheat prices? What social problems were experienced elsewhere in the world?

> *"The moment we choose to love we begin to move against domination, against oppression. The moment we choose love we begin to move towards freedom, to act in ways that liberate ourselves and others. That action is the testimony of love as the practice of freedom. "*
> ~ bell hooks, writer and educator

There are also many other examples. The depletion of resources in one country will affect another. For instance, the fall of the cod stocks in Newfoundland not only affected the Canadian market, but it also affected supplies for cod and other fish around the world. The spread of disease in one part of the world, for example H1N1, which was thought to have originated in Mexico, quickly became a global pandemic. The production, marketing, and sale of goods, which now occurs on a worldwide scale, is also an example. Clothes we buy in Canada, for instance, begin as raw materials in India, but may be sewn together in Bangladesh and then shipped to Canada for sale and final purchase. What results is that social problems may spring up in other countries that seem unrelated to the social and political context of Canada. Yet imagine what may happen if the factory in Bangladesh gets moved to another country. Or imagine if the chemicals used in the production of items in India were to leak out of the plant and pollute people's drinking water? And indeed, this was the case in Bhopal, India, where gas and other chemicals leaked out of the Union Carbide Plant and killed thousands of people. In these examples, how responsible is Canada for the creation of a social problem that exists halfway around the world?

Courtesy of Shutterstock.

Global citizenship perspectives see these questions as extremely relevant to any kind of social analysis. In addition, they stress the importance of analyzing the history of social frameworks and structures, so that we must consider the historical roots of a given situation or context. This is because social problems have a history. They appear because of other existing problems that were not dealt with or solved previously. Therefore, social problems are a sign or warning that if they are not solved as quickly as possible, they could extend into other problems.

Courtesy of Shutterstock.

Take the issue of poverty, as an example. We have to ask ourselves why it is a social problem and why it should be of concern to us. Does poverty affect us individually? Does it affect us globally? Some of you may argue that it does not. Others may argue that if you are not poor, then it does not affect you. On the other hand, poverty could contribute to homelessness, hunger, domestic violence, poor health, drug and alcohol addiction, physical and mental health problems, spread of diseases, illness, shorter life span, unemployment, increase in crime. How can these problems have an impact on all of us?

Recognizing the history of social problems and the interconnectedness of our globalized world, we begin to see that we cannot exclude ourselves from discussions of social problems. Instead, we must begin to investigate and evaluate social problems, because they *do* have a trickle down effect that influences us individually. More importantly, however, we must, as individuals, undertake social analysis so that we can become aware of how our *own* actions may inadvertently contribute to the ongoing oppression of people. In this way, we recognize our own responsibilities and can find ways to create social change.

Identify a social problem that concerns you. Why does this problem concern you?
_____
_____
_____
_____

Are you aware of the history of this social problem? If so, what is its history?
_____
_____
_____
_____

Why is it problematic to examine social problems without looking at their history?
_____
_____
_____
_____

EVENTS THAT CONTRIBUTED TO SOCIAL CHANGE

Event: The Incorporation of Disability Rights into the Canadian Charter of Rights and Freedoms

WHEN: 1982

WHERE: Ottawa, Canada

WHAT: A victory for the rights of Canadians living with disabilities

Compiled by Sarah Duffy

In the early 1980's Canada was going through a time of change. Under the leadership of Pierre Trudeau, a bill of rights for all Canadians was being created – the Canadian Charter of Rights and Freedoms. One area of rights, Disability Rights, was omitted from the draft Charter. Here is the story, told in first person by Disability Rights activist, David Lepofsky.

"... The 1980 draft Charter originally included equality rights but deliberately omitted persons with disabilities. Many voices contributed to our victory in getting the Charter amended to include disability equality.... Then-prime minister Pierre Trudeau, to whom we remain indebted, was pushing the Charter so hard that I never thought he would stop to listen to us.... When I heard that the Charter excluded disability, I asked the Canadian Institute for the Blind to appoint me as its "constitutional spokesman," whatever that was. The CNIB agreed. I immediately launched our campaign to the media. But the media ignored us. ...Then came an unexpected phone call. Parliament invited CNIB to appear before it within 36 hours. Hearings were televised nationally... It was a moment I'll never forget. In the background I heard thousands outside City Hall, singing "Imagine" in remembrance of Beatle John Lennon, murdered that week. Arguments made by various organizations before the parliamentary committee and elsewhere in 1980 were simple: If the Charter is to guarantee equal rights, it must include equality for all, including persons with disabilities, not just equality for some. Canadians with disabilities face unfair barriers when seeking employment, education, and opportunities that others take for granted. We needed and need equality. Canada planned to pass the Charter in 1981, which happened to be the International Year of the Disabled. Canada co-sponsored the U.N.'s declaration... After the public hearings, the federal government wouldn't budge, despite enormous pressure. At home, I watched live on television the government's presentation before the parliamentary committee rejecting our proposed disability amendment. I ran to the phone, called a newspaper minutes before its deadline, and denounced the government for being wrong and unfair. My words ran the next day on page 2, beside the government's speech. Trudeau wanted to win public support for the Charter over the heads of the holdout premiers. Advocates kept up the pressure. Then word came from a justice minister named Jean Chrétien that the government would support our disability amendment. The disability amendment was an enormous milestone on our road to equality."

Lepofsky, D. (2002, April). ODA Committee. Retrieved from ODA Committee website: http://www.odacommittee.net/

What are the Root Causes of Social Problems?

To conduct social analysis, we must analyze what are the root causes of social problems by critically examining the historical, socioeconomic, and political conditions that lead to, for example, poverty. By not examining these "roots" we will not be able to make an accurate diagnosis of why social problems exist in society. Consider the historic role of slavery, colonialism, wars, ethnic and religious conflicts, natural disasters, global warming and the market system as examples. What roles do they play in creating social problems and inequality in society? For example, slavery as a system supported the colonial economy by providing free labour. As a result, historic policies and traditions developed out of this system so that, for instance, segregation in the United States, and even current day racial tensions can ultimately be traced back to the history of slavery and its practices. In addition, another consequence of the enslavement of people was the emptying of Africa's prime labour force. This led to the underdevelopment of Africa. In both the colonial context, and in the African context, social problems therefore arose.

Photo by Jared Purdy

The example above demonstrates the importance of understanding the history and historical context of a given social problem. It is also relevant to identify and understand socioeconomic and political factors and how they contribute to social problems. For instance, if we think about poverty, what would we say are its root causes?

What do you think are the root causes of poverty? (Consider history, economy, politics etc.)
- not educated
- lack of jobs.
- growing up in a poor community.

To answer the question about the root causes of poverty, we must consider the ways in which the economy enables some people to accumulate wealth, yet limits or denies others the same possibilities. Those who have more wealth have a greater say in the distribution of power, both politically and socially. What this means is that those with political power are in power because they have access to a greater pool of financial support from those who are wealthy. In return, policies are developed that support the financial and social interests of those with wealth. In addition, one can argue that world poverty results from the control and monopolization of natural resources by a few multinational corporations who are able to influence the prices of products (such as sugar, coffee, cocoa, bauxite, and minerals) that are sold on the world markets to countries in Europe and North America. These prices are not decided by the sellers or producers (who often reside in poor countries) but by people and institutions based in Europe and the U.S. The role of international financial institutions, such as the World Bank, the International Monetary Fund (IMF), and powerful regulatory agencies such as the World Trade Organization (WTO), which was set up to regulate global trade, also contribute to the ongoing impoverishment of already economically poor, yet resource rich nations. Therefore, "in the face of such enormous external influence, the governments of poor nations and their people are often powerless. As a result, in the global context, a few get wealthy while the majority struggle." http://www.globalissues.org/issue/2/causes-of-poverty. For these reasons, disparities exist between the rich and the poor, and contribute to the underlying causes of poverty in our society.

SOCIAL ANALYSIS OF GLOBAL SWEATSHOPS

Think about global sweatshops? Why are sweatshops a social problem?
_____
_____

What are the root causes of the social problem?
_____
_____
_____
_____
_____
_____
_____
_____
_____
_____
_____
_____
_____
_____
_____
_____
_____

Social Structures in Society

In order to get at root causes of social problems, we must first recognize that society does not work based on the loosely connected decisions of a few individuals, and that instead, society operates according to a number of visible and invisible structures. **Social structures** describe how society is organized (who gets what or benefits the most). In social analysis, the concept structure "suggests that root causes are not individual, but rather institutional" (Michael, Czerny, & Clarke, 1994, p. 18). This means that an individual is not entirely responsible for the social positioning or location in which he or she finds him or herself. If a person is poor, it is not because that person necessarily "chooses" to be poor. Rather, social structure "involves discovering, describing, explaining, and ultimately challenging the structures that define social existence" (Michael, Czerny, & Clarke,1994, p.19).

Photo by Jared Purdy

Society is therefore organized around the economy, governments, religion, culture, education, family, traditions and customs. These social structures are well-established "institutions" that have existed for centuries. They are maintained and supported on a daily basis by the people who are themselves affected by the structures. In other words, people live within social structures, and perpetuate them, often without

> **Social Structure:** Refers to how society is organized, including relationships between various social institutions and socio-economic classes.

even realizing it. Some structures, such as the economy or government, are "visible" because we can point directly to the organizations and people who work in these areas, and therefore determine public policy. For instance, we know that the Canadian government is made up of a prime minister, his or her cabinet, in addition to the elected representatives that make up the legislature, and so on.

Photo by Jared Purdy

Other structures are "invisible", or less visible, because they don't operate in quite the same way as a large organization or body of policies. Culture, families, traditions, customs, and beliefs fall under this category. Thus, a society may believe that when a couple gets married, it is the responsibility of the bride's family to provide the bridegroom with a dowry. The dowry is a set of gifts that can range from cash, to farm animals, to linens and silverware, jewelry, or any other items the society views as valuable. Thus, the concept of a dowry is not written down, and is not codified as part of the law, or organization of a government. Yet the practice of giving a dowry can be a very integral part of a given society's structure, so that to get married without a dowry would be considered socially unacceptable.

Identify and explain social structures that influence your life.

Visible:

_____
_____
_____
_____
_____
_____
_____
_____
_____
_____

Invisible:

_____
_____
_____
_____
_____
_____
_____
_____
_____
_____
_____
_____

Social structures therefore determine the way people live, the actions and behavior of individuals and communities, and how groups interrelate with each other. The study of social structures in society provides an understanding of the distribution and access to power, resources and other essential services to the community. It also explains the root causes of 'structural' inequalities and how they contribute to exploitation, exclusion, discrimination, lack of access to education, food, shelter, water, sanitation services and health care.

> "Someone once said that you can measure the stature of a man by the size of his enemy... With that in mind, I say to our people, 'We have been and still are at odds with the most dangerous, well-funded, strongest military and political organization in the history of the world.' ... I am proud to be a Native American because my people before me stood up against overwhelming odds so that I might have a chance to exist. They were successful as I am living proof."
> ~ Leonard Peltier, Native American activist and writer

Courtesy of Shutterstock.

The organization or "structure" of "societies" is different around the world because of geography, language, culture, beliefs, traditions and practices, access to resources, environment, natural conditions and people's experiences. How a society looks in one context, and what are its most significant features, will not be the same or similar in another context. Even if we compared Canada with the United States, we would find that there are differences in the types of social problems occurring in each country because of the differences between our two nations, our political structures, our economies, our histories, our cultural fabric, and so on. Hence, it is essential to note that the social structure of "society" differs depending on where you live. Now that we understand why we should be concerned with social problems, and what social structures are, it is helpful to examine how to go about conducting social analyses.

Courtesy of Shutterstock.

Stop and Reflect

If we understand that social problems are caused by historical, economic, social, and political conditions, then is this understanding enough to explain why the majority of the world's population are poor and live on less than $2.50 a day?

_____
_____
_____
_____
_____
_____
_____
_____
_____
_____
_____
_____
_____
_____
_____
_____
_____
_____
_____

Did You Know?

"Worldwide 2.4 billion people do not have access to basic sanitation: they lack safe means of disposal of excreta and waste water."

~ World Health Organization, http://www.who.int/water_sanitation_health/sanitproblems/en/index1.html

Frameworks for Conducting Social Analysis

The Social Analysis Working Group here at Centennial developed the following three models for social analysis: 1) *The Iceberg Model*, 2) *Basic Critical Thinking/Questioning Model*; and 3) *Ways of Reading Social Problems Model*. Following these models, the authors of this chapter have provided one further model to help you in your discovery of social analysis frameworks. Taken together, these tools will guide you in your analysis of social problems and your path to discover solutions and possibilities for social action.

The Iceberg Model

Within this model, individual acts appear at the top of the pyramid because they are the ones that are most visible. Just like an iceberg, we imagine that the greatest part of the iceberg is what we see above the surface of the water. What scientists, researchers, and naval vessels have found, however, is that the majority of the iceberg actually floats beneath the surface of the water. So, using the metaphor of the iceberg, we must understand that what we see on the surface is only a small portion of the real, underlying components of social problems. If we dig further down to the bottom or root of a social problem, we find that social problems are perpetuated because of ideologies, and the social structures that work to maintain the inequities we find globally.

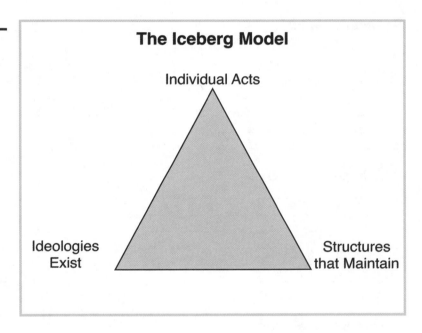

Ideologies exist as ideas, beliefs and opinions that provide us with a sense of how society functions. They serve as "screens through which we perceive the social world." (Marchak, 1975, p1) In other words, ideologies mask how we understand and see the world, and influence what we think is important. For instance, in the identity chapter, you will look at what it means to be "Canadian", and who gets to use that term. In a sense, we can say that there are certain *ideologies* that exist that shape how we understand the notion of being Canadian. Ideologies are not taught in the way that you might learn about math or spelling at school. Instead, we absorb and learn ideologies through the media, government, family, friends, and community. Ideologies are particularly important because they are often used to support one group over another, so that power imbalances and inequities in privilege are created.

Ideology: A set of beliefs, or way of thinking that shapes how a person sees the world.

In order to apply this approach to an analysis of a social problem, we might therefore ask ourselves the following questions: What are the individual acts that appear to contribute to the social problem? What are the collective acts that contribute? What are the ideologies that exist? Who perpetuates these ideologies? For whom are they useful? To whom are the ideologies applied? How do the ideologies work to structure our thinking around social problems? What institutional, state, or structural systems utilize the ideologies to maintain power? What are structures that maintain this problem?

Use the **Iceberg Model** to do a social analysis of homelessness.

Individual Acts:

_____
_____
_____
_____
_____
_____
_____

Ideologies that exist:

_____
_____
_____
_____
_____
_____

Structures that maintain:

_____
_____
_____
_____
_____
_____

Notes/Questions:

_____
_____
_____
_____
_____
_____
_____

Basic Critical Thinking/ Questioning Approach

Within the basic critical thinking approach, one approaches the social problem simply by asking critical questions about the nature of the problem. This critical thinking approach requires that the problem be analyzed from all sides and perspectives using critical thinking techniques. For instance, critical thinkers often will use a "3M" approach. This approach requires us to "Maximize, Minimize, and Modify". If you take the component parts of a social problem, what parts can you enlarge or maximize in order to further investigate? What parts should be minimized or made smaller because they have less relevance to the issue? What parts can or should be modified or changed because they require social action?

Or, imagine that the social problem is an object such as a fruit, a pen, a plastic bag, or other item that you can hold in your hand. How do you go about analyzing that object? Critical thinkers will tell you that it is necessary to identify all aspects of the object, and to look at it from a 360 degree perspective in order to fully analyze its composition. So, for instance, what does a pen look like? What does the texture of the fruit feel like? What does the plastic bag look like when it is full? What about when it is empty? These are practical examples for critically examining objects, but social problems are not objects. If we wanted to think more analytically about social problems, we could imagine that we are holding a cup of coffee. Thinking about coffee from a 360 degree perspective requires that we consider coffee production, the environment, world economies, demand, pricing, consumption, the benefits to the producers, and so forth. The following questions therefore are essential to an analysis based on this critical thinking approach: What is the social problem? Who defines it? Why is it considered a social problem? Who or what is affected? Who benefits? Who loses? What is the overall cost to society? What are possible solutions?

Basic Critical Thinking/ Questioning Approach

- What is the social problem?
- Who defines it?
- Why is it considered a social problem?
- Who or what is affected?
- Who benefits?
- Who loses?
- What is the overall cost to society?
- What are possible solutions?

CRITICAL QUESTIONING

What does it mean to ask critical questions? How do we ask critical questions?

_____
_____
_____
_____
_____
_____

Use the *Basic Critical Thinking/ Questioning Approach* to do a social analysis of coffee production?

What is the social problem?

Who defines it?

Why is it considered a social problem?

Who or what is affected?

Who benefits?

Who loses?

What is the overall cost to society?

What are possible solutions?

Notes/Questions

Ways of Reading Social Problems

Do you remember what it was like when you learned to read? Did you begin by looking at whole words? Or did you have to learn the alphabet, and its symbolic representation of sounds first? Chances are you began with the alphabet and the combination of letters such as "ch", "th", so that you were introduced to phonics. Just as you learned to read, therefore, you cannot conduct social analysis by looking at the entire problem as a whole. Instead, you must break down the problem to its most fundamental building blocks, and work your way up so that you find yourself looking at the entire puzzle and how the pieces all fit together.

Ways of Reading Social Problems

Taking this approach, you can begin to "read" a social problem by:

- Examining Commonly Accepted Beliefs
- Tracing History
- Identify Key Players and Perspectives
- Moving Back and Forth
- Focusing on the System

Socioeconomic political approach:

Earlier we identified the need to carefully examine what is a social problem. Who defines a problem as such? Why should a social problem be of concern to us as individuals? What are the root causes of social problems? We also argue that in social analysis it is very important to fully explore the historical, political and socioeconomic roots that contribute to social problems. By examining the interconnectedness of historical, political, and socioeconomic factors, we can see that social problems derive because of multiple, interlaced issues, practices, and structures that work together to make analysis of social problems a challenging task. Taking into consideration the role of the structures of society (which includes the political, social and economic factors that we discussed earlier) we must also fully explore the following questions:

- What are the historical roots of a social problem?
- How exactly does a social problem begin?
- What factors merge to create the problem?
- What was the situation like *before* the problem began? What was it like after?
- From whose perspective is the story told? How does that affect the *kind* of story that gets told?
- How would the story be different if it were told from another perspective?
- What other perspectives are available?
- Whose voices are heard? Whose are not heard?
- What is left out?
- Who are the major players? What role did they play and what was the impact?
- Who was affected?
- Is the problem connected or linked to other problems and issues?
- Is it linked to the context in which the problem began? If so, how?
- What is the importance of a particular event or incident that occurred? What followed?

Secondly in our opinion, the political aspect of society is integral in terms of the economic and social resources that people have access to. In the following, it is important to carefully consider these questions when conducting social analysis:

> *"The first problem for all of us, men and women, is not to learn, but to unlearn."*
> ~ Gloria Steinmen, author and feminist

- What system of political power exists in the society?
- Is it a dictatorship?
- A democratic government?
- A military government?
- How was it established?
- What are the key institutions? (e.g. courts, military, government)
- How is power distributed amongst the key institutions?
- What roles do they play in determining how policies are made?
- Are politicians elected into power?
- Do they represent the interests of the people who voted for them?
- Who has the greatest say in decision making?
- How are the interests of the people represented?

Integral in the distribution of power is the economy as it relates to how goods and services are distributed, as well as how policies are developed pertaining to the role of labour, private property, and capital. In this regard, it is useful to ask these questions:

- How is production organized in society?
- Who owns the means of production?
- How many people are dependent on it for a living?
- Is there a concentration of economic power in a few hands?
- What influence do they have on the rights of labour, local and foreign investments?
- Who controls and owns the sale and distribution of natural resources?
- If it is a foreign multinational corporation how much royalties are they paying to extract the resources?
- What connection do the rich have with those in political power?
- Explain the impact on decision making. Who wins or loses?
- Whose voices are being heard or left out?

- What are the social impacts of the economic structures?
- How is society affected by factors such as what kind of goods and services are produced in a particular area, or who controls the means of production?
- How does the community benefit or lose from the types of economic systems that are in place in a given context?
- And what happens to a community when that economic structure changes?

Use the *Ways of Reading Social Problems* framework to do a social analysis of world hunger.

Examining commonly accepted beliefs:

_____
_____
_____
_____
_____
_____

Tracing history:

_____
_____
_____
_____
_____
_____

Identify key places and perspectives:

_____
_____
_____
_____
_____
_____

Moving back and forth:

_____
_____
_____
_____
_____
_____

Focusing on the system:

_____
_____
_____
_____
_____

Notes/Questions:

_____
_____
_____
_____
_____

AGENTS OF SOCIAL CHANGE: GLOBAL CITIZENS IN ACTION

Activist: Martin Luther King Jr.

1929 - 1968
Activist for Civil Rights
United States of America

Compiled by Sarah Duffy

Martin Luther King Jr., was born in the United States in 1929 at a time of racial segregation. In Atlanta, where King was born, blacks were barred from white schools, parks, swimming pools and lunch counters. King was born to affluent parents and he had the opportunity to complete a college education, receiving a doctorate in 1955.

In 1955 civil rights activists decided to contest racial segregation on buses following the incident where Rosa Parks, an African American woman, refused to give up her seat to a white passenger and was arrested for taking this stand. The activists formed the Montgomery Improvement Association and decided to boycott the bus system, Martin Luther King Jr. was chosen as their leader. King led the boycott for over a year. During this time, his home was dynamited and his family was threatened. However, he continued to lead the boycott and eventually the city's buses were desegregated. After this, King toured the country speaking about race relations and civil rights. In October of 1960, King was arrested with 33 other people for staging a lunch-in at a segregated lunch counter in an Atlanta department store. Although these charges were dropped for King, he was held in prison on an offence related to traffic fines. His case was widely publicized and inspired public outcry. Finally, presidential candidate, John F. Kennedy stepped in and intervened to arrange King's release.

In the years from 1960 to 1965, King went on to lead a number of civil rights campaigns and gained much public support. His non-violent tactics were applauded and well received. In 1963, King and other civil rights leaders organized the March on Washington where over 200,000 individuals gathered demanding justice and equal rights. At this event, King delivered his famous 'I have a dream' speech. The rising profile of the civil rights movement resulted in the passing of the Civil Rights Act in 1964. This act authorized the federal government to enforce desegregation of public accommodations and outlawed discrimination in publicly owned facilities and in employment. Later, in December 1964, King received the Nobel Peace Prize. Martin Luther King Jr. was assassinated in April 1968. His death resulted in riots in 100 cities around the United States. In memory of King and his accomplishments many states now have a Martin Luther King day.

Davenport, H. (2003). Civil Rights. In H. Davenport, *Days that Shook the World* (pp. 120-144). London: BBC Worldwide Ltd.

Martin Luther King Jr. Biography. (Date Unknown). Retrieved September 25, 2010 from Biography.com: www.biography.com

Moving from Social Analysis to Social Action

"For to be free is not merely to cast off one's chains, but to live in a way that respects and enhances the freedom of others "
~ Nelson Mandela, former President of South Africa and anti-apartheid activist

Given what you have learned about social problems, it is important to state that each of us, individually and collectively, can contribute to social change. We can do this through critical analysis of social problems, creating awareness of the issues, advocating on behalf of the disadvantaged, and even more powerfully, building bridges with those affected by social problems to work collectively to create social change in people's lives. From a global citizenship perspective, we must be able to critically analyze the structures of power that contribute to the disparities of wealth, and how we benefit from these inequalities here in Canada.

In chapter 7, you will read about the strategies, activities, and possibilities that will enable you to conduct your own forms of social action. As you go forward to develop a plan for social action, you must keep in mind that it is important to always cycle back to your initial analysis of the social problem itself. As you proceed with social action, you will find that your preliminary analyses may change or be refined as new questions, new information, and new ideas surface in the process of conducting social action. In this way, your journey towards social action will become more comprehensive and therefore more meaningful for you as a global citizen as you proceed in your efforts to effect social change.

Courtesy of Shutterstock.

Getting Engaged: Activities

WHAT CONSTITUTES A SOCIAL PROBLEM?

What constitutes a social problem?

_____
_____
_____
_____
_____
_____
_____
_____

Create a list of major social problems that exist globally today.

_____
_____
_____
_____
_____
_____
_____
_____

What social problems exist in Canada?

_____
_____
_____
_____
_____
_____
_____
_____

Is inequality a social problem?

_____
_____
_____
_____
_____
_____
_____

THINKING ABOUT SOCIAL PROBLEMS

Think of social structures of where you live currently, or have lived previously. Compare and contrast your experience.

_____
_____
_____
_____
_____
_____
_____

What social problems exist in those places?

_____
_____
_____
_____
_____
_____

What are the root causes?

_____
_____
_____
_____
_____
_____
_____
_____
_____
_____
_____
_____

How would you solve them?

_____
_____
_____
_____
_____
_____
_____
_____
_____

WHAT'S IN A LESSON LEARNED?

Think about the words of Van Jones, environmental activist:

"When the colonizer came [to Africa] the colonizer said, 'All this is commodities; all this can be taken and sold.' And your great-grandmother said, 'No, no, no. This is sacred; this is precious... That tree is holy; that river is holy'... The colonizer said, 'That's not a tree; that's lumber. That's not God's creature; that's a pelt'... And your great-grandmother when she said, 'This tree is sacred,' it actually turns out now that she was speaking a high form of ecological science, a high form of scientific wisdom and genius."
(In Mack, T. & Picower, B. (2009). *Planning to Change the World: A Plan Book for Social Justice Teachers.*)

How does this quote relate to the importance of social analysis?

_____
_____
_____
_____
_____

Discuss with a partner or small group.

Social Analysis to Social Action

As part of your Social Action Plan you will need to analyze a social problem. (Refer to pg. 239 for a detailed explanation of the Social Analysis and Social Action Plan assignment)

In a small group: Euthanasia

Pick a social problem that you are interested in learning more about:
   Euthanasia
_____
_____

Why did your group choose this social problem to focus on?
   - Controversal,
_____
_____

Why is this a social problem?
   - Some countries don't have the right.
   - ethics + morals
   - baby boomers, getting old, put on machines
   - family / wealth
_____
_____
_____

Social Analysis to Social Action

Who or what does this social problem affect?

affects families

Use one of the frameworks to analyze the problem.

"We must reinvent a future free of blinders
so that we can choose from real options. "
~ David Suzuki, Japanese Canadian academic and
environmental activist

Portfolio Sharing Session

Make a list of the activities, assignments and course work you have completed during this unit:

Sweat-shop activity, the social analysis prop

Decide which artifact from the list above you would like to share with your classmates. Which of the things on this list had the most impact on you or provided the most learning?

Reflect on why this item was so meaningful: Why did you choose that item of learning? What did it tell you about yourself? What have you learned or discovered that you hadn't thought of before? How does it relate to your life, your own experiences? How will it affect your actions in the future? What do you still feel you need to learn?

Bring your portfolio to class, including your selected artifact and reflection, and be prepared to share them a group and/or the class.
Listen carefully to the feedback of others. Write points about that feedback here:

What insight does this feedback provide you with? How does it affect your thinking and what you might do in the future as you continue learning in this area?

Listen attentively to others as they share their artifacts with you. Provide them with respectful and thoughtful feedback. Make some notes here about anything they share that has particular meaning for you:

Developed by Gina Marshall, Stanley Doyle-Wood, Holly Baines, Julia Satov, Zabedia Nazim (2010) Centennial College, Toronto, ON.

Assignments

Social Action Project: Refer to pg. 239 in the text.

Social Action Project Rubric: Refer to pg. 241 in the text.

Chapter Summary

Definitions:

Ideology: A collection of ideas that form the basis of public opinion in a society.

Location: The term refers to how we identify ourselves in terms of socio-economic class, culture, gender, sexuality, religion, and so forth.

Social Problem: A social condition (such as poverty) or a pattern of behavior (such as violence against women) that people believe [requires] public concern and collective action to bring about change (Centennial College, 2009, p.7).

Social Structure: Refers to how society is organized, including relationships between various social institutions and socio-economic classes.

Main Concepts:

- Identifying social problems and their scope
- Recognizing the history of social problems and the interconnectedness of our globalized world
- Examining the social structures that exist in society and the implications of these structures
- Exploring the root causes of social problems
- Establishing frameworks for conducting social analysis
- Defining the connection between social analysis and social action

Additional Resources

Getting started on social analysis, by Jamie Swift, Jacquline Davies, Robert Clarke and Michael Czerny S.J.

> *Description:* This book examines social issues in Canada and provides an approach for social analysis.

Canadian Council on Social Development – www.ccsd.ca

> *Description:* "The Canadian Council on Social Development (CCSD) is a non-governmental, not-for-profit organization, which was founded in 1920. Our mission is to develop and promote progressive social policies inspired by social justice, equality and the empowerment of individuals and communities. We do this through research, consultation, public education and advocacy. Our main product is information." (CCSD/ About US (n.d.). Retrieved from http://www.ccsd.ca/aboutus.html)

Contemporary Canadian Social Issues, by Carmen Niessen

> *Description:* "Carmen Niessen and Rebecca Bromwich combine sociological theory with legal and practical expertise in this new edition of Contemporary Canadian Social Issues. They continue to offer instruction on how to identify social problems. This text examines ways of analysing these problems through various sociological perspectives, applying them to a variety of important issues in Canadian society. Students are encouraged to form responses to these issues, as well as respond to those of various social groups." (Edmond Montgomery Publications (n.d.). Retrieved from http:// www.emp.ca).

Canadian Centre for Policy Alternatives– http://www.policyalternatives.ca/

> *Description:* "The Canadian Centre for Policy Alternatives is an independent, non-partisan research institute concerned with issues of social, economic and environmental justice. Founded in 1980, the CCPA is one of Canada's leading progressive voices in public policy debates." (Policy Alternatives / Offices (n.d.). Retrieved from http:// www.policyalternatives.ca/offices)

References

Biography. (Date Unknown) Martin Luther King Jr. Retrieved on September 26, 2010 from
www.biography.com

Davenport, H. (2003). Civil rights. In Davenport, H. (2003). *Days that Shook the World*. London: BBC
Worldwide Ltd. p. 120-144.

hooks, b. Social Action Quote. In Mack, T. & Picower, B. (2009). *Planning to Change the World: A Plan Book
for Social Justice Teachers*. New York: New York Collective of Radical Educators and the Education
for Liberation Network. p. 39

Jones, V. Social Action Quote. In Mack, T. & Picower, B. (2009). *Planning to Change the World: A Plan Book
for Social Justice Teachers*. New York: New York Collective of Radical Educators and the Education
for Liberation Network. p. 107

Kendall D; Nygaard, V. T., E; (Ed.). (2008). *Social Problems in a Diverse Society* (2 ed.). Toronto: Pearson
Education Canada/3

Mandela, N. (Date Unknown) Social Action Quote. Retrieved on October 2, 2010 from
http://thinkexist.com/quotation/ for-to-be-free-is-not-merely-to-cast-off-one-s/357215.html

Marchak, P. (1975). *Ideological Perspectives on Canada*. Toronto: McGraw-Hill Ryerson.

Michael S.J, Czerny, J. S., Clarke, R, (Ed.). (1994). *Social Analysis Again: Getting Started on Social Analysis in
Canada* (3 ed.).

Michael S.J, C. J. S., Clarke, R, (Ed.). (2008). *Global Citizenship: From Social Analysis to Social Action*.
(2 ed.).

Mooney, L. A., Knox, D., & Schacht, C. . (2000). *Understanding social problems (2nd ed.)*. Cincinnati,:
Wadsworth.M.

ODA Committee. (2002) Lepofsky, David. Retrieved on October 2, 2010 from http://
www.odacommittee.net/20years-charter.html

Peltier, L. Social Analysis Quote. In Mack, T. & Picower, B. (2009). *Planning to Change the World: A Plan
Book for Social Justice Teachers*. New York: New York Collective of Radical Educators and the
Education for Liberation Network. p. 59

Shah, A. (2010) *Causes of Poverty*. Retrieved on September 24, 2010 from Global Issues http://
www.globalissues.org/issue/2/causes-of-poverty.

Steinem, G. (Date Unknown) Social Analysis Quote. Retrieved on September 26, 2010 from
http://feminist.com/resources/quotes/

Suzuki, D. (Date Unknown) Social Analysis Quote. Retrieved on September 26, 2010 from
    http://thinkexist.com/quotes/david_suzuki/

World Health Organization. (Date Unknown) *People and waste: The size of the problem.* Retrieved on
    September 26, 2010 from http://www.who.int/water_sanitation_health/sanitproblems/en/
    index1.html

Notes

CHAPTER 4

Media Literacy

Courtesy of Shutterstock.

CHAPTER OBJECTIVES:

- Learning to critically read the media

- Understanding media conglomeration, power, and control

- Analyzing the influence of media on self and collective

Renee M. Sgroi

Introduction

Imagine you are riding on a bus, streetcar, or subway train. You look around. Besides the other passengers, what do you see? Chances are you are looking at print or televised advertisements for everything from the latest movie or television show, to the newest shaving cream or chocolate bar. Now imagine your cell phone rings. If you answer the call, you might speak to a friend from another city, or even country. Or, you might find a text message waiting for you, inviting you to a party later that day. A passenger might walk by you with the sounds of the latest big sensation in music blaring from her headphones. Or you might lean over your seat to peer at your bus mate's laptop, and see an episode of a television program you watched last night.

> **Medium:** Is the means by which a message is sent. It is what enables a message to travel from a sender to a receiver.

The point of this scenario? Everywhere you go, you are surrounded by some form of media. **Media** is a broad term that can include everything from advertising, television, movies, internet, radio, books, newspapers, flyers, brochures, and blogs, as well as the technology we use to access those communications. When we talk about media, we can refer both to the **medium** of communication (the technology, such as TV or telephone) or the **messages** communicated.

> **Media:** Refers to television, internet, radio, advertising, newspapers, books, magazines, and any form of mediated communication.

> **Message:** The encoded information that is sent over a communications channel (e.g. a letter, an e-mail, a television transmission) and is then interpreted by a receiver.

"A point of view can be a dangerous luxury when substituted for insight and understanding."
~Marshall McLuhan

The term media can also be used in other ways. Often, the word refers to news media (print and online newspapers like *The Toronto Star*, news agencies such as Reuters or Canadian Press, television news channels and services such as CP24, or Fox News). It can also apply to talk shows, movies, online blogs, Wikis, social networking sites, radio programs, and other forms of mediated communication in which the latest issues are discussed. For example, when a high-profile celebrity or person in the news gets married or divorced, that person's relationship gets disputed (sometimes trashed) in all kinds of media forms. From the tabloids you'd find at the checkout stand in the grocery store, to the six o'clock news or the front page of a national newspaper, the same story will appear several times.

Photo by Alice Kieltyka

> "Media literacy is not just important, it's absolutely critical. It's going to make the difference between whether kids are a tool of the mass media or whether the mass media is a tool for kids to use."
> ~ Linda Ellerbee, producer/host, Nick News

Stop and Reflect

Think of the most recent example of a story you've heard involving a famous person, celebrity, or sports figure. What is the story?

_____
_____
_____
_____
_____
_____
_____
_____
_____

Where did you read about it or hear about it?

_____
_____
_____
_____
_____
_____
_____
_____
_____
_____
_____

Courtesy of Shutterstock.

Critical Media Literacy

Critical media literacy is an approach to thinking about media that asks us to "read" media through a critical lens. This approach developed from awareness that media affect and shape how we understand the world. With the speed of communications, especially given what is sometimes referred to as an internet "revolution", the world is flooded by more and more media images, sound bites, and memes.

What are we (as audiences, receivers, and interpreters of these messages) supposed to make of all the media forms around us? How do we navigate the complex webs of stories, images, and meanings all around us? How do we know what to believe and what not to believe? How do we know what issues to focus on? What stories, people, and factors should we pay attention to? What is worthy of our concentration? Critical media literacy gives us the tools to answer these questions, and to move from being passive receivers to active thinkers who can interpret the messages all around us.

Courtesy of Shutterstock.

Provide some examples of media text that you interacted with today:

_____
_____
_____
_____
_____
_____
_____
_____
_____
_____

With which communications medium were those texts circulated?

_____
_____
_____
_____
_____
_____
_____
_____
_____
_____
_____
_____
_____

Critical Media Literacy: Media literacy is the ability to sift through and analyze the messages that inform, entertain and sell to us every day. It's the ability to bring critical thinking skills to bear on all media— from music videos and Web environments to product placement in films and virtual displays on NHL hockey boards. It's about asking pertinent questions about what's there, and noticing what's not there. And it's the instinct to question what lies behind media productions— the motives, the money, the values and the ownership— and to be aware of how these factors influence content (Jane Tallim in Media Awareness Network; www.media-awareness.ca)

One of the best tools critical media literacy gives us is to think about how ALL media communications are put together as text. While we often think of the word "text" as it refers to textbooks, from a critical media literacy perspective, text actually refers to the ways in which meanings are created by combining words, music, images, stories, etc. into a cohesive whole. In this sense, a text can be a movie, a recorded interview, a printed article, a music video, a website – in short, anything that aims to: 1) communicate some kind of message; 2) has been created by a group or individual; and 3) is circulated or sent across some kind of communications medium, for example, the internet. So, if you think about the examples of celebrities or sports figures you wrote in the box above, think about *how* those stories are put together in the different media forms in which they appear. *How* was the story presented? *How* are people discussed? *What* gets said in the media about these people? Inevitably, the answers to how stories are framed by the media help to shape our thoughts about these people and their activities.

> ## Thinking About Framing
>
> If you think of a picture, photo, or a painting inside of a frame, what kind of image comes to your mind?
> What does the frame do to the picture?
> Think about what the frame contains, and what it leaves out.

Framed for Misrepresentation

Take a look at the framed image presented.
What does the image tell you? What information is provided? What message does the image portray?

_____
_____
_____
_____
_____
_____
_____

Courtesy of Shutterstock.

Now take another look, and this time at the entire picture. What does this image tell you? What information is left out in the framed image? How is the message portrayed in this image different from the framed image presented above?

_____
_____
_____
_____
_____
_____
_____

Courtesy of Shutterstock.

Did You Know?

Diversity: Women Are Still Missing as News Sources

Women make up slightly more than half of the population, but you would never know it if your news comes from television, the internet or newspapers.

Women are particularly absent in coverage of politics, the military, and foreign policy, according to a study released in 2005 by the Project for Excellence in Journalism, a Washington-based think tank affiliated with the Columbia University Graduate School of Journalism. Women are most likely to be included in feature stories about children, celebrities and homemaking.

The study examined nearly 17 000 news reports by 45 different news outlets during 20 randomly selected days over 9 months in 2004. Three-quarters of all stories studied contained at least one male source. Just one-third contained a female source. The sourcing gap widened as the number of sources in a story increased. Reporters were more than three times as likely to cite two or more men within a news story as to cite at least two women. "Finding a male as the best first source does not apparently lead a journalist to look for a female as the second or third source," the report said. The worst offenders were cable television and PBS, and newspapers gave women the most exposure.

The dismal trend of using few women as sources in news stories hasn't changed much since it was first studied in 1989. A series of studies beginning that year found that women were mentioned less than 25 percent of the time on the front pages of newspapers, and those who were mentioned were often of a lower socioeconomic status than male sources. A 2000 study of news coverage of the military found that civilian experts and politicians commenting on military stories almost never are women. Research by Canadians Gertrude Robinson and Armande Saint Jean for the International Federation of Journalists echoes the findings of these studies. Their 2001 investigation found that only 28 percent of print journalists and 37 percent of broadcast journalists are female.

The London-based Media Diversity Institute says that women are further discriminated against when they are

Authority Figure A United Nations representative, unusual in being a woman, addresses a refugee crisis in Jordan. Study after study of media coverage find women represented much less in the news than in their growing presence in political, research and academic leadership.

members of minority ethnic communities: "When individuals are mentioned in stories less than 3 percent of them are women, which is three and half times less than men at 35 percent. The majority of women appear in roles that comply with the dominant patriarchal pattern—women are mostly victims and witnesses of events."

Taken from *The Media of Mass Communication*, Fifth Canadian Edition, by John Vivian and Peter J. Maurin

Media Ownership and Regulation

Critical media literacy also asks us to think about commercial and political factors of media ownership and regulation. One of the key issues is the question of who controls the media. If you were to look at media in Canada, for instance, you would see that most of the newspapers, radio stations, and television channels are owned by a few, very large corporations. At time of writing, for instance, CTVglobemedia (which owned the broadcaster, CTV, as well as the national newspaper, *The Globe and Mail,* and numerous specialty channels such as TSN, Business News Network (BNN), Discovery HD, CTV

> *"The medium is the message"*
> ~ Marshall McLuhan
> Understanding Media

Photo by Alice Kieltyka

News Channel) was taken over by BCE Inc. As a result, CTVglobemedia was divided. *The Globe and Mail* returned to its previous owners, Woodbridge Co. Ltd. (which is owned by the Thomson family). According to *The Globe and Mail,* "The marriage of the country's biggest phone company and largest broadcaster is the latest move in an era of convergence among media firms and those who distribute their content" (Ladurantaye, 2010, p. A1). In the United States, the media are also controlled by a handful of corporations: News Corporation, Disney, Time Warner, General Electric, Viacom, and CBS. Disney, for instance, not only produces animated films such as *Toy Story,* but it owns the television network ABC, production companies such as Buena Vista, Touchstone, and Miramax, radio stations, print publications, online sites, and a host of other companies (see http://www.freepress.net/ownership/chart/main).

From a critical media literacy perspective, we have to ask: what issues arise when one company owns so many subsidiaries? One answer to this is called **vertical integration**. When a company produces a product, such as a film or television show, the process of production goes through

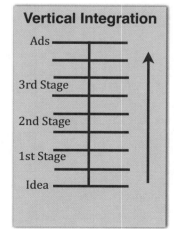

Vertical Integration

Ads

3rd Stage

2nd Stage

1st Stage

Idea

> **Vertical Integration:** Refers to corporate control over the production of media content through the acquisition of smaller media companies into the large corporations.

many stages, from the initial conception or idea for a magazine, TV program, or film, through to the final product that gets released on newsstands or in your local movie theatre. Generally, it takes a number of small companies to help in the process of making a film or TV show, but as more and more companies are taken over by larger corporations, the whole process essentially takes place "in-house". In other words, a corporation such as Disney might have complete control over *every stage* of the production of a new film because of the level of its vertical integration, and its control of so many smaller companies.

Photo by Jared Purdy

But what does all of this have to do with viewers and critical media literacy? The answer lies in the way that the forms of media ownership control the *kinds* of products that are produced. Successes such as Disney's *High School Musical*, for instance, reflect the values, beliefs, and norms so prevalent in all of Disney's products. If you are familiar with this film series, or have seen other Disney movies (animated or live-action), ask yourself: who are the people in these films? What voices are heard? What voices are excluded? Where do the characters live? What happens to them in the story? Chances are, if you scratch the surface of two Disney films, you'll find some of the same character types, storylines, and scenarios depicted in both. The similarities between different Disney products reveal the effects of vertical integration and of media ownership and control.

List your favorite movies and indicate why they are your favorite.

What was the last film or movie you watched?

_____

Who were the characters? Were they male or female?

_____

How many male characters were there compared to female characters and vice versa?

_____

What sorts of people did they portray?

_____

What were their races, cultures, classes, or ethnic backgrounds?

_____

What kinds of jobs or occupations did these characters have?

_____

Where did they live?

_____

Where did the story take place?

_____

What happened in the movie?

_____

Were there winners or losers? If so, who were the winners?

_____
_____

Did You Know? Spike Lee

Spike Lee

Spike Lee (far right)

Spike Lee, a bright, innovative young film director, was in deep trouble in 1992. He had persuaded Warner Brothers, the big Hollywood studio, to put up $20 million for a film biography of controversial black leader Malcolm X, one of Lee's heroes. He insisted on expensive foreign shooting in Cairo and Soweto, and now, not only was the $20 million from Warner gone but so was $8 million from other investors. To finish the movie, Lee put up his own $3 million upfront salary to pay, he hoped, all the production bills.

The crisis was not the first for Lee, whose experience as a moviemaker illustrates several realities about the U.S. movie industry, not all of them flattering:

- Hollywood is the heart of the U.S. movie industry, and it is difficult, if not impossible, for feature filmmakers to succeed outside of the Hollywood establishment.
- Hollywood, with rare exceptions, favours movies that follow themes that already have proven successful rather than taking risks on innovative, controversial themes.
- Fortunes come and go in Hollywood, even studio fortunes. Although Warner is a major studio and often flush with money, it was on an austerity binge when Spike Lee came back for more money in 1992.
- The U.S. movie industry has been taken over by conglomerates, which, as in the case of Warner Brothers, at the time a subsidiary of Time Warner, was being pressured in 1992 to maximize profits to see the parent company through a difficult economic period.

To hear Spike Lee tell it, his problem also was symptomatic of racism in the movie industry. Addressing the Los Angeles Advertising Club during the *Malcolm X* crisis, Lee, who is black, was blunt: "I think there's a ceiling on how much money Hollywood's going to spend on black films or films with a black theme."

Although studio executives would deny Lee's charge, his perceptions were born of experience in making five movies, all critically acclaimed and all profitable but all filmed on shoestring budgets and with little or no studio promotion.

Taken from *The Media of Mass Communication*, Fifth Canadian Edition, by John Vivian and Peter J. Maurin

What Do You Think?

Do you think that Spike Lee's claim of racism in the film industry is true? Why or why not? Think of examples of recent movies you have watched.

_____

_____

_____

_____

_____

_____

_____

_____

_____

> **Bias:** When one particular opinion or perspective takes one side over another. In media, bias refers to the selection of which events and stories are reported and how they are covered (Wikipedia).

Another effect of media ownership is bias. A **bias** is a person (or group of people's) perspective that takes one side over another. So, for instance, if you are a loyal Fido customer because you like the service you receive, but your friend is trying to convince you to switch over to Koodo because he thinks it's cheaper, you might find that your views on mobile services are *biased* by your experiences with Fido. However, when we talk about media bias, the meaning changes a bit. With regards to media, bias generally means that the media form (whether it be internet, TV, a magazine, etc.) contains within it a particular slant or perspective on certain issues. For example, we can state that American and Canadian news media might have certain biases that lead us to focus on particular news items of interest to Americans and Canadians. We might be more likely to hear about healthcare issues in Canada or the United States, than we would about those same issues in Ghana or Turkey, for instance. This is as a result of our media bias towards North American issues.

Photo by Alice Kieltyka

In this respect, bias is tied to issues of media ownership, because "who owns what" plays such a large part in shaping the kinds of images we see, and the sorts of stories that get told. Yet related to this is the issue of regulation. Regulation also determines what we are allowed to see and hear, and what we are not. In Canada, broadcast and telecommunications media are controlled by the Canadian Radio-television and Telecommunications Commission (otherwise known as the CRTC). The price you are charged for your cell phone, for instance, depends on rulings that come from the CRTC. In addition, the number of cell phone companies that are allowed to provide service and products in Canada is also regulated by the CRTC. In terms of broadcasting, companies that want to operate a radio or television station must first apply for a license

> ### The Difficulty of Ethics
>
> *"Mass media organizations have put together codes of ethics that prescribe how practitioners should go about their work. Although useful in many ways, these codes neither sort through the bedeviling problems that result from conflicting prescriptions nor help much when the only available options are negative."*
>
> In The Media of Mass Communication, by Vivian, J. & Maurin, P.J. (2007), Pearson Publishers, pg. 244.

from the CRTC. In addition, companies that want to buy or take over other companies must also get approval from the CRTC. For example, in 2007, the CRTC approved CTVglobemedia's purchase of CHUM (a Canadian company that owns many radio and television stations). Yet the CRTC wanted to limit the control CTVglobemedia had over broadcasting in Canada. Basically, the CRTC didn't want one company to own too much. So, the CRTC blocked CTV from owning *all* of CHUM. Many of CHUM's local television stations, including Toronto's CityTV, were sold to CTV's rival, Rogers Communications (see CRTC Broadcasting Decision 2007-165, http://www.crtc.gc.ca/eng/archive/2007/db2007-165.htm).

How much we pay for internet service, what we see and hear on our radios and televisions, and what we are given access to very much depends on how our government (through its regulatory arm, the CRTC) decides what we, as citizens and residents of Canada, can and cannot have access to. If we were to look critically at a basic television cable package, for instance, we would probably see that we have access to a number of Canadian television stations (CBC, CTV, Global, TVO, CityTV) as well as a number of American stations (Fox, CBS, ABC, NBC). Now ask yourself: what channels do you have to pay for? What channels are considered a necessary part of basic cable? What channels are left out? How the government regulates access to communication also affects how we learn about the world.

> As critical media consumers, why is it important to be aware of and consider media bias when interpreting media messages?
> _____
> _____
> _____
> _____
> _____
> _____
> _____
> _____

When **regulation** and media ownership are considered together, we enter another area central to any analysis of the media: **ideology**. An ideology can be viewed as a set of beliefs, or way of thinking that shapes how a person sees the world. Ideologies are always linked to power, because they give power to some groups, thoughts, actions, or behaviors while denying power to others.

Regulation: The rules and guidelines that set limits and determine policies relevant to the organization of media and communications.

Ideology: A set of beliefs, or way of thinking that shapes how a person sees the world.

Ideologies are also thought to be powerful because it is often difficult to see how they work, and to recognize when people are looking at the world from an ideological perspective. For instance, the CRTC requires that Canadian broadcasters maintain a minimum percentage of Canadian content on Canadian airwaves. What does this say about Canada's view of broadcasting? Why would Canada have this policy? What interests are being protected by this policy? Clearly, the CRTC regulation on Canadian Content (or "CanCon" as it is known) reveals an ideology in which Canada, and Canadian culture needs to be protected.

> *"I saw themselves as others had seen them. They had been formed by the images made of them by those who had the deepest necessity to despise them. "*
> ~ James Baldwin, writer and civil rights activist

Photo by Alice Kieltyka

Media regulations therefore show us that ideologies are at work in deciding what we can and cannot watch, listen to, or see. And to return to our discussion of bias, we can also think about how ideologies reveal bias. How is this possible? If the CRTC regulation on "CanCon" shows us that we need to protect Canadian culture, then is it possible that the media in Canada will be *biased* towards content, shows,

> *"Representation is the way in which meaning is given to the things depicted "*
> ~ Stuart Hall

programs, media sources, etc. that are *Canadian*? And then our next question might be: but what constitutes *Canadian*? This is an important question, for it leads us to another important topic regarding bias, and that is how the media illustrate certain biases in terms of representation.

Representation: (In Media) Refers to how people, events, places, and stories, are portrayed on television, the internet, on the radio, or in newspapers.

Representation in the media refers to how people, events, places, and stories, are portrayed on television, the internet, on the radio, or in newspapers. Think back to the celebrity story you identified above. How was the story first depicted in the media? How were people characterized or portrayed? Portrayal is one aspect of representation, but another aspect is the question of *who* gets talked about, what events are selected as newsworthy, and what are not. Representation therefore also shows bias because it's in the way people, events, and stories are portrayed, and what is included and what is not, that a slant towards one perspective or another is revealed.

Consider the example of Hurricane Katrina. When that story first broke, images of the tourist sections of New Orleans were shown. What wasn't shown (at first, at least) were images of the poorer areas affected by the disaster. The mainstream media were not yet interested in the stories of devastation that affected the poor, and predominantly Black communities. When the mainstream media *did* pick up on the stories, these communities were sometimes depicted as "dangerous" areas, characterized by looting and other criminal activities. One outcome of these media portrayals was that many of the mainstream media sources were strongly criticized for their biased reporting and presentation of the events and people affected. Yet the point about all of this is that the media contained certain inherent biases based on prejudice, stereotypes, and racism that pit some groups of people against others. Does this mean that people who work in the media are all biased and prejudiced? No, it does not. But as an institution, the media itself contains within it particular stories, and ways of looking at the world, so that people may consciously or unconsciously tell those stories, and *represent* the news along these biased lines.

JOURNALISTS' PERSONAL VALUES AND BIASES

"As gatekeepers, journalists make important decisions on which events, phenomena and issues are reported and which are not. The personal values that journalists bring to their work and that therefore determine which stories are told - and also how they are told - generally coincide with mainstream values."

In The Media of Mass Communication, by Vivian, J. & Maurin, P.J. (2007), Pearson Publishers, pg. 156.

Photo by Alice Kieltyka

Finally, we might ask ourselves why the media are impacted by regulation, ownership, representation, bias, and the production of text. Why do all these factors come into play when we think about the media? One of the most important things we can say about media, and a key factor that we should always keep in our minds, is that no matter what type of media we're thinking of (internet, radio, TV, movies, magazines, etc.), the media are always shaped and determined by commercial interests. That is, the media exist to make money. Even news programs and newspapers are affected by the importance of advertising sales for TV, radio, and internet, and print ads for newspapers. For instance, you can watch any given TV news station, and the newscast will be occasionally interrupted for commercial breaks. Why is this? Because the news wouldn't exist without commercials. Even all-news channels such as CP24 and CTVNewsNet are affected by the sale of advertising time. So, a basic premise in media production is the question of: will it sell? When we add this to the mix of factors regarding media and the production of meanings, images, and stories, we begin to realize that the media messages should not be taken at face value, and we should always be conscious of the kinds of messages the media have offered us.

Did You Know?

Television programming is all about bringing audiences to advertisers. What other kinds of commercial interests do you see in media?

Highlights about Canadian Television

Canadians could choose from 685 television services in 2007, including 456 English-language services, 103 French-language services and 126 services in other languages. In 2007, Canadians watched an average of 26.8 hours of television per week. Canadian television services attracted 98.5% of the French-language viewing audience in Quebec and 74.9% of the viewing audience in the rest f the country. Commercial television revenues increased 4.3%, or $218 million, from $5 billion in 2006 to $5.3 billion in 2007. This was largely due to increased subscriber revenues of $152 million.

From "Facts and Figures" page, CRTC website.

Calvin and Hobbes

by Bill Watterson

Courtesy of Universal UClick.

EVENTS THAT CONTRIBUTE TO SOCIAL CHANGE

Event: The Impact of Social Media on Traditional News Coverage

WHEN: 2004 +

WHERE: Globally

WHAT: Social media is changing the way news events are communicated, providing opportunities for new and multiple perspectives, and real-time transmission.

Compiled by Sarah Duffy

Facebook was launched in February 2004, Flickr in 2004, YouTube in 2005, Twitter in 2006 (Wikipedia, n.d.). We are living in a time that is influenced by social media. How have these and other forms of social media changed our lives and impacted the ways in which news is reported? According to mobile expert and CEO of Polar Mobile, Kunal Gupta, "Social media and news media have effectively merged into one continuum. In a world where the likes of Twitter, Facebook, email and mobile messaging services such as SMS connect people in real-time, most people can't imagine having to wait more than a day or so to receive their updates. The advent of social media broke the monopoly news media held on story-telling and has turned every consumer into a potential publisher offering much more timely access to certain types of stories." (Chris Hogg, 2010).

Social Media Strategist, Mark Evans, agrees with this perspective and discusses the impact of social media on the traditional media industry. In Evan's opinion, "It's important to explore the intersection of social media and traditional media because of the major structural changes that have happened over the past five years. Social media has democratized the creation and distribution of news, destroying the tight grip that traditional media had for decades. At the same time, social media has hammered the financial underpinnings of traditional media, forcing the major players to restructure to compete and remain viable." (Chris Hogg, 2010).

The use of social media is increasing. As found in a recent Neilson Company study, released in August 2010, Americans spend 22.7 percent of their time online on social networking sites and blogs, up from 15.8 percent in 2009 (a 43 percent increase). (What Americans Do Online, 2010).

While accuracy, objectivity and quality of news stories may be impacted by these quick, real time mediums, the accessibility and grass-roots nature of news coverage is proving to be popular and its impact will likely continue into the foreseeable future.

Hogg, Chris. (2010, August). *Experts weigh-in on future of media, impact of mobile devices.* Retrieved from Digital Journal's website: http://www.digitaljournal.com/article/296169.

What Americans Do Online: Social Media And Games Dominate Activity. (August, 2010). Retrieved from http://blog.nielsen.com/nielsenwire/online_mobile/what-americans-do-online-social-media-and-games-dominate-activity/

Evaluate the Message

Courtesy of Benetton USA Corp.

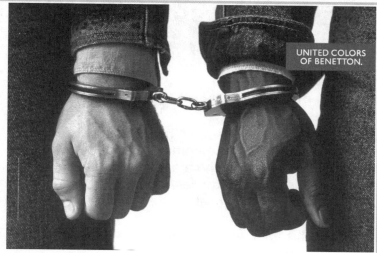

This photograph, produced by the United Colors of Benetton, was part of an advertising campaign to show that all of us are linked together regardless of skin color. However, many people's interpretation of this image points to the influence of their cultural biases. In their eyes, this picture shows a White police officer escorting a Black criminal.

© Copyright 1989 Benetton Group S.p.A.—Photo: Oliviero Toscani

What message do you get out of this advertisement?

_____

_____

_____

_____

What is it that makes you interpret this advertisement in such a way?

_____

_____

_____

_____

Why do you think that Benetton chose to use this kind of image to advertise its product? Benetton is an expensive clothing line. How does this ad sell the clothing? Or does it?

_____

_____

_____

_____

Critical media literacy helps us to ask these kinds of questions, and to interrogate the media and its messages. It is an approach that asks us to think about our own roles as audiences of the media, and to think about how we engage with media, the kinds of media forms we relate to, and the inherent biases, ideologies, commercial, and regulatory factors that come in to play in this array of media texts available to us. So next time you're watching a movie, looking for something online, or listening to the radio in your car or on the TTC, try to be more aware of what you're looking at and listening to. It just may be that you'll find yourself beginning to use your new critical media literacy awareness!

Getting Engaged: Activities

Deepening Your Media Literacy

How can you become more media literate?

Think of your favorite commercial on television

Dig Deeper: People who are media literate consume media with a critical eye. They evaluate sources, intended purposes, techniques and deeper meanings. Answer these questions about your favorite commercial:

Why is this ad effective? Write a list of the persuasive techniques used.

_____

_____

_____

_____

Who is the intended audience? Who will benefit from this commercial?

_____

_____

Does it sell more than a product?

_____

_____

Does it help you to identify any social values? Which ones? Does it glamorize a way of life? Does it bind a community?

_____

_____

_____

_____

How does it attempt to shape our perception of reality?

_____

_____

What is the elitist view of this TV ad? What is the populist view?

_____

_____

What signs (icons and symbols) are used in this ad?

_____

In Vivian, J. & Maurin, P.J. (2007) The Media of Mass Communication. Pearson, Toronto, p. 31.

What Do You Think?

Media are most powerful when they operate at an emotional level. Do you think most viewers would be able to separate fact from fantasy in your favorite commercial? Does your favorite commercial tell you anything truly useful about the product? Do you think it is fair for a commercial to attempt to shape our behavior or attitudes?

Discuss these questions in a small group.

Notes:

_____
_____
_____
_____
_____
_____
_____
_____
_____
_____
_____
_____
_____
_____
_____
_____
_____
_____
_____
_____
_____
_____
_____
_____
_____
_____
_____
_____
_____
_____
_____

In Vivian, J. & Maurin, P.J. (2007) The Media of Mass Communication. Pearson, Toronto, p. 31.

Prime Time Television and Racial Diversity Audit

In this activity you will be assessing how well prime-time television reflects racial diversity in Canada.

Step 1: Watch prime-time (i.e., evening) drama, action or comedy television shows (excluding sports and news) for a 2-3 hour period or watch multiple episodes of the same show. While you are watching, record the prominence of roles played by TV characters from various representation groups. Make one check mark for each character you find in each category. (See below for definitions of characters.) In addition, indicate whether the characters are male or female.

Representative Groups	Opening Credits		Main Characters		Secondary Characters (Characters that might not appear in every episode)	
	M	F	M	F	M	F

Adapted from Media Awareness Network, media-awareness.ca

Step 2: Review your data from the diversity audit. Consider the following questions:

What types of roles are played by different groups in the show(s) that you watched?

_____
_____
_____
_____

Did you notice any patterns in the roles played by certain ethnic groups?

_____
_____
_____
_____

How are men and women portrayed in these shows? Does this differ by ethnic group?

_____
_____
_____
_____

Do you think that the shows reflect the diversity in Canada?

_____
_____
_____
_____

When you're thinking about various representative groups of people in popular entertainment, consider the following:

- Are the portrayals realistic?
- Are positive and negative roles distributed equally?
- Do people of color have main roles, or are they only bit players?
- Where people of color are cast because of their race or ethnicity, is this casting appropriate or relevant to the story?
- Are non-white characters portrayed in a rich and complex manner, and shown in a variety of roles?
- Why is this important to think about?

_____
_____
_____
_____
_____
_____
_____
_____

Adapted from Media Awareness Network, media-awareness.ca

How to Detect Bias in the News (mediaawareness.ca)

At one time or other we all complain about "bias in the news." The fact is, despite the journalistic ideal of "objectivity," every news story is influenced by the attitudes and background of its interviewers, writers, photographers and editors. Not all bias is deliberate. But you can become a more aware news reader or viewer by watching for the following journalistic techniques that allow bias to "creep in" to the news

Instructions:

1. Review the following descriptions of the types of bias that can be found in the news.
2. In your group, review the newspaper or magazine provided by your instructor.
3. Identify 3-5 examples of bias and be prepared to share with the class.

Bias through selection and omission - An editor can express a bias by choosing to use or not to use a specific news item. Within a given story, some details can be ignored, and others included, to give readers or viewers a different opinion about the events reported. If, during a speech, a few people boo, the reaction can be described as "remarks greeted by jeers" or they can be ignored as "a handful of dissidents." Bias through omission is difficult to detect. Only by comparing news reports from a wide variety of outlets can the form of bias be observed.

Bias through placement Readers of papers judge first page stories to be more significant than those buried in the back. Television and radio newscasts run the most important stories first and leave the less significant for later. Where a story is placed, therefore, influences what a reader or viewer thinks about its importance.

Bias by headline - Many people read only the headlines of a news item. Most people scan nearly all the headlines in a newspaper. Headlines are the most-read part of a paper. They can summarize as well as present carefully hidden bias and prejudices. They can convey excitement where little exists. They can express approval or condemnation.

Bias by photos, captions and camera angles - Some pictures flatter a person, others make the person look unpleasant. A paper can choose photos to influence opinion about, for example, a candidate for election. On television, the choice of which visual images to display is extremely important. The captions newspapers run below photos are also potential sources of bias.

Bias by photos, captions and camera angles - Some pictures flatter a person, others make the person look unpleasant. A paper can choose photos to influence opinion about, for example, a candidate for election. On television, the choice of which visual images to display is extremely important. The captions newspapers run below photos are also potential sources of bias.

Adapted from Media Awareness Network, media-awareness.ca

How to Detect Bias in the News (mediaawareness.ca)

Bias through use of names and titles News media often use labels and titles to describe people, places, and events. A person can be called an "ex-con" or be referred to as someone who "served time twenty years ago for a minor offence." Whether a person is described as a "terrorist" or a "freedom fighter" is a clear indication of editorial bias.

Bias through statistics and crowd counts To make a disaster seem more spectacular (and therefore worthy of reading about), numbers can be inflated. "A hundred injured in air crash" can be the same as "only minor injuries in air crash," reflecting the opinion of the person doing the counting. Bias by source control To detect bias, always consider where the news item "comes from." Is the information supplied by a reporter, an eyewitness, police or fire officials, executives, or elected or appointed government officials? Each may have a particular bias that is introduced into the story. Companies and public relations directors supply news outlets with puff pieces through news releases, photos or videos. Often news outlets depend on pseudo-events (demonstrations, sit-ins, ribbon cuttings, speeches and ceremonies) that take place mainly to gain news coverage.

Bias through word choice and tone Showing the same kind of bias that appears in headlines, the use of positive or negative words or words with a particular connotation can strongly influence the reader or viewer.

Notes:

_____
_____
_____
_____
_____
_____
_____
_____
_____
_____
_____
_____
_____
_____

Adapted from Media Awareness Network, media-awareness.ca

Chapter Summary

Definitions:

Bias: When one particular opinion or perspective takes one side over another. In media, bias refers to the selection of which events and stories are reported and how they are covered (Wikipedia).

Critical Media Literacy: Media literacy is the ability to sift through and analyze the messages that inform, entertain and sell to us every day. It's the ability to bring critical thinking skills to bear on all media— from music videos and Web environments to product placement in films and virtual displays on NHL hockey boards. It's about asking pertinent questions about what's there, and noticing what's not there. And it's the instinct to question what lies behind media productions— the motives, the money, the values and the ownership— and to be aware of how these factors influence content (Jane Tallim in Media Awareness Network; www.media-awareness.ca)

Ideology: A set of beliefs, or way of thinking that shapes how a person sees the world.

Media: Refers to television, internet, radio, advertising, newspapers, books, magazines, and any form of mediated communication.

Medium: Is the means by which a message is sent. It is what enables a message to travel from a sender to a receiver.

Message: The encoded information that is sent over a communications channel (e.g.. a letter, an e-mail, a television transmission) and is then interpreted by a receiver.

Regulation: The rules and guidelines that set limits and determine policies relevant to the organization of media and communications.

Representation: (In Media) Refers to how people, events, places, and stories, are portrayed on television, the internet, on the radio, or in newspapers.

Vertical Integration: Refers to corporate control over the production of media content through the acquisition of smaller media companies into the large corporations.

Main Concepts:

- Exploring the term "media" and the importance of media literacy for Global Citizens
- Developing an understanding of critical media literacy and its scope
- Identifying the implications of media ownership and the impact of regulation
- Recognizing the prevalence of bias and stereotypes in many forms of media

Additional Resources

Media Awareness Network (Canadian) www.media-awareness.ca

Description: This website is home to one of the world's most comprehensive collections of media literacy and digital literacy resources (source: www.media-awareness.ca).

The Association for Media Literacy (Canadian) - www.aml.ca

Description: The Association for Media Literacy is made up of teachers, librarians, consultants, parents, cultural workers, and media professionals concerned about the impact of the mass media on contemporary culture. This website provides links to articles and other resources on the topic of media literacy (source: www. aml.ca).

Media literacy.com (American) - www.medialiteracy.com

Description: The mission of this website is to increase awareness of the need for media literacy education and of the many resources available for teaching it (source: www.medialiteracy.com).

Centre for Media Literacy (American) - www.medialit.org

Description: The Center for Media Literacy (CML) is dedicated to a new vision of literacy for the 21st Century: the ability to communicate competently in all media forms as well as to access, understand, analyse, evaluate and participate with powerful images, words and sounds that make up our contemporary mass media culture. Indeed, we believe these skills of media literacy are essential for both children and adults as individuals and as citizens of a democratic society (source: www.medialit.org)

References

Andersen, N. (2010). "Media Literacy and Media Education". Retrieved July 5, 2010 from Media Awareness Network http://www.media-awareness.ca/english/teachers/media_literacy/what_is_media_literacy.cfm

Bucher, R.D. (2008) *Building Cultural Intelligence (CQ): Nine Mega Skills.* New Jersey: Pearson Publishers, p. 58.

Baldwin, J. Media Quote. In Mack, T. & Picower, B. (2009). *Planning to Change the World: A Plan Book for Social Justice Teachers.* New York: New York Collective of Radical Educators and the Education for Liberation Network. p. 85

CBC. (1999) Out of Orbit: The Life and Times of Marshall McLuhan. Retrieved on October 2, 2010 from http://www.cbc.ca/lifeandtimes/mcluhan.html

CRTC. (Date Unknown) Broadcasting Decision 2007. Retrieved on September 8, 2010 from http://www.crtc.gc.ca/eng/home-accueil.htm

CRTC. (Date Unknown) Facts and Figures. Retrieved on September 8, 2010 from http://www.crtc.gc.ca/eng/home

Digital Journal. (2010) Experts weigh in on future of media, impact of mobile devices. Retrieved on October 2, 2010 from http://www.digitaljournal.com/article/296169

Ellerbee, L. (Date Unknown) Media Quote. Retrieved on October 1, 2010 from http://www.frankwbaker.com/Media_Lit_Quotes.html

Free Press. (Date Unknown). Ownership Chart: The Big 6. Retrieved on September 8, 2010 from http://www.freepress.net/ownership/chart/main

Gibson, T. (2000) Marshall McLuhan: The Three Fundamental Innovations in Technology. The McLuhan Program in Culture and Technology, University of Toronto. Retrieved on October 2, 2010 from http://www.utoronto.ca/mcluhan/tsc_mcluhan_basic_innovations.htm

Hall, S. (1997). [video] *Representation and the Media.* Dir. Sut Jhally. Media Education Foundation

History by the Minute. (Date Unknown) Innovators: Marshall McLuhan. Retrieved on October 2, 2010 from http://www.histori.ca/minutes/minute.do?id=10226

Ladurantaye. (2010) Globe and Mail, p. A1.

McLuhan, M. Media Quote. Retrieved October 1, 2010 from http://www.brainyquote.com/quotes/quotes/m/marshallmc135184.html

McLuhan, M. (1964/1997). *Understanding Media: The Extensions of Man.* Cambridge: The MIT Press.

Media Awareness Network. (Date Unknown) *Prime Time Television and Diversity Audit Activity*. Retrieved on September 20, 2010 from www.media-awareness.ca

Media Awareness Network. (Date Unknown) *How to Detect Bias in the News*. Retrieved on September 20, 2010 from www.media-awareness.ca

Nielson Wire. (2010). What Americans do on-line: Social media and games dominate activity. Retrieved on October 2, 2010 from http://blog.nielsen.com/nielsenwire/online_mobile/what-americans-do-online-social-media-and-games-dominate-activity/

Tallim, J. (Date Unknown) Critical Media Literacy. Media Awareness Network. Retrieved on October 1, 2010 from www.media-awareness.ca

Vivian, J. & Maurin, P.J. (2007). *The Media of Mass Communication*. Toronto: Pearson Publishers, p. 31, 53, 156, 161, 215, 244.

Wikipedia. (Date Unknown) Bias definition. Retrieved on September 25, 2010 from http://en.wikipedia.org/wiki/Bias

Notes

CHAPTER 5

Who Am I? Who Are We?: Exploring Our Identities as Global Citizens

Renee M. Sgroi and Khalid Ali

Courtesy of Shutterstock.

CHAPTER OBJECTIVES:

- Exploring dimensions of identity and identity construction

- Understanding the intersectionality of identity

- Investigating how identity and values are connected

Introduction

In today's world, we often hear the words "identity" and "identification" used in different ways. We have to protect ourselves from credit card and online identity theft. We may hear about a crime in which the identity of the victims or criminals is not revealed. At school, you are not allowed to write an exam without proper identification or "ID". If you are nineteen, you may be asked for ID when going to a club or having a drink in a bar. You might read about a celebrity's social activities in the news and discover that this person is undergoing an "identity crisis". While these examples all relate to the term "identity", the concept of identity is different in each example. How then can we begin to define identity? What *is identity?*

The self is "a subject in process, a subject as verb."
~Bronwyn Davies (1997, p. 274)

Let's start by considering the following scenario: You are at an airport in a country that is unfamiliar to you. You do not speak the language, and you are lost. There are many people around you, all speaking a foreign language. All of a sudden, you hear someone speaking your native tongue. Not only does this person speak your language, but it is the same regional dialect that you speak. You automatically turn to talk to this person. Why? What is it that draws you to this person? What is it about this person that makes you feel comfortable, so that you have no hesitations about saying "hello"?

"In common sense language, identification is constructed on the back of a recognition of some common origin or shared characteristics with another person or group, or with an ideal."
~Stuart Hall (1996, p. 2)

First, you are drawn by the language. Region and geography come next, then there's history, culture, and socio-economic structures. For example, chances are that if you are from the same geographical region, you will speak the same regional dialect and may share knowledge of similar slang words or phrases. There will also be other identifiable markers, such as dress or appearance, the way you might walk quickly or slowly, your body language and so on. You might be of the same gender, race, and/or ethnicity. Perhaps you share the same sexual orientation.

Courtesy of Shutterstock.

You might have been born in the same place. You will share an understanding of the events that have taken place in this area. You will also have been exposed to similar kinds of social and economic policies that have influenced how you were raised. These factors contribute to a sense of familiarity.

But what if the scenario changed? What if you did not encounter this person in this busy airport? What factors would contribute to the sense of difference you feel? How would you deal with the sense of isolation and unfamiliarity that you experienced from the start? Once again, you're faced with the issue of language. What about culture? Region? Geography? Dress? Appearance? Body language? What about the history of this country? Do these factors convey *similarities* or *differences*?

Stop and Reflect

Think of a situation in which you were around individuals from your racial, ethnic, or cultural background. How did you feel? What made you feel this way?

_____
_____
_____
_____
_____
_____

Now think of a situation in which you were around individuals who were from a racial, ethnic, or cultural background that was different from your own. How did you feel? What made you feel this way?

_____
_____
_____
_____
_____
_____
_____
_____
_____

Courtesy of Shutterstock.

Identity: Some Definitions

Whether or not you have actually found yourself in this type of scenario, the issue here is about how we, as groups and as individuals, make identifications in our lives. In other words, how do we know who we are? Who am I? What am I? Why? What helps us to know who we are? What helps us to say, "I am this, but I'm not that"? To answer these questions, we have

> **Identity:** The distinguishing character or personality of an individual (Merriam-Webster Dictionary).

to think about **identity**, and how we define or explain that term. Identity is not about your legal standing as a citizen or landed immigrant. It is not about your social insurance number, your height, your eye or hair colour, or your address. What is identity then?

Photo by Alice Kieltyka

According to Rummens (1993), "The term identity comes from the French word identité that has its linguistic roots in the Latin noun *identitas* ... meaning 'the same.' The term is thus essentially comparative in nature, as it emphasizes the sharing of a degree of sameness or oneness with others of a particular characteristic." (qtd. in Rummens

> Think of a time when you may have travelled to your country of birth or your parents' country of birth. How were you perceived by the locals?
>
> _____
> _____
> _____
> _____
>
> What kinds of privileges were you seen to possess?
>
> _____
> _____
> _____
>
> What kinds of privileges were you thought to lack?
>
> _____
> _____
> _____
> _____

2003, p. 12).   In other words, identity is concerned with whether or not we see ourselves as similar to others or different. Woodward (1997) argues that there are several components that explain the concept identity. She believes that identity involves: 1) the idea that identities are based on difference; 2) the belief that identities can be defined in relation to the kinds of materials we buy or use, and how we feel those products express our identities; 3) social and political processes, such as an identification with a region, or language group that does not have political representation at a state level (for instance, in Canada the French language as it gets represented outside of Québec); 4) a recognition that identities are never fully formed, and can change over time; and 5) an awareness that our identities have an impact on our emotional and psychological health, because identity provides a sense of belonging (p. 12).

By looking at identity in these ways, as global citizens we can add further dimensions to the concept of identity. First, we can talk about the social process we all go through in defining who we are. Consider, for instance, some of the categories mentioned above: language, history, culture, dress, body language, and geography. What about other categories such as religion? Nationality? Traditions? Customs? Faith? Symbols? Sexuality? Race? Ethnicity? Gender? Let's think about how we learn these categories. Take language, for example. How do we learn to talk? Do we acquire language by ourselves? Or do we learn it from others? What about clothing? Where do we learn what is appropriate and not appropriate in terms of the clothes we put onto our bodies? What about traditions? Where do we learn what traditions to follow? Where do we learn how to prepare that special, once-a-year dinner for a particular religious holiday or festival? Why do we do these things?

Courtesy of Shutterstock.

Now that you have been given a definition of identity, think about what identity means to you.

_____
_____
_____
_____

How would you define identity?

_____
_____
_____
_____
_____
_____

The Social Construction of Identity

We learn about aspects of our identities in social contexts, from family, friends, and our communities. This is a process we call *socialization*. Thus, we can say that we *adopt* our identities in relation to the kinds of traditions, languages, customs, clothing, and practices that we grow up with. In other words, we can define identity as a *social* process, as one that occurs in a *social* context, and is socially **constructed**. Although the construction of identity occurs in a social context, we can also speak about identity as it relates to personal aspects of our beings. In this sense, **social identity** is about how we see ourselves as individuals who are members of *groups,* and how we are perceived by *others* both inside and outside the group, whereas personal identity has more to do with how we see ourselves as individuals.

Social Identity: How we see ourselves as individuals who are members of *groups*, and how we are perceived by *others* both inside and outside the group.

Construction: The way in which something is created or formed. *Social construction* of identity refers to the ways in which society contributes to and shapes the formation of your identity.

Forming one's *social identity* is an evolving process that goes through different phases of development as one goes through life. From this basis we develop our independence as individuals. In addition, our identities change over time, as we change and grow across the span of our lifetimes.

Photo by Alice Kieltyka

We are also subjected to external, social influences independent of groups or communities. For instance, do the media have an influence on how we define ourselves? How do we shape our identities in relation to the clothes we wear, the hairstyles that are considered fashionable, the shoes we wear, or the cars we drive? What about the technological gadgets we purchase? What does it say about you if your cellphone is outdated? Or if you've never heard of an iPhone or iPad? The choices we make with regards to clothing, fashion, cars, technology, and so on, very much reflect how we understand our emerging personal identities (especially in relation to consumption).

Photo by Jared Purdy

Thinking about ourselves in terms of our social identities helps us to see that we are made up of multiple different aspects, such as: culture, religion, ethnicity, consumer patterns, family, nation, sexual identity, race, gender, class, language, place of origin, region, and so on. When you think about your own identity, would you say that you identify with only one of the characteristics listed here? Or would more than one apply to you? If you found that your place of origin, your first language, or your family's first language, and your race, for instance, have something to do with how you see yourself, then you are recognizing that your identity is not permanent, or stamped upon you in a fixed way, and that instead, it is made up of several different parts.

THE SOCIAL FORMATION OF YOU

Make a list of the parts of your identity that have been shaped by your family, friends, and community.

_____

_____

_____

_____

_____

_____

_____

> *"To be revolutionary is to be original, to know where we came from, to validate what is ours and help it to flourish, the best of what is ours, of our beginnings, our principles, and to leave behind what no longer serves us."*
> ~ Inés Hernández-Ávila Native American/Chicana writer and activist

If our identities are not fixed, that is, if they change, then we also have to recognize that there are other, external factors that work to shape how we see ourselves, and how we identify ourselves. One of these aspects of social identity is the state, that is, the geographical and political boundaries that define a place, such as Canada. State and institutional policies shape how we see ourselves as citizens of a particular country. For example, we can think about patriotism, and the kinds of symbols and rituals we practice and engage in, that make us feel patriotic towards our country.   In Canada, for instance, we sing our national anthem, "O Canada", and we stand at attention when the Canadian flag is raised. In the United States, slogans such as "the land of the free" and "the home of the brave" are circulated within the media and popular culture to encourage that spirit of patriotism to the U.S. state.

But what if we start to consider for whom and for what purpose this patriotism plays out? Think, for example, about the Molson Canadian ads that centered on the phrase "I am Canadian". How do we know what is Canadian? How can we define this term? What is the *Canadian* way?

Courtesy of Shutterstock.

CANADIAN IDENTITY

What does it mean to be Canadian?

_____

_____

_____

_____

_____

Canada is a multicultural country. In light of this comment, do you think that there is one specific Canadian identity?

_____

_____

_____

_____

_____

_____

Who decides what it means to be Canadian?

_____

_____

_____

_____

_____

Courtesy of Shutterstock.

Answering this question is difficult. Aboriginal peoples were here long before European explorers arrived, and the history of Canada's development as a country is characterized by the immigration of peoples from around the world. Given this history, it may be difficult to define a "Canadian" way, except to say that Canada is a country very much defined by multiculturalism. *Multiculturalism*, as a policy, was adopted in Canada in the late 1960s and early 1970s, and opened the immigration rules so that people from all over the world could settle in Canada. As a social policy, multiculturalism promotes diversity, and respect for the cultures, languages, and traditions that people have brought to our country, so that we have the freedom to retain our cultural identities while still remaining Canadian. Yet, in English-speaking Canada (as opposed to Québec), many people nevertheless make reference to a *dominant culture*. A dominant culture refers to the group or groups who represent the majority of people in a particular region. For instance, we would say that in Canada, the dominant culture is English speaking (as opposed to French, which is primarily spoken in Québec as a first language). But what if you came to Canada from a place where English was not the first language spoken? How would you feel? How would you try to fit in with the dominant culture around you? Or, imagine that you have come to Toronto from a smaller community in Ontario, or elsewhere in Canada. What would you do to make yourself fit in with the people around you? Or would you even attempt it?

It is important to consider these questions as they speak to other, significant aspects of identity. When people come to a new country or new community, do they see themselves as: *assimilated, hyphenated, or separated/isolated*? Someone who *assimilates* into the dominant culture

Assimilate: To fully become a part of the dominant culture; taking on the culture, language, and customs of the dominant group, to a greater or lesser extent.

Hyphenate: To merge together the cultures of more than one cultural, enthic, and or linguistic group.

becomes a part of it, and does not necessarily see cultural, racial, or ethnic differences between him or herself and the mainstream culture. Consider, for instance, that in the United States, the metaphor used to describe patterns of immigration is referred to as a "*melting pot*". What this means is that people who immigrate to the U.S. become American, and this identity takes precedence over any other national or ethnic identity. By contrast, Canada has been referred to as a "*mixing bowl*" where people maintain the identities of their places of origin. Thus, in Canada, many people identify themselves as *hyphenated* Canadians, such as Jamaican-Canadian, Greek-Canadian, Tamil-Canadian,

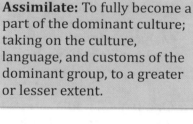

and so on. The third possibility is that people do not assimilate fully, and they do not see themselves as hyphenated either. Instead, they view themselves as completely *separate* or *isolated* from the dominant culture.

Separate/Isolate: To be completely apart from or feel unassociated with a cultural, ethnic, and/or linguistic group.

Courtesy of Shutterstock.

Regardless of whether people see themselves as assimilated, hyphenated, or separated/isolated, there will no doubt be a period when people feel alienated and alone from mainstream culture. Can our social identity contribute to differences between people? Consider for a moment how you felt when you were not recognized, accepted, treated equally, marginalized, valued or empowered. What does it feel like to be overlooked, ignored, shunned, left out, rejected, discriminated against, insulted, or denied opportunities to move forward in life?

Courtesy of Shutterstock.

I Am Proud to Be Bilingual
by Monica Thao, 4th grade student

I am very proud to be bilingual and do not agree with the idea of having to give up my first language and culture. I live in a home where I eat different food, listen to different music and speak a different language. I am my grandparents' little angel who talked to them in Hmong everyday when I was young. At age four, I had a fever that affected my language ability. My teacher worried about me pronouncing English wrong. Mommy referred me to speech, and Daddy didn't let me take Hmong class. I was supposed to speak only English.

One night, I had a dream that my eighty-year-old grandmother was dying. I said I loved her, but it was in English. I struggled word by word in Hmong. She was gone before I finished saying I loved her. I cried in my dream. I told Daddy I must go to Hmong class. I was born bilingual from the beginning. My first language and culture give me strength to make up myself. How can I live in two cultures and speak only one language? My life will be more beautiful and interesting if I speak both Hmong and English.

In Rethinking Our Classrooms: Teaching for Equity and Justice, Volume 2, Bigelow, B., Harvey, B., Karp, S., & Miller, L. (2001). Rethinking Schools Ltd., p. 32.

Stop and Reflect

An individual's identity is made up of so many different parts. When you are in a new environment where your identity does not match that of the dominant group, how do you feel?

_____
_____
_____
_____
_____
_____
_____
_____
_____

How do your feelings impact on your sense of yourself as an individual?

_____
_____
_____
_____
_____
_____
_____
_____
_____
_____
_____

AGENTS OF SOCIAL CHANGE: GLOBAL CITIZENS IN ACTION

Activist: Emily Howard Stowe

1831 - 1903
Activist for Woman's Rights, First Canadian Female Doctor
Canada

Compiled by Sarah Duffy

Emily Howard Stowe was born in Ontario in 1831. She was educated at home by her mother and went onto become a school teacher and the first female public school principal in Upper Canada (Ontario). She left teaching to raise a family but needed to return to work after her husband became sick with tuberculosis. In 1865, she decided she would like to become a doctor and applied to the Toronto School of Medicine. She was not accepted and was told by the university's Vice-President, ""The doors of the University are not open to women and I trust they never will be." (Dr Emily Howard Stowe). She was, however, able to attend college in New York and completed her degree in 1867 at the New York Medical College for Women, a homeopathic institution in the city of New York. After returning to Canada, she set up practice but was forced to return to medical school to obtain additional credits prior to receiving her Canadian license. She applied to do this but was turned down again by the University of Toronto. In 1871 she was eventually allowed to attend the school along with another female and the two became the first women to attend lectures at the Toronto School of Medicine.

Following her struggles to gain acceptance in the medical field, Stowe became a leading figure in the feminist movement in Toronto. She helped to found the Toronto Women's Literary Guild, which was Canada's first suffragette group. This group was established to fight for women's rights and improvements in working conditions. They lobbied successfully to make Toronto higher education available to women. In 1883, the club was renamed the Canadian Women's Suffrage Association.

Dr. Emily Howard Stowe is remembered as the first Canadian woman to practise medicine in Canada and a lifelong champion of women's rights. Her tireless campaign to provide women with access to medical schools led to the organization of the women's movement in Canada and to the foundation of a medical college for women.

Dr. Emily Howard Stowe. (n.d.). Retrieved from http://www.collectionscanada.gc.ca/physicians/030002-2500-e.html

Personal Identity

Social identity thus plays a key role in shaping how we define ourselves. Yet the experiences and knowledge we learn from social settings may not always affect how we see ourselves. For instance, do we always do _exactly_ what we learn in childhood? Do we _always_ follow along with the traditions, languages, and customs that our parents, family, and friends teach us? And what if we do not? How will we feel? Isolated? Lonely? Different? What are the consequences for not following along with the traditions, norms, beliefs, and practices learned in childhood? Do we lose a sense of belonging if we do not practice the same beliefs, traditions, etc. as our families, friends or communities? And does identity then depend on some sense of community or group belonging?

> **Personal Identity:** Refers to how individuals see, understand, and shape their own identities.

In contrast to social identity, **personal identity** "is the result of an identification of self, by self, with respect to other. It is, in other words, a self-identification on the part of the individual" (Rummens, 2003, p. 23). What this means is that personal identity refers to how we see, understand and shape our _own_ identities. It is about the control we have in determining and creating our own identities, and in defining who we are.

Second, whether or not we follow along with the traditions, beliefs, and values we learned in childhood, we should acknowledge that we are defining identity based on a comparison. We look for similarities and differences between ourselves and others in what is sometimes referred to as a process of "_othering_". In other words, identities "are formed in relation to other identities, to 'the outsider' or in terms of the 'other': that is, in relation to what they are not" (Woodward, 1997, p. 423). To give an example, if you define yourself as Italian-Canadian, it is because you are **not** Chinese-Canadian, Hungarian-Canadian, Kenyan-Canadian, Liberian-Canadian, and so on. Deciding to define yourself as

Courtesy of Shutterstock.

Italian-Canadian, you are actually making a choice against all the other possibilities that exist. In this way, you make a choice to be seen as _one_ possibility of Canadianness, against, or in opposition to, or "other" from the remaining choices available to you. Furthermore, Woodward (1997) explains that identity is not entirely about seeing yourself as opposite to something else, and that identity "_depends on,_ difference" (p. 417, italics original). This suggests that we can only ever define our identities _in relation to something else_, through the marking of difference. Thinking back to the example of being Italian-Canadian, this category, or "marker" is placed beside all other possible markers (Chinese, Hungarian, Kenyan, Liberian, etc.). Therefore, the only way we can know that someone is Italian-Canadian is because that person is not Chinese-Canadian, Hungarian-Canadian, and so on. Sometimes, the marking of difference happens through social exclusion. For instance, imagine you are not part of the "in" crowd at school. How do you define yourself? As an outsider? And if so, what are you outside of? This kind of scenario sets up an "us" versus "them" situation.

Courtesy of Shutterstock.

What is important about "othering" is that it involves **power** relationships. So, for instance, if you were to define yourself as a student here at college, you do so by making a comparison between student and professor. Because you are a student, that means you are necessarily not a professor. You define yourself by what you are not, by what is "other". At the same time, if you are a student, then you recognize that in the context of the classroom, there are certain power dynamics at work. For instance, if your professor is lecturing, what is your expected behavior in the classroom? Would it be alright to listen to your iPod during the lecture? The point is that there are expected behaviors, attitudes, norms, practices that are assumed by both students and professors in a classroom setting because there are certain relations of power at work.

> **Power:** Refers to the control people may have over individuals, groups of people, resources, territories, wealth, institutions, to name a few.

In other scenarios, othering can have powerful consequences. For example, in Rwanda, the conflict between the Hutus and Tutsis led to genocide, while the conflict between Catholics and Protestants in Northern Ireland led to years of terrorist attacks, fighting, and death. How do people decide to classify one another, and pit themselves against one another? How do people decide on what distinguishes them? What are the justifications for one group trying to gain control over another? Or think about the ethnic conflicts in the former Yugoslavia between the ethnic Serbs, Croats, and Bosnians. Not only did these conflicts lead to the demise of the nation, it also led to war and killing of thousands of people.

You could also think of this in terms of workplace practices. If you are an employee, your identity is shaped in relation to your position as *employee* (and <u>not</u> *employer*). As an employee, you have little choice but to adopt the attitudes, behaviors, and workplace ethic expected of you by your employer. Therefore, there's always a certain relation of power that affects how we understand identity, and this applies whether or not we are talking about employers and employees, professors and students, parents and children, or any other power dynamic.

> *"I resolutely believe that respect for diversity is a fundamental pillar in the eradication of racism, xenophobia and intolerance. There is no excuse for evading the responsibility of finding the most suitable path toward the elimination of any expression of discrimination against indigenous peoples."*
> ~ Rigoberta Menchu Tum, Guatemala Mayan human rights activist

Courtesy of Shutterstock.

IDENTITY and POWER

Think of a situation in which you felt a sense of power. How did this influence your feelings about yourself, your position, and your identity?

Now think of a situation in which you felt you were lacking in power. How did this influence how you felt about yourself, your position, and your identity?

Why is it important to think about power dynamics when looking at identity formation?

Intersectionality

The relationship between power and identity is significant because our identities cannot be reduced to just one characteristic. For instance, we cannot say that our families of origin are the only determining factors that help us shape our identities. As we have seen, our identities can be influenced by multiple factors, including race, religion, culture, class, ethnicity, gender, age, ability, language, place of origin, sexual orientation, in addition to the experiences we gain in social settings.

> **Matrix:** A grid, or graph, with X and Y axes, upon which you can plot things visually.

Photo by Alice Kieltyka

Andersen and Hill Collins (2008) describe race, class, and gender as a "matrix of domination". A **matrix** is a grid, or graph, with X and Y axes, upon which you can plot things visually (see below). For instance, if you wanted to plot how fast a car travels in time and space, you could use a matrix to measure how fast a car travels in time, and the space the car can cover (distance) using X and Y axes. If we apply this image of a matrix to factors that shape our identities, then we begin to see that categories such as race, class, and gender *combine* to shape the way people identify themselves and experience their daily lives (p. 114). As Andersen and Hill Collins explain, "A matrix of domination posits multiple, interlocking levels of domination that stem from the societal configurations of race, class, and gender relations" (p. 114). In other words, if you imagine that different factors such as race, ethnicity, class, gender, ability, and so on could be plotted along a matrix, you would find that in some contexts, intersecting points, such as race and class, would be most significant, while in other contexts, ability and gender would be most significant.

For instance, let's imagine we wanted to think about a white, disabled, single woman with only a high school education who lives in social housing. In what contexts would her gendered identity make it

Courtesy of Shutterstock.

difficult for her to access services or resources? In what contexts would that same identity make it easy to access other opportunities? What about her race? In what contexts would her identity as a white woman be an advantage? And would that same identity create disadvantages for her? Now what if we think about her identity as a disabled person? Does that diminish her social status? What if we think about the intersection of her identities as a gendered *and* disabled person? Would she be treated the same way as a disabled man? Does her gender make a difference?

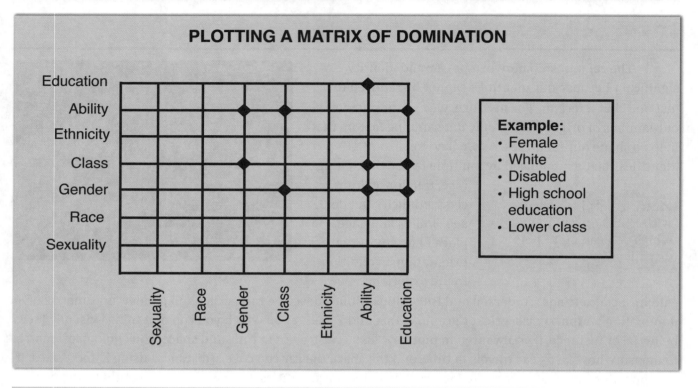

PLOTTING A MATRIX OF DOMINATION

Example:
• Female
• White
• Disabled
• High school education
• Lower class

Step 1: List the factors that make up this woman's identity:

_____

_____

_____

Step 2: Plot the factors of difference that make up this woman's identity. Mark the spot on the matrix where these factors intersect. For example, where gender intersects with education place a dot.

Which intersections would provide her with power and/ or privilege? Why?

_____

_____

_____

_____

Which intersections would limit her power and/ or privilege? Why?

_____

_____

_____

_____

_____

_____

PLOTTING YOUR MATRIX OF DOMINATION

Categories of Difference:
- Education
- Ability
- Ethnicity
- Class
- Gender
- Race
- Sexuality
- Language
- Place of origin
- Age
- Culture
- Nationality
- Religion/Creed
- Marital status
- Family status
- Citizenship
- Record of offense

List the factors that make up your identity. Write these factors in the blank spots along the matrix.

_____

_____

_____

At which points do you feel that you would have a greater degree of power and/ or privilege?

_____

_____

_____

_____

_____

_____

At which points do you feel that you would be limited or denied power and/ or privilege?

_____

_____

_____

_____

_____

_____

This example helps to explain the importance of the concept of **intersectionality.** Because our identities are formed through multiple sources and influences, we can say that we possess intersectional identities that give or take away a certain degree of power and privilege.

> **Intersectionality:** Occurs when different facets of our identities merge or connect.

Bias and Stereotypes

Unfortunately, while we can see that our identities are multiple, and intersecting, often people judge us on one or two characteristics resulting in significant **bias**. Henry and Tator (2005) define bias as "an opinion, preference, prejudice, or inclination formed without reasonable justification that then influences an individual's or group's ability to evaluate a particular situation objectively or accurately; an unfounded preference for or against." (p. 348) This means that people make decisions about others based on limited amounts of information, or preconceived ideas. It is particularly dangerous and unfair because it denies people the right to claim their full identities, based on who they really are. It can also limit people's abilities to function in the world, and limit their access to resources and opportunities, because those in power and with **privilege** perpetuate discrimination and therefore make biased decisions. For instance, a recent UK study found that job applicants with non-English sounding names fared much worse than those with English-sounding names. The study revealed that those with English-sounding names were given job interviews roughly fifty-percent more often than those with non-English sounding names. ("Race *bias* among UK employers").

> **Privilege:** Refers to a benefit that people can accumulate, be born into, or be given based on their place of origin, class status, community or professional affiliations. Often people are not aware of the privileges that they have access to.

Courtesy of Shutterstock.

> **Bias**: When one particular opinion or perspective takes one side over another.

Stop and Reflect

Do you think this kind of bias exists in Canada?

_____
_____
_____

Have you ever felt this kind of bias in Canada? If so, what was it like?

_____
_____
_____

What was the context of your experience?

_____
_____
_____

How did it make you feel?

_____
_____
_____
_____

Biases are therefore influenced by who we are, and can also have an effect on how we see ourselves and how we live in the world. In the example above, do you think a person with a non-English sounding name might consider changing his or her name in order to get a job? Is this right? Is it equitable for a person to feel that he or she has to change his or her name in order to get a job, or to be accepted in society? What effect does this have on a person's being or identity? Does bias cause people to question who they really are? And if so, do people then feel isolated?

Photo by Jared Purdy

EXAMINING BIASES

Take a few moments to write down what you think are your biases. Be honest and open about your biases.

_____

_____

_____

_____

_____

_____

_____

_____

_____

_____

In small groups, or with a partner, share your biases. What do you think others will feel about you when they discover what your biases are?

_____

_____

_____

What about the people who would be impacted by your biases?

_____

_____

_____

How do you feel if you are impacted by someone else's bias?

_____

_____

_____

Related to the issue of bias is that of **stereotypes**. Stereotypes are commonly held beliefs or notions that include generalizations and assumptions about individuals or groups of people based on their social identity, appearance, and behavior. Stereotypes begin when people take one characteristic or attribute of a particular group, and apply it to the whole group. For instance, some people might believe that all members of an ethnic group act or behave in a certain way. While it may be true that some people from that ethnic group might act that way, or *appear* to act that way, it is not necessarily true that all people do. Nor can the ethnic group be reduced to that one characteristic, so we can't simply say, "All people from X are like this". Thus stereotypes reduce people's identities into flat, one-dimensional portraits that deny the roundedness and complexities of human identities.

> **Stereotype:** Commonly held beliefs or notions that include generalizations and assumptions about individuals or groups of people based on their social identity, appearance, and behavior.

It is especially significant to examine stereotypes, as they have often been used to justify the oppression of others. Stereotypes are quite dangerous in that they can be used to support political and economic decisions by the ruling class that result in the control and domination of people and resources. For example, in the United States and the Caribbean, slavery was, in part, rationalized and perpetuated using stereotypes of the enslaved peoples as inferior, lazy, unintelligent, and so on. In a related way, in Canada, the oppression of Aboriginal peoples was justified using similar stereotypical ideas that people were primitive, uncivilized, barbaric, and unworthy of looking after themselves. The consequences of stereotypes in these various contexts resulted in the historic exploitation and oppression of peoples, based on their race and ethnicities.

> **Stop and Reflect**
>
> *What can we do to avoid stereotypes? Getting to know each other through dialogue, discussions and exchanges can break down negative stereotypes.*
>
> _____
> _____
> _____
> _____
> _____
> _____
> _____
> _____
>
> *It is also important to question where we learn those generalizations, assumptions or images of people. Is it from the media, friends, TV, movies, school?*
>
> _____
> _____
> _____
> _____
> _____
> _____
> _____
> _____
> _____
> _____

> *"About all you can do in life is be who you are. Some people will love you for you. Most will love you for what you can do for them, and some won't like you at all."*
> ~ Rita Mae Brown, author and activist for gay rights

At the same time, the people who are being stereotyped themselves may continue to promote the stereotypes because they are made to believe that these false characterizations are true. Consider what would happen to a person who has **internalized** a stereotype. What does this do to a person's identity or sense of him or herself? Does the imposition of the stereotype diminish a person's sense of self-respect? Dignity? Authenticity?

> **Internalization:** Refers to a process whereby people incorporate external ideas, thoughts, or beliefs into their own sense of self or their beliefs about the world. Internalization can create risks when those external influences are negative, and are repeatedly stated and circulated by those in power. In other words, if you constantly heard someone tell you as a child that you were bad, then chances are you would grow up believing this. A consequence might be that you would act out your belief in your own "bad" self, and this might lead to aggressive behavior and even criminal activity.

Values and Norms: The Link to Identity

Values are powerful reminders of who we are, and are linked to our identity because they help to determine our relationship to the world. **Values** are deeply held personal beliefs and ideas that we feel very strongly about, and they help us to define what we think is good, bad, right, wrong, desirable, undesirable, appropriate or not appropriate.

> **Values:** Deeply held personal beliefs and ideas that we feel very strongly about, and they help us to define what we think is good, bad, right, wrong, desirable, undesirable, appropriate or not appropriate.

Values are important because they help guide our actions, behavior and attitudes towards one other as global and local citizens. They serve as standards for how we evaluate and judge ourselves and others. Through our values we are able to make decisions that impact our lives and relationships with others.

At one level, we share certain values as a nation, community, or group of individuals; however, our values are not all the same. They are socially constructed and differ depending on culture, religious beliefs, gender, place of birth, ethnicity, and other influences. From our childhood, our values are also influenced by our parents, family, teachers, friends, the media, religious leaders, celebrities, community leaders, school, level of education and peers. For example, two children, who attend the same elementary school with its own set of values, will not necessarily have the same beliefs on a particular topic or issue, because these children may also be influenced by the different media they engage with, by their different families of origins and ethnicities, their religions, and so on. On the other hand, our values also change over time depending on our life experiences and age. What were your sets of values when you were in high school? If you are a parent, what are your values now? Have they changed? What are your values now that you are a college student?

Photo by Alice Kieltyka

EXAMPLES OF VALUES

Values might include sincerity, loyalty, caring, consideration, truthfulness, honesty, reliability, trustworthiness, dependability, kindness, thoughtfulness, courtesy, warmth, helpfulness, respect, politeness, open-mindedness, conscientiousness, morality, discipline.

Attributes or characteristics that might not be considered as accepted values include: Craftiness, mean-spiritedness, dishonesty, greed, cunning, gullibility, superstition, bad, uncaring, troubled, moody, pompousness, aggression, unsympathetic, uncompromising, hot-tempered, antisocial, rude, unfriendly, unforgiving, selfish, arrogant, malicious, deceiving, envious, intolerant, insensitive, inconsiderate, thoughtless, petty and pretentious.

Stop and Reflect

As global citizens, what are our commonly-held values?

_____
_____
_____
_____
_____
_____
_____

How do we see our identities in a global context?

_____
_____
_____
_____
_____
_____
_____

What types of norms should global citizens promote?

_____
_____
_____
_____
_____
_____
_____
_____

"The value systems of those with access to power and of those far removed from such access cannot be the same. The viewpoint of the privileged is unlike that of the underprivileged."

~ Aung San Suu Kyi, Nobel Peace Prize winner and pro-democracy activist in Burma

Photo by Jared Purdy

Courtesy of Shutterstock.

It is important to note that values by definition are very ambiguous concepts of what is desirable, good, bad, right wrong, etc. They do not necessarily tell us how to behave or to act. In contrast **norms** can be seen as socially acceptable or established rules of behavior of individuals, groups and society. They are social agreements commonly accepted within a society. They are based on agreed-upon traditions and beliefs that everyone in the society is expected to

> **Norms:** Socially acceptable or established rules of behavior of individuals, groups and society.

uphold and follow. For instance, in Canada, we might say that one of our norms is that we are not supposed to drink and drive, or speed on the highway, or both. Yet individuals sometimes commit these acts contrary to the socially-held norms that go against these practices. How would an individual who was accused of drunk driving be perceived by the general public? Our social response to these infractions tells us what we, as a society, uphold as our norms. Therefore, norms dictate certain patterns or expected standards of behavior.

The question we should pose around the issue of norms has to do with the relationship between norms and identity. In other words, do socially-determined norms conflict with an individual's identity? Think of wanting to have a different hair style that is spiked or colored. Or what about piercing a part of your body that contradicts the accepted norms of your family or community group? What would be the reaction of your parents, family or friends? What about wearing baggy pants to a job interview? What are the social norms that dictate against doing this? How would that affect an individual's sense of him or herself? Can norms violate your sense of identity? Where do we draw the line? Are norms internalized through the expectations or reactions of others? And how do we use these internalized norms to shape our identities?

Think of past and current leaders of the world and make a list of what you think are their values for example, George W. Bush, Dick Cheney, Tony Blair, Stephen Harper, Robert Mugabe.

_____

_____

_____

_____

As global citizens make a list of global leaders who you think have made a difference in making the world a better place. For instance, you might mention one or more of the following: Unas Khan, Nelson Mandela, Martin Luther King Jr., Rosa Parks, Viola Desmond, Agnes MacPhail, Mahatma Gandhi, Malcolm X, Terry Fox, Pierre Trudeau, Tommy Douglas. What are their values?

_____

_____

_____

_____

Consider how our values contribute to the formation of our identity. What are the essential characteristics that help to define each of us? Are your values evolving or are they the same as a few years ago? Are our values independent of who we are? Are we forced to share the same values within our families or community? Are there contradictions in our values? What are the consequences for our identities?

VALUES AND YOUR IDENTITY

Make a list of values in the following categories (Social, personal, family, national, political, community and work oriented) that you think best represent your identity.

_____
_____
_____
_____
_____
_____
_____

Who has influenced your values?

_____
_____
_____
_____

Are there socially determined norms that conflict with your identity?

_____
_____
_____
_____
_____

Why do you think this conflict exists?

_____
_____
_____
_____
_____

Global Citizenship, Identity, Values, and Norms

Photo by Jared Purdy

One of the key principles of global citizenship is that in order for us to exist in the world *as* global citizens, we must first be able to understand and define ourselves and our own identities. Global citizenship advocates for diversity, social justice, sustainable environments, equity and equality, human rights, and respect. To achieve these goals, we must also comprehend who we are, how our identities are formed, and what factors influence and shape what we claim as our identities. We must be able to recognize our own intersectionality so that we become aware of the moments of power and privilege we have access to, and those we do not. Seeing ourselves as intersectional beings also allows us to witness the vulnerability of our own humanity, so that we understand that, like others, we, too are composed of multiple identities that are at times conflicting, complex, and yet combine to form the persons that we are.

Untangling our own biases, norms, and values is also significant because in order for us to define who we are, we must also pinpoint the external influences that shape how we see ourselves and how we act in the world. Our values, in particular, determine the practices, thoughts, actions and ways of being that we perceive to be important. This will have an influence on how we look at others, and the extent to which we can achieve some of the goals of global citizenship because it is only by challenging our existing values that we can move forward to treat others with the respect and dignity that global citizenship upholds as fundamental human rights.

Doing so enables us to determine the levels of bias in our own thinking and actions, and the ways in which we might reproduce stereotypes and discriminatory approaches in our jobs, communities, and home lives. It will allow us to reformulate and rethink practices that may have stemmed from our preconceived notions and biases about others, so that our actions and behaviors towards others recognize and honor the diversity and dignity of each individual. In order for us to respect diversity in a global context therefore, we must first see the gaps in our perspectives and knowledge that limit our abilities to see the world, and the individuals who exist within it, as a place and people defined by difference.

Identity, values, norms, biases and stereotypes are therefore critical elements in the movement forward to become global citizens. By recognizing the importance of these elements and their interconnectedness, we achieve a better sense and understanding of our own identities, which can enrich our lives as individuals. We also strengthen and broaden the possibilities for creating social change globally by developing our awareness of the need to respect diversity, and each individual's human right to dignity, authenticity, self-respect, and the right to live in a world characterized by sound environmental practices, fairness, equity, social justice, and equality. In this way, it would become possible to achieve the freedom to determine one's own sense of identity and self, and the freedom to express that identity without fear of political, economic, social or cultural discrimination. As global citizens therefore, understanding our own identities is a critical first step forward on the path to social justice and transformation.

EVENTS THAT CONTRIBUTED TO SOCIAL CHANGE

Event: Same-sex Marriage is Legalized in Canada

WHEN: July 20, 2005

WHERE: Canada

WHAT: Canada becomes the fourth country in the world to legalize same-sex marriage, advancing the fight for equality by same-sex Canadian couples.

Compiled by Sarah Duffy

In 1965, the Supreme Court of Canada upheld a ruling that labelled Everett Klippert, an individual who was being questioned as part of an arson investigation, as a "dangerous sexual offender." Klippert was imprisoned for admitting he was gay. Subsequently, Macleans magazine published an article that was sympathetic to homosexuality and this led to a time of national debate regarding Canada's homosexuality laws. In 1969, homosexuality was decriminalized in Canada under the leadership of Prime Minister, Pierre Trudeau.

A number of advances in LGBT rights were made over the next thirty-five years until July 20, 2005 when same-sex marriage became legal in Canada under Prime Minister, Paul Martin. This ruling made Canada the fourth country in the world to legalize same-sex marriage, ensuring that same-sex Canadians would have the same rights of marriage as opposite-sex couples.

The Supreme Court and same-sex marriage. (2005, June). CBC News. Retrieved from http://www.cbc.ca/news/background/samesexrights/

Gay marriage critics, supporters lobby MPs ahead of free vote. (2006, October). CBC News. Retrieved from http://www.cbc.ca/canada/story/2006/10/24/samesex-opponents.html

> *"No government has the right to tell its citizens when or whom to love. The only queer people are those who don't love anybody"*
> ~ Rita Mae Brown, author and activist for gay rights

Getting Engaged: Activities

WHO AM I?

Pretend you are writing a personal advertisement to look for a life partner. Using 100 words describe yourself.

What aspects of your identity or values did you include? Why?

_____
_____
_____
_____
_____
_____
_____

What aspects of your identity or values did you leave out? Why?

_____
_____
_____
_____
_____
_____
_____

At times, we focus on first impressions when meeting someone. Why is this problematic?

_____
_____
_____
_____
_____
_____
_____

Author Unknown. Date Unknown.

WHO ARE YOU?

Your answers to the following shed light on your identity formation at this point in your life.

Who am I?

_____
_____
_____
_____
_____

With whom do I identify?

_____
_____
_____
_____
_____

What are my values?

_____
_____
_____
_____
_____

How do others see me?

_____
_____
_____
_____
_____

Retrieved from Bucher, R.D. (2008) Building Cultural Intelligence: Nine Megaskills. Pearson Publishers: New Jersey, p.36-37.

WHO ARE YOU?

What do others want me to be?

_____

_____

_____

_____

_____

With whom do I spend my time?

_____

_____

_____

_____

_____

What do the media say I am?

_____

_____

_____

_____

_____

Where and when do I feel like I belong?

_____

_____

_____

_____

_____

_____

Retrieved from Bucher, R.D. (2008) Building Cultural Intelligence: Nine Megaskills. Pearson Publishers: New Jersey, p.36-37.

IDENTITY CONFLICTS

Identify the aspects of your identity that conflict.

Past experience conflicts with _____

_____ conflicts with _____

_____ conflicts with _____

_____ conflicts with _____

_____ conflicts with _____

_____ conflicts with _____

Why do these conflict?

_____
_____
_____
_____
_____
_____
_____
_____
_____
_____
_____

How do you resolve these conflicts?

_____
_____
_____
_____
_____
_____
_____
_____
_____
_____
_____

Your Values

Identify where your values come from by filling in the chart below. For each group indicate the group in which you are a member (example: family, religious group) and beside it write which of your value(s) came from that group.

DIRECTIONS: This is an **eco-map**, a drawing that represents relationships connecting you and some of the groups that make up your cultural silo. Within each numbered circle, identify a group to which you belong. Then next to each circle, write the most important value you have learned from that group.

Taken from *Building Cultural Intelligence (CQ): Nine Megaskills*, by Richard D. Bucher

My Eco-Map

GROUP **1** value
GROUP **2** value
GROUP **6** value
ME
GROUP **3** value
GROUP **5** value
GROUP **4** value

Analysis of Your Eco-Map

DIRECTIONS: Next, examine the groups you identified in your eco-map. Place an "X" beside the answer that best describes each group's cultural diversity.

Group #1 _____
Very Diverse _____   Somewhat Diverse _____   Very Little Diversity _____

Group #2 _____
Very Diverse _____   Somewhat Diverse _____   Very Little Diversity _____

Taken from *Building Cultural Intelligence (CQ): Nine Megaskills*, by Richard D. Bucher

How do these values shape your identity?

_____
_____
_____
_____
_____
_____
_____
_____

Bucher, R.D. (2008) Building Cultural Intelligence: Nine Megaskills. Pearson Publishers: New Jersey, p.40.

Describe one stereotype of a group with which you identify. If you internalize this stereotype, how might it affect your behavior? (Question retrieved from Bucher, R.D. (2008) Building Cultural Intelligence: Nine Megaskills. Pearson Publishers: New Jersey, p.44.)

_____
_____
_____
_____
_____
_____
_____
_____
_____

OUTSIDE THE ZONE

Have you ever spent time with a family member or friend and they behaved differently than usual in a situation where they were out of their comfort zone? Did their identity and values change to suit the new context? How?

_____
_____
_____
_____
_____
_____

Think of a situation in which you were outside of your comfort zone.

How did you feel?

_____
_____
_____
_____
_____

What made you feel this way?

_____
_____
_____
_____
_____
_____

Did you alter your behavior? Why or why not?

_____
_____
_____
_____
_____
_____

Adapted from Bucher, R.D. (2008) Building Cultural Intelligence: Nine Megaskills. Pearson Publishers: New Jersey, p.120.

Male versus Female

Do you believe that there are differences between males and females?
If so, identify them:

Male	Female

Why do you believe that gender differences exist?

_____

_____

_____

_____

_____

_____

Where do your ideas about gender come from?

_____

_____

_____

_____

_____

_____

How did you learn about the gender differences? (ex: family, media etc.)

_____

_____

_____

_____

_____

_____

Adapted from Bucher, R.D. (2008) Building Cultural Intelligence: Nine Megaskills. Pearson Publishers: New Jersey, p.142

What groups in society maintain gender differences?

_____
_____
_____
_____
_____
_____

For whom is it useful to maintain gender differences? (gender differences connect to power)

_____
_____
_____
_____
_____
_____

Do these ideas about gender influence your identity and values?

_____
_____
_____
_____
_____
_____

Adapted from Bucher, R.D. (2008) Building Cultural Intelligence: Nine Megaskills. Pearson Publishers: New Jersey, p.142

SEX versus GENDER

What do you think is the difference between sex and gender?

_____
_____
_____
_____
_____
_____
_____
_____
_____
_____
_____
_____
_____
_____

Portfolio Sharing Session

Make a list of the activities, assignments and course work you have completed during this unit:

_____
_____
_____

Decide which artifact from the list above you would like to share with your classmates. Which of the things on this list had the most impact on you or provided the most learning?

_____
_____
_____

Reflect on why this item was so meaningful: Why did you choose that item of learning? What did it tell you about yourself? What have you learned or discovered that you hadn't thought of before? How does it relate to your life, your own experiences? How will it affect your actions in the future? What do you still feel you need to learn?

_____
_____
_____
_____
_____
_____

Bring your portfolio to class, including your selected artifact and reflection, and be prepared to share them a group and/or the class.
Listen carefully to the feedback of others. Write points about that feedback here:

_____
_____
_____
_____

What insight does this feedback provide you with? How does it affect your thinking and what you might do in the future as you continue learning in this area?

_____
_____
_____

Listen attentively to others as they share their artifacts with you. Provide them with respectful and thoughtful feedback. Make some notes here about anything they share that has particular meaning for you:

_____
_____
_____

Developed by Gina Marshall, Stanley Doyle-Wood, Holly Baines, Julia Satov, Zabedia Nazim (2010) Centennial College, Toronto, ON.

Assignments

Identity and Values Assignment: Refer to pg. 245 in the text (Note: Choice of 3 versions).

Identity and Values Assignment Rubric: Refer to pg. 251 in the text.

Chapter Summary

Definitions:

Assimilate: To fully become a part of the dominant culture; taking on the culture, language, and customs of the dominant group, to a greater or lesser extent.

Bias: When one particular opinion or perspective takes one side over another.

Construction: The way in which something is created or formed. *Social construction* of identity refers to the ways in which society contributes to and shapes the formation of your identity.

Hyphenate: To merge together the cultures of more than one cultural, ethnic, and/ or linguistic group.

Identity: The distinguishing character or personality of an individual (Merriam-Webster Dictionary).

Internalization: Refers to a process whereby people incorporate external ideas, thoughts, or beliefs into their own sense of self or their beliefs about the world. Internalization can create risks when those external influences are negative, and are repeatedly stated and circulated by those in power.

Intersectionality: Occurs when different facets of our identities merge or connect.

Matrix: A grid, or graph, with X and Y axes, upon which you can plot things visually.

Norms: Socially acceptable or established rules of behavior for individuals, groups and society.

Personal Identity: Refers to how individuals see, understand, and shape their own identities.

Power: Refers to the control people may have over individuals, groups of people, resources, territories, wealth, and institutions to name a few.

Privilege: Refers to a benefit that people can accumulate, be born into, or be given based on their place of origin, class status, community or professional affiliations. Often people are not aware of the privileges that they have access to.

Separate/Isolated: To be completely apart from or feel unassociated with a cultural, ethnic, and/ or linguistic group.

Social Identity: Refers to how we see ourselves as individuals who are members of groups, and how we are perceived by others both inside and outside the group.

Stereotype: Commonly held beliefs or notions that include generalizations and assumptions about individuals or groups of people based on their social identity, appearance, and behavior.

Values: Deeply held personal beliefs and ideas that we feel very strongly about, and they help us to define what we think is good, bad, right, wrong, desirable, undesirable, appropriate or not appropriate.

Main Concepts:

- Understanding the social construction of identity
- Identifying personal identity and its components
- Examining the intersectionality of identity
- Tracing bias and stereotypes
- Examining values and norms, including their link to identity
- Uncovering the importance of an understanding of identity, values, and norms for global citizens

Additional Resources

A networked self identity, community and culture on social network sites by, Zizi Papacharissi. (Centennial College Libraries).

Description: "A Networked Self examines self presentation and social connection in the digital age. This collection brings together new work on online social networks by leading scholars from a variety of disciplines. The focus of the volume rests on the construction of the self, and what happens to self-identity when it is presented through networks of social connections in new media environments,"(Editorial Review (n.d.). Retrieved from http://www.amazon.com/Networked-Self-Identity-Community-Culture/dp/0415801818).

We are more - http://www.youtube.com/watch?v=zsq68qRexFc

Description: Canadian poet, Shane Koyczan, delivers his poem about being Canadian, which was part of the 2010 Olympic Game's opening ceremonies.

Canadian values boil down to liberal democracy, by Clifford Orwin, http://www.theglobeandmail.com/news/opinions/article1131777.ece

Description: This article comments on the difficulty of describing Canadian values and describes fundamental Canadian values today.

References

Andersen, M.L. & Hill, C.P. (2008) Why race, class, and gender still matter. In *Global citizenship: From social analysis to social action.* 2nd ed. (pp. 111-123). Toronto: Pearson Custom Publishing.

Brown, R.M. (Date Unknown) Identity Quote. Retrieved on September 20, 2010 from http://www.brainyquote.com/quotes/authors/r/rita_mae_brown.html

Brown, R.M. (Date Unknown) Identity Quote. In Mack, T. & Picower, B. (2009). *Planning to Change the World: A Plan Book for Social Justice Teachers.* New York: New York Collective of Radical Educators and the Education for Liberation Network. p. 35

Bucher, R.D. (2008) Building Cultural Intelligence (CQ): Nine Mega Skills. New Jersey: Pearson Publishers. p. 36-37, 40, 44, 120, 142,

CBC News. (2005) In Depth: Same Sex Rights. The Supreme Court and same-sex marriage. Retrieved on September 26, 2010 from   http://www.cbc.ca/news/background/samesexrights/

CBC News. (2006) Gay marriage critics, supporters lobby MPs ahead of free vote. Retrieved on September 26, 2010 from http://www.cbc.ca/canada/story/2006/10/24/samesex-opponents.html

Davies, B. (1997). The subject of post-structuralism: A reply to Alison Jones. *Gender and Education, vol 9*: 3, pp. 271-283.

Hall, S. (1996). Who needs identity? In Hall & Du Gay (Eds) *Questions of Cultural Identity.* (pp. 3-17) London: Sage.

Henry, F. & C. Tator. (2005) *The Colour of democracy: Racism in Canadian society.* 3rd ed. Toronto: Nelson.

Hernández-Ávila, I. Identity Quote. In Mack, T. & Picower, B. (2009). *Planning to Change the World: A Plan Book for Social Justice Teachers.* New York: New York Collective of Radical Educators and the Education for Liberation Network. p. 10

Library and Archives Canada. (Date Unknown) Famous Canadian Physicians: Dr. Emily Howard Stowe. Retrieved on September 29, 2010 from http://www.collectionscanada.gc.ca/physicians/ 030002-2500-e.html

Merriam Webster (Date Unknown) Identity Definition. Dictionary. Retrieved on September 26, 2010 from http://www.merriam-webster.com/dictionary/identity?show=0&t=1286337028

Menchu Tum, R. (Date Unknown) Identity Quote. Retrieved on September 8, 2010 from http:// www.betterworldheroes.com/pages-m/menchu-quotes.htm

Race *bias* among UK employers. *The Statesman.* n.p. Oct 19, 2009.

Rummens, J.A. (2003). Conceptualizing identity and diversity: Overlaps, intersections, and processes. *Canadian ethnic studies,* 35:3, pp. 10-25.

San Suu Ky, A. (Date Unknown) Identity Quote. Retrieved on September 20, 2010 from http://

Woodward, K. (1997) Concepts of identity and difference. In Woodward, K. (ed) *Identity and difference: Culture, media, and identities.* (pp. 7-61). London: Sage.

Notes

CHAPTER 6

Moving to Equity and Advancing Inequality

Courtesy of Shutterstock.

CHAPTER OBJECTIVES:

- Understanding the factors that contribute to and perpetuate inequalities

- Analyzing social issues using the frameworks of inequality and equity

- Discussing why power, privilege, and inequality exist in society

- Examining the difference between equality and equity

Kisha McPherson

Introduction

In this chapter, we will explore the concepts of inequality, equality and equity. We will investigate why inequalities exist and how inequalities impact individuals and communities. We will be curious and begin to ask questions about why the right to marry has not universally been extended to same-sex couples, why women worldwide continue to earn less than their male counterparts, why people with disabilities are often unable to access public spaces, why new Canadians are restricted from employment in their fields of expertise and why economic poverty is most prevalent amongst indigenous peoples in Canada. We will illuminate factors that contribute to inequality by drawing on definitions, theoretical frameworks and everyday examples from our lives and the world around us. While recognizing the complexity of these issues, we will consider our role as global citizens in identifying spaces for responsible action and strategies to advance equality for all.

> *"There may be times when we are powerless to prevent injustice, but there must never be a time when we fail to protest."*
> ~Elie Wiesel, Nobel Peace Prize winner and Holocaust survivor

What is Inequality?

Inequality can be described as any difference in the treatment of people on the basis of class, gender, age, ability, race, ethnicity, sexuality, or citizenship. This treatment could be unfair as it involves restricting people's full participation in society and limiting resources and opportunities, hence, affecting overall quality of life.

Inequality: Refers to any difference in the treatment of people on the basis of class, gender, age, ability, race, ethnicity, sexuality, or citizenship.

In Canada, we have the Charter of Rights and Freedoms that extends specific rights to Canadian citizens. For example, Canadian citizens are entitled to run and vote in an election, practice freedom of speech, hold certain government jobs, and travel internationally on a Canadian passport.

Inequalities exist throughout the world and they persist over time. They have historical roots, they exist currently and they will exist in the future (Currey, 2007). If you consider slavery, you will notice that slavery has its long history that ties to modern slavery today. Slavery existed in ancient times and continued to exist in ancient Greece and Rome. It persisted through the 18th and 19th century and it is present in today's society in the form of modern slavery which involves human trafficking, exploiting live-in care givers, child labour, and prostitution to name a few.

> "I would like to be remembered as a person who wanted to be free... so other people would be also free."
> ~ Rosa Parks, African American civil rights activist

Stop and Reflect

Do you feel that these rights are universally applied to all Canadians? If not, explain.

_____
_____
_____
_____
_____
_____
_____
_____
_____
_____
_____
_____
_____
_____
_____
_____
_____
_____

Did You Know?

Around the world, millions of people are living in bondage. They labor in fields and factories under brutal employers who threaten them with violence if they try to escape. They work in homes for families that keep them virtually imprisoned. They are forced to work as prostitutes or to beg in the streets, fearful of the consequences if they fail to earn their daily quota. They are women, men, and children of all ages, and they are often held far from home with no money, no connections, and no way to ask for help.

(Hillary Clinton, Secretary of State, U.S. State Department Trafficking in Persons Report, 2009, http://www.state.gov/secretary/rm/2009a/06/124872.htm)

Case Study

In this scenario, identify the differential treatment and how has access to opportunities and resources been limited to different students.

In planning an international youth leadership conference, young people from East Africa are invited to Canada to participate in the exchange of knowledge and ideas. Based on past experience, the visa process began six months before the scheduled conference date. The visa process for the East African students involved a valid passport, full medicals, financial assurance, resumés, letters of reference, and a full background check. If any of the students had a communicable disease, they were automatically denied a visa. The following year, students from Canada were invited to attend a similar conference in East Africa. For Canadian students, the visa process involved only photos, passport and an application form and it began a month before the conference.

_____
_____
_____
_____
_____
_____
_____
_____
_____
_____
_____
_____
_____
_____
_____
_____
_____
_____
_____
_____
_____

> *"I've run into more discrimination as a woman than as an Indian."*
> ~ Wilma Mankiller, the first woman elected Chief of the Cherokee Nation

EVENTS THAT CONTRIBUTED TO SOCIAL CHANGE

Event: Gandhi begins a hunger strike as a form of protest

WHEN: 1932
WHERE: India
WHAT: A step forward in the fight for civil rights in India

Compiled by Sarah Duffy

Mohandas Karamchand Gandhi was a civil rights activist and one of the major political and spiritual leaders of his time. Gandhi is known for his non-violent activism. He led many protests against the British rule in India and inequality in Indian society. He was jailed a number of times for these activities. During one of these jail sentences on September 16, 1932 Gandhi began a hunger strike in protest of British support for a new Indian constitution that would have resulted in separate political representation for India's lowest social caste, the "untouchables". After six days of his hunger strike, the British agreed to reverse the decision and also accepted the terms of an agreement between the higher caste Indians and the "untouchables".

Mahatma Gandhi. (Date Unknown) Retrieved from http://www.biography.com/articles/Mahatma-Gandhi-9305898.

Lee, U. (2010, September). September 16, 1932 : Gandhi Begins Hunger Strike. Retrieved from the Take Part website: http://www.takepart.com/news/2010/09/15/september-16-1932-ghandi-begins-hunger-strike

"You must be the change you wish to see in the world."
~ Mahatma Gandhi, political and spiritual leader, civil rights activist

Why Do Inequalities Exist?

As global citizens, we will apply our skills in critical literacy and draw on the social analysis frameworks from chapter 3 to understand why inequalities exist in communities and countries around the world.   In this chapter, we identify 4 factors that work together to organize the production and reproduction of inequalities. We will begin with an examination of social stratification. This theory is concerned with the emergence of social divisions and social hierarchies based on identity. The second factor contributing to inequality is power and privilege. We make the explicit link between relations of power, social identities in a stratified society and inequalities experienced by marginalized groups.   The third contributing factor is that those deeply rooted and common sense ideas that shape what a society looks like and what it considers valuable. We link dominant ideologies back to the production and reproduction of inequality. Last, we focus attention on the visible and invisible barriers that restrict access and full participation for some groups within a society.

Social Stratification

> **Social Stratification:** Refers to "the hierarchical arrangement of large social groups on the basis of their control over basic resources" (Kendall, 2010, p.214).

The first factor explores how the differences in social identities (Chapter 5) have been structured, organized and reinforced in one way or another by the society we live in (Grabb, 2007, p.3-7). Within our society, social identities have been further divided through a process described as **social stratification**. "Social stratification is the hierarchical arrangement of large social groups on the basis of their control over basic resources" (Kendall, 2010, p.214).

> **Dominant Group:** Those who are disproportionately at the top of the hierarchy of class.

Let's take a closer look at the social category of class. Within the category of class stratification is based on "the ownership and control of resources and on the type of work people do" (Kendall, 2006, p. 219). This class category has been stratified and ranked as lower, middle and upper class. The upper class would be considered the

> **Non-dominant Groups:** Those whose members are not in positions of power with limited access to power.

dominant group within this category; all other groups are referred to as non-dominant. **Dominant groups** are those who are disproportionately at the top of the hierarchy of class. They have "maximal access to the society's power resources, particular political authority and control of the means of economic production" (Kendall, Nygaard, & Thompson, 2007, p. 7). **Non-dominant groups** are those whose members are not in positions of power with limited access to power.

Courtesy of Shutterstock.

AGENTS OF SOCIAL CHANGE: GLOBAL CITIZENS IN ACTION

Activist: Helen Keller

1880 - 1968
Activist for Disability Rights
United States of America

Compiled by Sarah Duffy

Helen Keller was born in 1880 in Alabama, USA. She was born with full sight and hearing; however, an illness at the age of 19 months resulted in Helen becoming both blind and deaf. In an effort to help their daughter learn despite her disability, Helen's parents hired a teacher to work with her. This teacher was called Anne Sullivan. Upon meeting Helen, Anne taught her how to finger-spell. Over time, Helen made incredible progress and was able to read with both raised letter and Braille, in addition to typing with a regular and Braille typewriter. Helen's ability to learn was more advanced than had been previously seen in someone with her disabilities and, as a result, Helen began to gain publicity, appearing in national newspapers.

In the fall of 1900, Helen entered Radcliffe College. She was the first deaf-blind person in the United States to have ever enrolled at a college. During her time at Radcliffe, Helen wrote her first book, "The Story of My Life", which was published in 1903 and in 1904, she graduated and became the first deaf-blind person to earn a Bachelor of Arts degree. Helen went on to learn to read in many languages, to write 13 books and author many articles. She also devoted her life to social reform and was known as an active suffragist, pacifist and socialist. During her life, Helen lectured to audiences around the country about her experiences as a disabled person and advocated on the behalf of the disabled. In addition, Helen helped to start a number of foundations that focused on helping people with disabilities. She continued her advocacy work until she was in her 70's and actively promoted a change in image of the blind and deaf-blind from people with disabilities to people with abilities.

Helen Keller. (Date Unknown). Retrieved from http://www.afb.org/Section.asp?SectionID=1

Helen Keller. (Date Unknown). Retrieved from http://www.rnib.org.uk/aboutus/aboutsightloss/famous/Pages/helenkeller.aspx

Hierarchy of Class

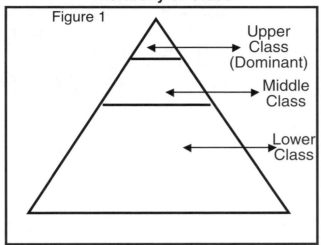

Figure 1

In *Figure 1*, we have illustrated the hierarchy of class. We can observe that those who belong to the upper class are placed at top. Those at the top of the hierarchy tend to have more resources, opportunity and are fewer in number.

The resources and opportunities that are available to some groups based on wealth and denied to others create an inequality. These inequalities produce disparities in food security, education, health care, life expectancy, among others. This class hierarchy is entrenched and reproduced from one generation to another.

Many of the categories such as, race, class, gender, ability, etc. that we use to describe ourselves, have been stratified into hierarchies similar to the one used to organize class. Inequality is experienced when the outcome of a situation in which a person is treated unfairly is based on aspects of social identity and their position within these categories as you have learned in chapter 5.

Stop and Reflect

Has inequality impacted you? If so, how?

_____

_____

_____

_____

_____

_____

_____

_____

_____

_____

_____

_____

_____

_____

_____

_____

Did You Know?

In 1980, 25% of recent immigrants to Canada were living in low income. By 2000, this proportion had increased to 36% of Canadian immigrants. Among Canadian-born people, the rate fell from 17% in 1980 to 14% in 2000.

(The Daily, Thursday February 12th, 2005. Statistics Canada)

Photo by Jared Purdy

Power and Privilege

The second factor contributing to inequality is power and privilege. In this section, we will first explore how power and privilege shapes relationships and the lived experiences of individuals and groups within a stratified social system. **Power** is the capacity to control resources, which allows structures of dominance and subordination to be created and maintained among social groups (McMullin, 2004 p. 29). Power creates conditions in which inequalities are reproduced in society. Power is associated with individuals and groups at the top of any social hierarchy. These groups can be referred to as dominant.

> **Power:** The capacity to control resources, which allows structures of dominance and subordination to be created and maintained among social groups (McMullin, 2004 p. 29).

Dominant groups are "people whose social identity confers on them unearned power and privilege. Most of us have one or more dominant identities. In most parts of Canada, dominant identities are White, male, English-speaking, heterosexual, able-bodied, Christian, affluent and middle class, thirty to sixty-five years of age, university educated, from central Canada" (Lopes & Thomas, 2006, p. 266). Membership in the dominant groups grant individuals privilege. "**Privilege** is gained through unearned power that gives dominant group members economic, social, and political advantage" (Lopes & Thomas, 2006, p.266). Privilege ensures this group's opportunities, rights and ways of being that afford them certain freedoms, choices, resources or materials that are categorically denied to others.

> **Privilege:** "Is gained through unearned power that gives dominant group members economic, social, and political advantage" (Lopes & Thomas, 2006, p.266).

Courtesy of Shutterstock.

For example, an individual who is able bodied compared to a disabled individual is considered to be privileged. It is likely that an able bodied individual will have easier access to resources than someone who is visually impaired or physically disabled. An able bodied person can easily enter a building, climb the stairs and access any floor within that building. This ensures the able bodied person an ease of access that may be denied to a person with a physical disability. Focusing on the definition of inequality, the able bodied person does not face any physical barriers that may restrict their access or limit their resources. Privilege is often invisible to those who have it, because privileges are experienced on a daily basis and become normalized overtime. Therefore, as global citizens our challenge is to make power and privilege visible in order to disrupt it.

Privilege in Every Day Life

Peggy McIntosh wrote a now famous article, which challenges people to consider their daily routine and uncover aspects of privilege in their own lives. The article was written in 1992 and a few of the outlined factors may not apply to as many people today however, there are still a number of relevant points that should be debated and discussed. Each point highlights an area of invisible privilege that is a common experience for many individuals (McIntosh, 1988).

To summarize the basic theme of McIntosh's article consider these points and respond to whether the statement is true or false.

True   False

☐ ☐   If you are sick and have to miss some time at work you do not have to worry about how you will afford to take the time needed to recuperate.

☐ ☐   Most of the people in high governmental positions are of the same race or ethnic background as you.

☐ ☐   The standards used to evaluate you in a position generally do not consider gender as factor of your ability.

☐ ☐   You do not run the risk of having your entire identity being reduced to the single aspect of your sexuality.

☐ ☐   You do not have to worry about being excluded from a position or work assignment based on physical ability.

☐ ☐   Your religion is not judged and condemned based on the actions of a small group of people (Johnson 2006, p. 25-32).

What motivates those who benefit from privilege and power to joint in the fight against inequality?

_____
_____
_____
_____
_____
_____
_____

Adapted from Mack, T. & Picower, B. (Eds.) (2009) Planning to Change the World. New York Collective of Radical Educators and the Education for Liberation Network, p. 16.

THINKING ABOUT PRIVILEGE

What are the privileges that you experience?

_____
_____
_____
_____
_____

What are the privileges that you lack? Why do you not have these privileges?

_____
_____
_____
_____
_____
_____
_____
_____
_____
_____
_____
_____
_____
_____

Ideology

To further examine inequalities, the third factor we will explore is how our ideas, beliefs and opinions are formed and perceive the social world. As outlined in chapter 3, ideologies mask and influence what we think is important. As a result, they are reinforced in the systems and structures that guide our actions, practices and policies.

Ideologies are rooted in history and are maintained through social structures that dictate the order of our society. The belief that certain groups are more superior to others has been entrenched in social structures for generations. For instance, the social construction of a female's position within society is considered to be nurturing, caring, weak and subordinate to men. This understanding has been manifested historically, reinforced over time and continues to marginalize women. The example reinforces the prevailing ideologies that benefit members of a dominant group (in this case men), and women's economic and social inequality.

Courtesy of Shutterstock.

Photo by Jared Purdy

We can also look at the history of Aboriginal peoples in Canada in order to demonstrate how ideologies informed behaviors and shaped social structures controlled by Canadian settlers.   The history of Canada has been marked by a deeply held and prevailing idea that Aboriginal peoples needed to be saved and integrated into a more civilized culture.   Underlying this move to assimilate Aboriginals was the belief that Christianity and European culture were superior. This belief led to the creation of the residential school system that relied on the forced removal and relocation of Aboriginal children from their homes and communities to remote schools. This displacement of Aborginal children compromised local economic systems, and led to the fragmentation of community networks, and loss of language and ways of knowing. Inequalities between Aboriginal peoples and Canadian settlers and newcomers continue to exist today. Ideology and history provide some clues about the causes of this present day reality.

Inequalities Throughout History

Identify three examples of inequalities throughout history. (Something that happened in the past that is no longer taking place i.e. Trans-Atlantic slavery). Discuss why the examples you provide are inequitable.

1) _____
_____
_____
_____
_____

2) _____
_____
_____
_____
_____

3) _____
_____
_____
_____
_____

Barriers

The final factors that contribute to inequalities are barriers that restrict access and full participation in society for some groups. Ideologies, supported by everyday actions, can lead to barriers that are effective in producing inequalities within society. Barriers can be understood as *visible or invisible* obstacles that prevent or limit people's access to the resources, opportunities and benefits of membership in society. These barriers are largely encountered by individuals and groups who are non-dominant through one or more of their social identities.

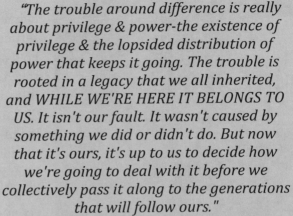

"The trouble around difference is really about privilege & power-the existence of privilege & the lopsided distribution of power that keeps it going. The trouble is rooted in a legacy that we all inherited, and WHILE WE'RE HERE IT BELONGS TO US. It isn't our fault. It wasn't caused by something we did or didn't do. But now that it's ours, it's up to us to decide how we're going to deal with it before we collectively pass it along to the generations that will follow ours."
~ Allen G. Johnson, In Privilege, Power, and Difference

Visible barriers include those public and private spaces that are inaccessible to individuals who have a physical disability. This is a literal interpretation of the term barrier but remains a very real restriction on the mobility of people. Thinking back to our work in Chapter 3, we also know that visible barriers include the documented policies and practices in any economic, political or social institution. These policies and practices largely represent the interest of members of dominant groups. As a result, those in non-dominant groups are restricted from participating and are not represented within public policy. For example, Canada accepts internationally trained immigrants based on a points system. This system admits individuals on the basis of educational credentials, length of work experience, and knowledge of one of the official languages (Reitz, 2006). This system demonstrates a visible barrier because immigration policies are in place to favor a certain category of individuals and deny access to others.

Courtesy of Shutterstock.

Alternatively, *invisible barriers* are not outlined and defined in the form of laws and policies; however, they are still maintained within social structures. Continuing with the previous example, this immigration policy illuminates invisible barriers to internationally trained immigrants once they arrive to Canada. They encounter significant challenges when they try to access employment in their area of expertise and training. Therefore, many are underemployed, unemployed or seek re-training.

INVISIBILITY OF PRIVILEGE

Imagine waking up tomorrow and being a different sexual orientation. Consider how your life will be different. Consider what adjustments you will need to make. More specifically, as this new person, will:

You have more of less privilege and power? Why or why not?

_____
_____
_____
_____
_____
_____

You have more of less difficulty finding the job of your choice? Why or why not?

_____
_____
_____
_____
_____
_____
_____

You feel safe to be open and honest with others regarding your new identity? Why or why not?

_____
_____
_____
_____
_____
_____
_____

Your close circle of friends remains the same? Why or why not?

_____
_____
_____
_____
_____
_____

From Bucher, R.D. (2008) Building Cultural Intelligence (CQ): Nine Megaskills. Pearson Publishers: New York. p. 112.

AGENTS OF SOCIAL CHANGE: GLOBAL CITIZENS IN ACTION

Activist: Kim Dae-Jung

1925 - 2009
Activist for democratic reform and Nobel Peace Prize Recipient
South Korea

Compiled by Sarah Duffy

Kim Dae-Jung was born in South Korea on December 3, 1925. In response to the dictatorial rule in South Korea, Kim Dae-Jung entered politics in 1961. He became a junior leader within his party, speaking out publicly against President Park Chung Hee and his regime. Subsequently, Kim was chosen as the presidential candidate for the new Democratic Party in 1971. He ran against the incumbent (President Park Chung Hee) and gained 46 per cent of the votes. As the opposition leader, Kim experienced an attempt on his life by his political opponents and was seriously injured. In President Park's subsequent term, he imposed a law banning all political activities, giving him power for life. Kim Dae-Jung opposed these measures and again led campaigns against President Park. In response to this, he was abducted by the Korean Central Intelligence Agency and, after international outcry, was placed under house arrest.

On March 1, 1976, he joined other activists in issuing the "Independence Day Declaration for Democratization." This initiated pro-democracy demonstrations in South Korea and he was subsequently sentenced to five years in prison. He was released but, again, placed under house arrest. Following the assassination of President Park in 1979, Kim had his rights restored; however, he was placed in prison again in 1980 after a group of soldiers took power and charged him with treason. A military court sentenced him to death, which was changed to life imprisonment and then a 20-year prison term. Subsequently, his prison term was suspended and he was allowed to travel to the United States where he remained in exile until 1985.

Kim returned to Seoul in 1985 and was successfully cleared of all charges and had all his rights restored. He ran for presidential election in 1987, 1992 and was then elected to president in 1997. At this time, the country was in a financial crisis. As president, Kim worked on economic recovery and was able help the country recover. He was also instrumental in helping to strengthen the relationship between North and South Korea. Kim was awarded the Nobel Peace Prize in 2000. He passed away in 2009 and is remembered for advancing democratic reform in South Korea and helping the country through the 1997-1998 financial crisis.

The Nobel Peace Prize, 2000 – Biography, Kim Dae-Jung (Date Unknown) Retrieved from http://nobelprize.org/nobel_prizes/peace/laureates/2000/dae-jung-bio.html

Kim Dae-Jung (Date Unknown) Retrieved from http://en.wikipedia.org/wiki/Kim_Dae-jung

Moving to Equity, Advancing Equality

As members of a global community, we continue to be inspired by a desire for meaningful and enduring equality in local and global contexts. Equality can be understood as the same treatment of people. Equality is concerned with providing universal access to opportunities and resources within a society and ensuring the full participation of all members within that society.

In this chapter, we rely on the concepts of social stratification, power and privilege, ideologies and barriers to understand why inequalities exist and to document their impacts on individuals and groups around the world. As global citizens, we have engaged in social analysis, described in Chapter 3, in order to better understand inequality as a global social problem. With this foundational knowledge, we are ready to explore visions for change and strategies for action.

Equity: Focuses on fairness and refers to fair access to resources, opportunities and outcomes.

Courtesy of Shutterstock.

If we consider the definition of equality, it becomes difficult and, perhaps even impossible, to imagine a world in which full equality or same treatment of all individuals can be achieved. This is where we turn to equity as a strategy to move societies to a place of greater and deeper equality. **Equity** focuses on fairness and refers to fair access to resources, opportunities and outcomes. In contrast, equality has an overemphasis on the idea of sameness. In an effort to treat everyone the same, equality fails to consider history, current contexts and circumstances of individuals and groups. Equity pays attention to how power is working in society and challenges unfair systems and practices. Any effort to dismantle unfair systems demands an analysis of societal stratification, the distribution of power and privilege, the influence of dominant ideologies, and the visible and invisible barriers that limit access and participation. In doing so, we create the conditions for equality that exists beyond declarations and charter documents.

"Human rights is a universal standard. It is a component of every religion and every civilization."
~ Shirin Ebadi, activist for women's, children's, and refugee rights

Equity allows us to work towards reducing the levels of inequality by applying fair solutions in any given situation. It forces systems to consider differences of individuals when creating just solutions. The face of equity can be confusing. It can mean treating people differently in order to ultimately treat them fairly (Lee, 2002).

Courtesy of Shutterstock

What shoe size do you wear?

Let's pretend all the students in the class were asked to take off their shoes and place them in the centre of the room. Once all the students have removed their shoes, the instructor is given the task to redistribute the shoes to the students. If the instructor were to use equality, every student would receive one pair of shoes, any pair of shoes. Equality requires all students to be treated the same. Equity on the other hand, would require the instructor to ensure that the pair of shoes that each student received fits the student who receives it.

Equity takes into consideration our differences because we do not live in a one size fits all world.

Globally, there is a need for achieving equity in all areas of life. "We must always remember that equity is a human issue, affecting real, individual human beings. Equity and inequality have personal repercussions, and are not simply abstract statistics or broad social issues" (Lee, 2003, p. 2). In order to effectively move towards an equitable society we must go through the process of social analysis and take action that will help lead us to social justice.

"How can one not speak about war, poverty, and inequality when people who suffer from these afflictions don't have a voice to speak. "
~ Isabel Allende, author

Photo by Jared Purdy

Thinking About Equality and Equity

Imagine for a second that there was a system that provided clothing for every person in the world. If our goal were to use equality and treat everyone the same, each person would receive the same items of clothing. A person living in Alaska, USA would receive exactly the same items of clothing as another person living in Mumbai, India. In this situation if equality is applied, do you think the clothing needs of a person in Mumbai are the same as a person in Alaska? Why?

_____
_____
_____
_____
_____

What might be a better approach in an effort to give people what they need?

_____
_____
_____
_____
_____
_____

IN YOUR OWN WORDS

Explain the meaning of equality using your own words and provide an example from your own life.

_____
_____
_____
_____
_____

Explain the meaning of equity using your own words and provide an example from your own life.

_____
_____
_____
_____
_____

What is the main difference between the two?

_____
_____
_____

Stop and Reflect

Can a system of **equality** continue to perpetuate **inequality**? If so, how and why?

_____
_____
_____
_____
_____
_____
_____
_____
_____
_____

How can society reach equity for all?

_____
_____
_____
_____
_____
_____
_____
_____
_____
_____
_____
_____
_____
_____
_____
_____
_____

"If you have come here to help me, then you are wasting
your time...But if you have come because your liberation is
bound up with mine, then let us work together."
~ Lila Watson, Indigenous Australian visual artist and Woman's
Rights activist

Getting Engaged: Activities

A Quick Recap

After reading this chapter, reflect on and summarize:

What do you know about:

Privilege:

_____
_____
_____

Power:

_____
_____
_____

Inequality:

_____
_____
_____

Equality:

_____
_____
_____

Equity:

_____
_____
_____

What would you like to know more about? What questions do you have?

_____
_____
_____
_____
_____
_____
_____
_____

TAKE A STAND: Equality or Equity

For each of the short cases decide if equality or equity would apply and explain why.

CASE A:
A man and a woman have the same level of education, experience, and qualification for a position. How should their wage be reflected? Why?

_____
_____
_____
_____
_____
_____

CASE B:
A 14 year old female and a 20-year-old female are charged with first-degree murder. How should their sentence be applied?

_____
_____
_____
_____
_____
_____

CASE C:
Two female students who are competing for a co-op position are required to write an exam at the end of a course. There is a time limit for the test as one of the skills being tested is speed. One of the students has a reading disability. Should she be given more time?

_____
_____
_____
_____
_____

CASE D:
Two patients come into the emergency room of a hospital with life threatening injuries at the exact same time. One of the patients is 4 years old and the other is 72 years old. You do not have enough staff to adequately treat both. Who do you treat?

_____
_____
_____
_____
_____

Equity in the Workplace

What is your designated profession?

_____
_____
_____

When you finish school, what do you intend to do as a career choice?

_____
_____
_____

Why is equity important in your profession?

_____
_____
_____
_____
_____
_____
_____
_____
_____
_____
_____

How can you make a difference in your designated profession to work towards social justice?

_____
_____
_____
_____
_____
_____
_____
_____
_____
_____
_____
_____
_____
_____
_____
_____
_____

UNDERSTANDING THE NATURE OF POWER

Getting results is very different for the powerful and powerless. Think back to the last time someone with power over you asked you to do something. What was your response?

_____
_____
_____
_____
_____
_____

Now imagine how you would react if the person making the request had little or no power. Would your response have been different? Why?

_____
_____
_____
_____
_____

From Bucher, R. D. (2008). Building Cultural Intelligence (CQ): Nine Megaskills. Pearson Publishers: New Jersey, pg. 231.

Power and Privilege

Discuss how and why power and privilege are related.

Why does an individual who has privilege also have power?

_____
_____
_____
_____
_____

In what ways does power provide benefits in society?

_____
_____
_____
_____
_____

INVISIBILITY OF PRIVILEGE

Person One	Person Two	Person Three
Tall White Male Average weight Age in 40's	Very short White Female Average weight Age in 70's	Average height Black Female Overweight Age in 30's

Think about the differences of these three individuals.
• How often do you think about your height?
• How often do you think about your race?
• How often do you think about your gender?
• How often do you think about your weight?
• How often do you think about your age?

Take some time to think about the possible responses of the three individuals:

1. Which person do you think thought about height most often?

_____

2. Which person do you think thought about race most often? Why?

_____

3. Which person do you think thought about gender most often? Why?

_____

4. Which person do you think thought about weight most often? Why?

_____

5. Which person do you think though about age most often? Why?

_____

Examine your answers to each of these five questions. Why do you think you answered the way you did?

_____
_____
_____
_____
_____
_____

From Bucher, R. D. (2008). Building Cultural Intelligence (CQ): Nine Megaskills. Pearson Publishers: New Jersey, pg. 240-241.

INVISIBILITY OF PRIVILEGE

What types of privileges did each of the three individuals have?

_____
_____
_____
_____
_____
_____

Explain how each of these individuals were oblivious to their privileges (privileges were invisible to them)?

_____
_____
_____
_____
_____
_____

Why is it problematic when we are oblivious of our privileges?

_____
_____
_____
_____
_____

From Bucher, R. D. (2008). Building Cultural Intelligence (CQ): Nine Megaskills. Pearson Publishers: New Jersey, pg. 240-241.

Are you more aware of those situations in which you have privileges or those in which you lack privileges? What might account for this? Provide examples of your experiences.

_____
_____
_____
_____
_____
_____
_____
_____
_____
_____

From Bucher, R. D. (2008). Building Cultural Intelligence (CQ): Nine Megaskills. Pearson Publishers: New Jersey, pg. 239.

FROM EQUITY TO SOCIAL JUSTICE

Think about what you have learned in this chapter and the concepts covered. Discuss why and how equity leads to social justice.

_____
_____
_____
_____
_____
_____
_____
_____
_____
_____
_____
_____
_____
_____
_____
_____
_____
_____
_____
_____
_____
_____
_____
_____
_____
_____
_____
_____
_____
_____
_____
_____
_____
_____
_____
_____
_____
_____
_____
_____
_____
_____
_____
_____
_____
_____

Portfolio Sharing Session

Make a list of the activities, assignments and course work you have completed during this unit:

_____
_____
_____

Decide which artifact from the list above you would like to share with your classmates. Which of the things on this list had the most impact on you or provided the most learning?

_____
_____
_____

Reflect on why this item was so meaningful: Why did you choose that item of learning? What did it tell you about yourself? What have you learned or discovered that you hadn't thought of before? How does it relate to your life, your own experiences? How will it affect your actions in the future? What do you still feel you need to learn?

_____
_____
_____
_____
_____

Bring your portfolio to class, including your selected artifact and reflection, and be prepared to share them a group and/or the class.
Listen carefully to the feedback of others. Write points about that feedback here:

_____
_____
_____
_____

What insight does this feedback provide you with? How does it affect your thinking and what you might do in the future as you continue learning in this area?

_____
_____
_____

Listen attentively to others as they share their artifacts with you. Provide them with respectful and thoughtful feedback. Make some notes here about anything they share that has particular meaning for you:

_____
_____
_____

Developed by Gina Marshall, Stanley Doyle-Wood, Holly Baines, Julia Satov, Zabedia Nazim (2010) Centennial College, Toronto, ON.

Chapter Summary

Definitions:

Dominant Group: Those who are disproportionately at the top of the hierarchy of class.

Equity: Focuses on fairness and refers to fair access to resources, opportunities and outcomes.

Inequality: Refers to any difference in the treatment of people on the basis of class, gender, age, ability, race, ethnicity, sexuality, or citizenship.

Non-dominant Groups: Those whose members are not in positions of power with limited access to power.

Power: The capacity to control resources, which allows structures of dominance and subordination to be created and maintained among social groups (McMullin, 2004 p. 29).

Privilege: "Is gained through unearned power that gives dominant group members economic, social, and political advantage" (Lopes & Thomas, 2006, p.266).

Social Stratification: Refers to "...the hierarchical arrangement of large social groups on the basis of their control over basic resources" (Kendall, 2010, p.214).

Main Concepts:

- Identification and discussion of inequality
- Reasons for the existence of inequalities
- Social stratification and inequality
- Power and privilege and inequality
- Ideology and inequality
- Barriers and inequality
- Moving past inequality to equity
- Equity locally and globally - How do we achieve it?

Additional Resources

The social construction of difference and inequality: race, class, gender, and sexuality 3rd ed., by Tracy Orr (Centennial College Libraries)

Description: "This anthology examines the social construction of race, class, gender, and sexuality and the institutional bases for these relations. The editor's goal is to help students see race, class, gender, and sexuality as both sources of identity and systems of social stratification." (Goodreads. (n.d.) Retrieved from http://www.goodreads.com)

Human Rights Watch http://www.hrw.org/

Description: This is the website for Human Rights Watch, an independent organization that focuses on defending human rights around the world.

Aboriginal History Did you know? Parts 1-4 – YouTube.com

Description: This series of video discusses the injustices in Aboriginal history in Canada.

Social inequality in Canada: patterns, problems, and policies, by Edward Grabb (Centennial College Libraries)

Description: "Social Inequality in Canada is a collection of twenty-eight articles that cover all of the major aspects of social inequality. The text covers two broad components: objective or structural conditions of social inequality (power, poverty and wealth, occupations, and educational attainment, in particular) and ideologies that help support these differences." (mypearsonstore. (n.d.) Retrieved from www.mypearsonstore.ca)

References

Allende, I. (Date Unknown). Equity Quote. In Mack, T. & Picower, B. (Eds.) (2009) *Planning to Change the World: A Plan Book for Social Justice Teachers.* New York Collective of Radical Educators and the Education for Liberation Network, p. 29

Biography. (Date Unknown). Mahatma Gandhi Retrieved from http://www.biography.com/articles/Mahatma-Gandhi-9305898.

Bucher, R.D. (2008) *Building Cultural Intelligence (CQ): Nine Megaskills.* Pearson Publishers: New York. p. 112, 231, 239, 240, 241.

Clinton, H. (2009) *Remarks at Release of the Ninth Annual Trafficking in Persons Report Alongside Leaders in Congress.* Retrieved on September 30, 2010 from http://www.state.gov/secretary/rm/2009a/06/124872.htm

Currey, F. (2009). In *Global Citizenship: From Social Analysis to Social Action.* Pearson Publishers, p. 107.

Dae-Jung, K. (Date Unknown). Retrieved on September 26, 2010 from http://en.wikipedia.org/wiki/Kim_Dae-jung

Ebdai, S. (Date Unknown) Equity Quote. Retrieved on October 6, 2010 from http://www.brainyquote.com/quotes/authors/s/shirin_ebadi.html

Gandhi, M. (Date Unknown) Social Action Quote. Retrieved on October 6, 2010 from http://www.brainyquote.com/quotes/quotes/m/mohandasga131253.htm

Grabb, E. G (2006). *Theories of Social Inequality,* 5th ed. Toronto, Canada: Harcourt Brace & Company.

Johnson, Allan G. (2006). *Privilege, Power and Difference*, 2nd ed. New York, NY: McGraw-Hill.

Keller, H. (Date Unknown). Retrieved on September 26, 2010 from http://www.afb.org/Section.asp?SectionID=1

Keller, H. (Date Unknown). Retrieved on September 26, 2010 from http://www.rnib.org.uk/aboutus/aboutsightloss/famous/Pages/helenkeller.aspx

Kendall, D. (2010). *Sociology in Our Times: The Essentials.* Belmont, CA: Wadsworth, Cengage Learning.

Kendall, D., Nygaard, V.L. & Thompson, E. (2004). *Social Problems in a Diverse Society.* Toronto, Canada: Pearson Education Canada.

Lee, E. (2002). Coaching For Equity. *New Teacher Centre Reflections, 5*, 1-2.

Lee, U. (2010, September). September 16, 1932 : Gandhi Begins Hunger Strike. Retrieved on September 26, 2010 from the Take Part http://www.takepart.com/news/2010/09/15/september-16-1932-ghandi-begins-hunger-strike

Lopes, T. & Thomas, B. (2006). *Dancing on Live Embers: Challenging Racism in Institutions.* Toronto, Canada: Between the Lines.

Mack, T. & Picower, B. (Eds.) (2009) *Planning to Change the World: A Plan Book for Social Justice Teachers.* New York Collective of Radical Educators and the Education for Liberation Network, p. 16.

Mankiller, W. (Date Unknown) Equality and Equity Quote. Retrieved on September 30, 2010 from http://www.brainyquote.com/quotes/authors/w/wilma_mankiller.html

McIntosh, P. (1988). In *Global Citizenship: From Social Analysis to Social Action.* Pearson Publishers.

Nobel Peace Prize. (Date Unknown). Biography, Kim Dae-Jung. Retrieved on September 26, 2010 from http://nobelprize.org/nobel_prizes/peace/laureates/2000/dae-jung-bio.html

Parks, R. (Date Unknown) Equality and Equity Quote. Retrieved on October 5, 2010 from http://www.brainyquote.com/quotes/keywords/remembered_3.html

Reitz, J. (2006). Does Canadian experience in immigrant incorporation have lessons for Europe? Text of keynote address presented to third annual conference of the IMISCOE (International Migration, Integration and Social Cohesion) network of excellence in European migration research, Vienna, Italy.

Statistics Canada. (2005). The Daily, Thursday February 12th, 2005. Retrieved from the world wide web on October 5, 2010 from http://www.statcan.gc.ca/pub/75-001-x/2009112/article/11055-eng.htm#a1.

Watson, L. (Date Unknown) Equity Quote. Retrieved on October 4, 2010 from http://www.ssc.wisc.edu/~oliver/soc220/Lectures220/General/AntiRacism%20Quotes.htm

Wiesel, E. (Date Unknown) Equality and Equity Quote. Retrieved October 4, 2010 from http://thinkexist.com/quotation/there_may_be_times_when_we_are_powerless_to/205068.html

Notes

CHAPTER 7

Making a Difference Through Social Action

Courtesy of Shutterstock.

CHAPTER OBJECTIVES:

- Defining social action and its importance

- Defining social justice

- Exploring institutional and grassroots approaches and responses to inequality

- Understanding why equity leads to social justice

- Explore ways in which you can become actively involved in social change

Doug Kerr and Sarah Duffy

Introduction

In this chapter you will learn about social action. We will examine different forms of social action and ways in which people are working to change society. We will look at various approaches, including individual actions, community organizations, and social movements. We will highlight historical and current activists who have made a difference in the fight for human rights and social justice. We will discuss social justice and charity, which are both types of social action. Finally, at the end of this chapter we will discuss how each of us can get involved in social change.

What is Social Action and Why is Social Action Important?

Sophia is the founder of Snug as a Bug, Kids Helping Kids. This year alone, her organization has organized packaged and delivered 3,000 care packages to children living in Toronto's homeless shelters. This is the organization's sixth year of operation. Today, Sophia is 17 years old.
(Daubs, 2010)

M.C Mehta is an environmental lawyer and activist who has won a series of high profile cases in India. The outcomes of these cases have significantly contributed to the health of the environment in India, including acts such as forcing companies to stop polluting sites like the Ganges River and Taj Mahal and introducing bylaws that ensure the 700,000 rickshaws in New Delhi run on clean natural gas instead of gasoline. Mehta makes less in one year than other lawyers make in a single court hearing but he continues with his work and has developed credibility with numerous judges in the country because he is known to act selflessly and in the best interest of society.
(Westhead, 2010)

Asafa is a Toronto taxi driver. He has been fighting for two years against the City of Toronto's taxi licensing policies which he says have created a two tier system that discriminates against minorities and newcomers. He has taken his case to the Human Rights Tribunal and hopes that his work will result in system changes that will remove the barriers that currently limit some groups from making a successful living as a taxi driver. (Javed, 2010)

Dave is described as a social entrepreneur. His goal in life is to make the city of Toronto a better place to live. He is committed to community activism, leading and participating in a range of actions such as guerrilla gardening (planting flowers in gaps of parking lots as a way of transforming space) and hosting City Idol (a competition for city councillor hopefuls). Dave as he is known, doesn't get paid for his work. He has slept in 26 homes over 14 months but he continues with his mission.
(Porter, 2010)

These are stories of individuals who are making a difference, individuals who are taking action - social action. Social action involves doing something to make the world a better place and is something that anyone can participate in. We do not need to be activists to take social action. Social action starts with an understanding of social problems, then moves towards an analysis of those problems, and concludes with the most important step - acting. Social action is about caring. It is about doing. It is about giving – time, money, energy, passion

Courtesy of Shutterstock.

and commitment. It is about addressing inequalities and issues that concern us. Social action is about change, social change. It is about trying to solve or reduce the issues that our community and the planet face today: poverty, disease, malnutrition, addictions, racism, homophobia, gender inequality, war, economic inequality, environmental destruction and climate change, to name a few. Social action is something you can integrate into your everyday life, devote your free time towards, or even something you can build your career upon.

Social Action: Individual or group behavior that involves interaction with other individuals or groups, especially organized action towards social reform (Dictionary.com).

Effective action requires planning. Effective social action begins with social analysis – raising questions about society and seeking possible answers or solutions. As we discussed in Chapter 3, social analysis helps us develop a critical awareness of the world, an awareness that identifies how society operates, how the "deck is stacked, how the rules are bent or broken for whose benefit." (Clarke, Czerny, & Swift, 2009, p. 178). Social action requires that we analyse how society works, examine who has power and why power dynamics exist. We should also understand our own positions of power and privilege, in addition to identifying our own biases. By doing this type of analysis first, we can gain a better understanding of the root causes of issues, which helps us focus our action on areas that will lead to greater social justice.

Social action may have a global reach.
As global citizens, the issues that concern us can be global in nature, linked to the countries and communities of others. As the world becomes smaller due to faster and easier communication, we are all increasingly aware of how issues in other parts of the world can impact our lives in Canada. We may have a friend living in a country devastated by civil war or we may have a personal experience visiting another country and seeing extreme poverty on the streets. With the internet, we can easily communicate with friends and strangers in all corners of the planet. Our awareness can lead to the asking of questions about why inequality and injustice continues in the world. Such questions may inspire us to action. As global economies become more closely linked, our actions here in Canada have a direct impact on the lives of people on the other side of the world. For instance, the rights of child workers in China or Bangladesh become connected to our own actions in Canada as a result of the products we purchase or endorse. The affordability of everything from clothes, to food, to electronic gadgets is connected to mass production of goods by cheap labour around the world. Increasingly, people around the world are asking critical questions about their own role in the global economy and this is leading to new forms of social action, such as the **fair trade** movement.

> *"Peace is not this utopian idea of dashing through a field of dandelions. You know, its hard work. Sometimes the peacemakers lose their lives in the process."*
> ~ Aqeela Sherrills, campaigner against gang violence and former Crip

Stop and Reflect

How often do you stop and think about who made the clothes you wear? What would you do if you knew that a 12-year old child was forced to work in a sweatshop to make your jeans? Would you change your purchasing habits if you knew this? Consumers concerned about global inequality may decide to take personal action through choosing to purchase fair trade products and goods to ensure that more money stays in the hands of people who produce the product.

What is your response to this?

_____
_____
_____
_____
_____
_____
_____
_____
_____
_____
_____
_____
_____
_____
_____
_____

Fair Trade: An alternative approach to conventional international trade. It is a trading partnership which aims at sustainable development for excluded and disadvantaged producers. It seeks to do this by providing better trading conditions, by awareness raising and by campaigning (Oxfam).

Courtesy of Shutterstock.

Social action is also local. Social action can happen when people try to effect change at a neighbourhood level. For example, a group of people in Scarborough might organize their own community gardening project to get to know their neighbours, share their food costs, and improve the local environment or they might organize a food drive to help those in their community. Individuals can also try to achieve change at a provincial or national level by getting involved in advocacy organizations or political parties. People might become active in a group such as Greenpeace Canada, which is trying to encourage the government to set targets to reduce greenhouse gas emissions. Some people get involved in public protest movements to raise awareness around the issues they are concerned about.

The results of social action are all around us. Your right to health care, your right to vote, sending your children to free public schools, all these rights and privileges are the result of people who worked to improve the lives of their communities. Canada has a long history of social action leading to progressive social change.

WHAT WOULD YOU DO?

What would you do if you knew that a toxic waste site existed near your neighbourhood? Would you organize your neighbors to demonstrate outside the company that owned the site? Would you call your local politicians to share your concerns? People often become active in social change when issues of inequality or injustice are outside their doorsteps.

What is your response to this?

_____
_____
_____
_____
_____
_____
_____
_____
_____
_____
_____
_____
_____
_____
_____
_____

AGENTS OF SOCIAL CHANGE: GLOBAL CITIZENS IN ACTION

Activist: MC Mehta

October 12, 1946 -
Activist for Environmental Justice
India

Compiled by Sarah Duffy

Mahessh Chandra (MC) Mehta was born in 1946 in a small village in district Rajouri in the Indian state of Jammu and Kashmir. Mehta completed his education and then went onto get a law degree and started his practice in the Jammu and Kashmir High Court. During this time, he was active in social and political issues and encouraged other students to take a stand against discrimination in the Jammu region.

In 1983, Mehta moved to Delhi and began his career as a Supreme Court Lawyer. In 1984, he visited the Indian landmark, the Taj Mahal, for the first time and he saw that the building's marble had turned yellow and had become pitted due to pollutants from nearby industries. As a result of this, Mehta filed his first environmental case in the Supreme Court of India. In 1985, Mehta learned that the Ganges River had caught fire due to industrial waste that was discarded into the river. He filed a petition with the Supreme Court against the polluting factories and any neighbouring municipalities.

In 1993, after a decade of court battles, the Supreme Court ordered 212 small factories around the Taj Mahal to close due to lack of pollution control devices. In the Ganges case, 5,000 factories have been told to install pollution controls and a number of factories have been closed. In addition, 250 towns and cities along the Ganges have been ordered to set up sewage treatment plans.

Over time, Mehta has obtained approximately 40 landmark judgements and other orders from the Supreme Court and he continues to fight against industries that create hazardous wastes and have other damaging impacts on the environment.

MC Mehta. (Date Unknown). Retrieved September 24, 2010, from MC Mehta Environmental Foundation: mcmef.org

MC Mehta. (Date Unknown). Retrieved September 24, 2010, from Goldman Prize: goldmanprize.org

Photo by Alice Kieltyka

Throughout the 20th century, Canadian workers have advocated for better working conditions, pensions, health insurance, and safer work environments. The women's movement led to some Canadian women receiving the right to vote in 1919 and later continued to advance women's roles in society, politics and business. Social action is often a struggle against the status quo as it challenges existing power structures. There are many social problems in Canada that **activists** are advocating to change today, such as the rights of migrant workers, the health of aboriginal Canadians, and homelessness.

> **Activist**: An individual who devotes their time, either paid or unpaid, to social change work.

A current example of social action is the change in environmental regulations. We are also seeing increased expectations of personal responsibility with regard to the environment. The environmental movement - once considered on the fringes of society - has become more mainstream as organizations involved in environmental issues become larger and more influential. In Canada, many municipalities and provinces have adopted new environmentally-friendly policies and laws. Energy efficient cars, recycling programs, investment in green energy systems such as solar, wind and geothermal, are just some of the examples of how the environmental movement is propelling social change today in Canada. Citizens' advocacy groups such as the Sierra Club Canada, Evergreen, Environmental Defence, and the David Suzuki Foundation have engaged people across Canada in advocating for more policies that lessen our impact on the environment. Despite this progress, there are still social issues and inequalities in Canadian society.

> Social action is important because we are making the world a better place for each of us and, in turn, for our children. Social action is important because it makes our lives richer, fuller, more meaningful and more connected.

Grassroots and Institutional Approaches to Change: Who is Making a Difference?

Many movements and organizations around the world are committed to social change, as they work to address economic and social inequalities. Social change can occur at different levels. Change is possible when people organize at a micro, mid-level or macro level (Clarke, Czerny, & Swift, 2009, p. 163). Each of these levels of change is important; each plays a role in creating long-term, sustainable social change. Individuals are making a difference through personal action, getting involved at the **grassroots** level in community organizing, joining or volunteering for non-profits, charities or social enterprises, or becoming active in politics.

> **Grassroots:** A term used to describe social activism at a local or community level.

Courtesy of Shutterstock.

Some forms of social change are at the **micro** or individual level. This type of change focuses on individuals working with small groups and trying to remedy a problem that affects them. Usually, individuals turn to their primary groups when they are having personal problems. This group includes family, close friends and other peers with whom we share our personal experiences. For example, if you help someone who is unemployed by working with them to update their resume you are helping to address unemployment at the individual level.

Micro: Basic or small scale (Free Dictionary Online by Farlex).

Other forms of social change are at the **mid**-range or community level. This includes secondary groups or formal organizations that assist individuals in overcoming problems by either helping them cope with their problems or creating community change. Grassroots groups are one form of mid-range social action. Grassroots means that the agenda is usually driven by a specific community and that it focuses on local issues. It also means that the group operates in a spontaneous and informal way and grows organically through word-of-mouth or through internet-based activism. Activities of grassroots movements could include hosting house meetings, putting up posters, using online social networks to set up virtual communities, distributing petitions, creating videos, mobilizing letter-writing, phone calling and emailing campaigns, and organizing demonstrations. An example of grassroots organizing could include a group of residents in a high-rise tower in Vancouver coming together to advocate to their landlord to improve the quality of the building or address health and safety concerns.

Mid: Medium or middle scale.

Stop and Reflect

Do you know of any grassroots movements in your community?

_____

_____

_____

_____

Do you think that these social movements have achieved their goals? Why or why not?

_____

_____

_____

What is the impact of their action?

_____

_____

_____

Can grassroots movements create long-lasting change? Why or why not?

_____

_____

_____

_____

Over time, these grassroots movements may develop into more formal groups called non-profit organizations, with a broader reach and focus. These organizations are also operating at the mid-range or community level. In Canada, there are over 160,000 non-profit organizations working in a wide diversity of areas, such as sports and recreation, religion, social services, arts and culture, fundraising, environment and housing. These organizations may also include publicly funded bodies such as hospitals or

Courtesy of Shutterstock.

universities and colleges. They also include smaller organizations with limited or no staff, yet they work on local environmental or social justice issues. Just over half of all non-profit organizations in Canada are registered as charities, which allows them to be exempt from taxes and provides their donors with tax credits for the money they give to the organization. (Statistics Canada, 2003).

A new concept in the non-profit sector is social entrepreneurship. This term is used to describe non-profit organizations or activists with social change goals who are using business principles and the market economy to achieve change. An example of a social enterprise might include a community centre in Toronto that starts an Arts and Craft store run by people with mental health challenges. Some social enterprises have been started by successful businesspeople. For example, UK chef and television personality, Jamie Oliver, launched a global chain of restaurants, Fifteen, that employs disadvantaged and jobless young people and trains them in cooking healthy and nutritious food (Fifteen/Mission, Date Unknown).

Did You Know? Social Action in the Business World

In the business world, corporate social responsibility (CSR) is increasing in importance. Many corporations partner with non-profit organizations to achieve their corporate social responsibility goals. Recent studies have shown that corporate social action impacts employee morale and is linked to higher organizational performance. In Canada, many companies participate in United Way campaigns, recruiting fundraising volunteers and raising money to support local charities. National corporations, including all the major banks, sponsor dozens of charitable events from the arts, the environment to social services. Organizations may have entire departments organized to co-ordinate the linking of public relations with corporate social responsibility goals. The Canadian magazine, *Corporate Knights*, has an annual list of the best corporate citizens in Canada, and looks at such environmental indicators as carbon emissions or social indicators such as the percentage of women, aboriginal people or people of colour on corporate Boards of Directors. (Corporate Knights, Date Unknown, http://www.corporateknights.ca/)

Finally, there are some forms of social change that are at the **macro**, institutional or systemic level. When a number of groups, organizations, and individuals begin to collaborate and organize around an issue, a **social movement** may be

> *"If there is a book that you want to read, but it hasn't been written yet, you must be the one to write it."*
> ~ Toni Morrison, Nobel and Pulitzer Prize winning African American author

Macro: Large scale (Free Dictionary Online by Farlex).

initiated. Social movements may include many non-profit organizations, individuals and grassroots groups working toward a common goal. The goal of social movements is usually at the systemic level. They are about changing an entire system, a way of life, or our collective values and beliefs. These movements engage and pressure institutions such as the media, government and corporations, with the goal of addressing the root causes of a social issue through political, legislative or cultural change. Some examples of well-known social movements in Canada include the women's suffrage movement of the early 20th century, the gay rights movement, the pro-environment movement, or the anti-drunk driving movement of recent years. Today around the world there are many social movements for social justice or social change. In much of Latin America and in Australia and New Zealand, there are movements by indigenous peoples for more political representation. In many countries around the world, especially in Africa and South Asia, there are movements for the rights of people living with HIV and AIDS.

Courtesy of Shutterstock.

Social Movement: A group of people with a common ideology who try together to achieve common goals (Free Online Dictionary).

Stop and Reflect

When we look back at history, we can see several large social movements that have pushed for the equality and civil rights of various groups of people, including workers, women, aboriginal people, African Canadians, Asian Canadians, and Lesbian, Gay, Bisexual, Transgender (LGBT) Canadians.

Do you think that those social movements are over now? Why or why not?

_____
_____
_____
_____
_____
_____

Do you think that these social movements have achieved their goals? Why or why not?

_____
_____
_____
_____
_____

MICRO, MID, AND MACRO SOCIAL ACTION

Provide an example of social action at each of the levels:

Micro	Mid	Macro

SOCIAL CHANGE AT THE MACRO LEVEL: THINK ABOUT IT

Why is it important to create change at the macro level?

_____

_____

What influence do institutions such as government and media have over society? Provide an example.

_____

_____

_____

_____

How is this linked to inequality?

_____

_____

_____

Is change at this level long-lasting? Why or why not?

_____

_____

_____

_____

_____

_____

Social action at any level can contribute to real and lasting social change. If we volunteer to teach a newcomer English so that they can get a job, we are contributing to social change. If we hand out flyers for a grassroots movement for greater rights for migrant works we are contributing to social change. If we participate in the social movement to bring stricter environmental guidelines for corporations and individuals, we are contributing to social change.

EVENTS THAT CONTRIBUTED TO SOCIAL CHANGE

Event: The Women's Suffrage Movement

WHERE: Canada

WHAT: The suffrage movement raised awareness and initiated changes in women's rights that benefit all Canadian women today

Compiled by Sarah Duffy

Definition: Suffrage – the right to vote or run for office.

Note: The women's suffrage movement originated in France during the 18th century. The movement was happening in many countries throughout the world and women gained the right to vote in different countries during different years. To date, in some countries, women still do not have the right to run for office.

The women's suffrage movement in Canada began in Toronto with a group led by Emily Stowe. The Toronto Woman's Suffrage Association was formed in 1877. In western Canada, the suffrage movement was initiated in the 1890's. The activities of the suffrage groups included holding meetings, leading demonstrations and sending petitions to parliament. In 1911, the western-Canada group began to make progress under the leadership of Nellie McClung, who helped to organize the Political Equality League, a group that focused on increasing support for the suffrage campaign. As a result of these activities, a number of men and politicians began to support the suffrage movement. Subsequently, during World War 1, women played an active role in supporting the war effort and suffrage received support across the country. In 1916, Manitoba passed a law granting women the right to vote in provincial elections. Other provinces followed and then in 1918 the Women's Franchise Act was passed, permitting all female Canadian citizens over the age of 21 the right to vote in federal elections effective January 1919.

The suffrage movement formed the roots of today's women's movement, which continues to address issues of inequality for women across Canada.

Women's Suffrage. (n.d.). Retrieved from the Canadian Encyclopaedia website: http://www.thecanadianencyclopedia.com/PrinterFriendly.cfm?Params=J1ARTJ0008687

Leadership is a key part of social movements.
Every day people take up causes that are meaningful to them and become leaders for social change. Mahatma Gandhi was an Indian lawyer living in South Africa in 1893 when he was thrown off a train after refusing to move from a first class compartment, which was reserved for white people, to third class, where Asians were required to sit. He went on to become a leader for the rights of Asians in South Africa. After his return

Photo by Jared Purdy

to India, he eventually became a social leader for millions of people and used non-violence and peaceful resistance in his fight for the independence of India from Britain. Individuals like Gandhi are known as social activists, people who take up a cause and devote their time and energy towards its achievement. Throughout history, numerous social activists have worked to address significant inequalities, inspiring others to fight for a common cause and make a contribution towards positive social change.

Did You Know? Activists Who Have Made a Difference

Tracing History - Historical Activists:

Activist: Mahatma Gandhi (1869-1948)
Issue Addressed: Racial equality in India

Activist: Martin Luther King Jr. (1929-1968)
Issues Addressed: Racial equality and poverty in the USA

Activist: Harvey Milk (1930-1978)
Issue Addressed: Equality of homosexuals in the USA

Activist: Nellie McClung (1873-1951)
Issue Addressed: Women's equality in Canada

Creating Change Today – Current Global Activists

Activist: Muhammad Yunus (Bangladesh), Nobel Peace Prize winner
Issue: Works to advance economic and social opportunities for the poor, especially women, through pioneering micro-finance

Activist: Rigoberta Menchu (Guatamala), UNESCO Goodwill Ambassador
Issue: Works to advance the rights of indigenous peoples' rights in Guatemala and around the world

Activist: Shirin Ebadi (Iran), Nobel Peace Prize winner
Issue: Human rights lawyer who works to support women's, children's and refugee rights

Activist: David Suzuki (Canada), Zoologist and broadcaster
Issue: Works to increase environmental awareness and to reduce effects of climate change

Did You Know? Many Types of Organizations are Making a Difference

Charity - Habitat for Humanity - http://www.habitat.ca/

Habitat for Humanity is a faith-based charity that believes in making affordable housing accessible to working families who earn less than the low-income cut off. The organization builds homes by using volunteer labour and donated materials. Homes are then "sold" to families with no money down payment, other than 500 volunteer hours. Families then receive an affordable no-interest mortgage with monthly payments based on 25% to 35% of the family's monthly income.

Charity - Evergreen - http://www.evergreen.ca/

Evergreen is a national Canadian charity that works to make cities more livable through improving the relationship between people and the natural environment. The organization brings together schools, municipalities and other community organizations to improve their local environment, through greening projects, environmental education and training.

Advocacy Group - Amnesty International - http://www.amnesty.ca/

Amnesty International is a network of organizations around the world that work to support people whose human rights are under attack. The organization carries out education and public awareness programs to encourage governments around the world to adhere to international standards of human rights and demand justice for individuals whose rights have been violated.

Grassroots - No One Is Illegal - http://www.nooneisillegal.org/

No One Is Illegal is a grassroots group of citizens that advocates for the rights of temporary migrant workers and fights the deportation of non-status immigrants from Canada. The organization believes that Canada's immigration system is unjust and exploits workers. It conducts public actions including demonstrations and media campaigns to raise awareness of immigration and migrant labour issues.

Social entrepreneurship – Eva's Phoenix Print Shop http://phoenixprintshop.ca/

Eva's Phoenix Print Shop is a socially and environmentally responsible commercial printer. The shop maintains an award-winning training program for homeless youth and is located at a transitional housing facility. Funds raised from the social enterprise go back into the operations of the organization.

Corporate social responsibility - RBC Blue Water Project http://bluewater.rbc.com/

Royal Bank of Canada's Blue Water Project is a corporate project to help protect fresh water in Canada and around the world through charitable grants to protect watersheds or ensure access to clean drinking water. The initiative also promotes responsible water use with employees and clients, and encourages the commercialization of businesses working on water issues.

The Difference Between Social Justice and Charity: Why Does Equity Lead to Social Justice?

Social justice and charity are both forms of social action. They are related concepts but are quite different in the way they attempt to address social inequality. Both are valuable tools that can be used by global citizens to improve their world and communities.

One goal of social action is charity. Traditionally, **charity** is motivated by the desire or pressure to do good and to help those who are less fortunate. Many Canadians make financial donations to organizations that they care about or that are working on important social, cultural and environmental issues. In addition, many Canadians volunteer their time helping to mentor newcomers, to provide rides for the elderly, or support a local church in their outreach with the homeless.

Charity is a theme across all major religions and faith traditions. In Christian theology, the term "caritas" refers to an unlimited kindness towards others. In Islam, sadaqah refers to voluntary acts of compassion and zakat, is one of the five pillars of Islam, the obligation of giving to the poor. In the Jewish faith, tzedakah refers to the obligation to perform charitable acts. In Sikhism, seva is the service performed to benefit the community.

Photo by Jared Purdy

Charity: Generosity and helpfulness especially towards the needy or suffering; aid given to those in need. Also; an institution engaged in relief of the poor (Merriam-Websters Dictionary).

But the question is, how much of a difference does charity make? Are we spending our charitable dollars and volunteer time effectively? We give in order to help the poor, but poverty is widespread. We try and lessen our own impact on the environment but we hear daily of continuing damage and environmental destruction. Millions of people on every continent face discrimination, racism and **xenophobia**. Militarization and war divert tremendous resources away from improving the lives of people around the world. Girls and women on every continent encounter discrimination and challenges in terms of equality of rights, employment, health and education levels. And while Canada is one of the wealthiest nations on earth, there are still many social problems facing our country. Close to two million Canadians struggle with housing affordability while between 200,000 and 300,000 are homeless (CBC, 2007) and many of Canada's aboriginal communities lack basic access to an adequate standard of living compared to that of other Canadians.

Xenophobia: A very strong fear or dislike of individuals who are different from the self or foreign.

Did You Know? Canadian Charities are Registered with the Canada Revenue Agency

The first $200 you donate in a year is eligible for a federal tax credit of 15%. After the first $200, the federal tax credit increases to 29% of the amount over $200. To receive this credit, donors declare their contributions to charity on their annual tax return (Canada Revenue Agency, Date Unknown).

> *"Charity is no substitute for justice withheld"*
> ~ Saint Augustine, 5th Century Philosopher

Social justice is different. It is about addressing the root cause of an issue, not its symptoms. In addition, **social justice** initiatives often raise questions about how society is arranged and whether people in positions of privilege and power owe something to those who are not. (Clarke, Czerny, & Swift, 2009, p. 163). Social justice is often political in nature and refers to seeking a more just and equitable world. In contrast, charity alleviates the symptoms of an issue, leaving the root cause unaddressed. As an example of this difference, charity is giving a poor person some food or clothing, while social justice is advocating to change the economic system so that people have more employment opportunities, to better feed and clothe themselves. Charity is giving to cancer research, while social justice is giving to a group that is organizing to clean up the toxins in our environment. Charity is establishing a scholarship fund for a low income student, while social justice is funding a student group that is organizing to ensure that higher education is affordable for everyone (Collins, Rogers, & Garner, 2000, p. 36.) By looking at these examples, we can see how social justice can alleviate the need for charity over time. For example, if we can change the system so that everyone can afford higher education, we would no longer require scholarship funds to help lower income students. However, if we just continue to develop additional scholarship funds, we help individual students but do not create any enduring, self-sustaining changes that would impact more students in the long term.

Social Justice: A concept based upon the belief that each individual and group within a given society has a right to civil liberties, equal opportunity, fairness, and participation in the educational, economic, institutional, social and moral freedoms and responsibilities valued by the community (Degan & Disman, University of Toronto).

CHARITY OR SOCIAL JUSTICE?

Compare and contrast charity and social justice. Provide examples of each.

Charity	Social Justice

Stop and Reflect

受人以鱼,不如授人以渔"

"Give a man a fish and he will eat for a day. Teach a man to fish and he will eat for a lifetime." ~ Chinese Proverb

What does this quote say about the difference between charity and social justice?

_____
_____
_____
_____
_____
_____
_____

Is the impact of charity and social justice different? How?

_____
_____
_____
_____
_____
_____

In your opinion, is one more effective than the other? Why?

_____
_____
_____
_____
_____

We have all witnessed social changes that have led to increased social justice.

An example in Canada over the past forty years includes advances in the civil rights of the lesbian, gay, bisexual and transgender (LGBT) communities. Not long ago in Canada, LGBT people were viewed as diseased or criminals because of their sexual orientation. In the past thirty years, homosexuality has been decriminalized (1969), sexual orientation has been added to the Canadian Human Rights Act (1996) and same sex marriage has been made legal (2005). These are changes that were made possible because of social activists who believed that all people, regardless of their sexual orientation, deserved equal rights. Activists fought for greater visibility in society and in the media, and pushed for legislative change as well. While homophobia still exists, attitudes towards LGBT people are significantly different than just a few years ago.

Did You Know? Social Justice Milestones in Canadian History

- Slavery of African Canadians was formally abolished in Canada in **1834**
- Women gained the right to vote in federal elections in **1919**
- Chinese Canadians were allowed to vote and become lawyers, accountants and pharmacists after **1947**
- Aboriginal people were allowed to leave reserves without the permission of the federal government in **1951**
- Homosexuality was decriminalized in **1969**
- The Charter of Rights and Freedoms was enacted in **1982**
- The Canadian government apologizes to Aboriginal Canadians for the residential school system in **2008**

When we understand social justice, we begin to see the links between social justice and equity. Equitable initiatives or programs are fair because they treat people differently based on underlying needs. The goal is to create an equal playing field for everyone. An example of this is the Ontario Student Assistance Program (OSAP). This program provides funding to post-secondary students who qualify based on their income level. Lower income students qualify for OSAP, while higher income students do not. The goal of OSAP is to provide access to post secondary education for all individuals regardless of their socio-economic background. This program leads to greater social justice because it ensures that the inequalities between students do not create barriers or impact a student's ability to further his or her education and, in turn, be better positioned for a variety of career and job options.

Courtesy of Shutterstock.

It is important to remember that social action in itself is not sufficient – in fact, not all social action leads to social justice. Social action can be undertaken by any group of people in society. There are groups in society such as xenophobic or racist groups that organize and advocate against equity. The rise of the Nazi Party in Germany or the Ku Klux Klan in North America are examples of these types of group.

While both charity and social justice are forms of social action, their goals and impact are different. Charity addresses symptoms while social justice addresses root causes. It's important to be aware of these differences when choosing the type of social action we want to participate in.

The Difference Between Social Justice and Charity: Why Does Equity Lead to Social Justice?

We are all impacted by injustices in the world around us. Most days, we see, hear or read of situations that are unfair, that go against human rights and human dignity. But many of us don't take action. Why?

Perhaps some of us feel overwhelmed by the social problems facing our society and planet, and we feel that we can't do anything to make a difference. If this is the case, it may help to view social action at three different levels (Kielburger & Kielburger, 2004, p. 122).

Stop and Reflect

"When I gave food to the poor, they called me a saint. When I asked why the poor had no food they called me a communist." Dom Helder Camara, Brazilian Roman Catholic Bishop (1909-1999)

Why do some groups respond negatively to individuals who are focused on social justice?

_____
_____
_____
_____

What motivates this reaction?

_____
_____
_____

Does this type of response make it more difficult to focus on social justice versus charity? Why or why not?

_____
_____
_____
_____
_____

Courtesy of Shutterstock.

The first level of action involves simple, daily personal decisions. This can be as easy as packing garbage-free lunches by using reusable packaging for our sandwiches, drinks and snacks. It could also mean recycling and placing our glass bottles or newspapers in the recycling bin and not littering on the streets. It may involve making a donation to a charity we are passionate about or speaking up if you hear a friend say something racist, sexist or homophobic.

The second level of action involves more significant and long-reaching decisions such as introducing environmentally-friendly products into our homes and encouraging others in our lives to do the same. It could involve joining a community organization or volunteering for a project in your neighbourhood that contributes to environmental well-being.

"Never doubt that a small group of thoughtful, committed citizens can change the world; indeed, it's the only thing that ever does."
~ Margaret Mead, anthropologist

The third level involves major, life changing acts that have a lasting impact on ourselves and others involved. This could mean making a career change to work in the social or environmental sectors. Or it could involve taking a leadership role by organizing your community around an issue, starting your own grassroots initiative or running for public office.

"Every great dream begins with a dreamer. Always remember, you have within you the strength, the patience, and the passion to reach for the stars to change the world."
~ Harriet Tubman, abolitionist and humanitarian

By looking at social action in this way, we begin to see how each of us can play a role in creating change. We can all participate in social action. Not all of us are social activists, and many of us will never lead a grassroots movement but we can participate in social action through the small, daily decisions that create change. Such action may lead us to places we never imagined possible.

Did You Know? Social Action can have a Positive Impact on You Too

From their experiences Craig and Marc Kielburger, co-founders of the non-profit organization Free the Children, found that young people who took social action felt an incredible and lasting impact on their lives. They describe this impact in the following section from their book, *Me to We* (2004) "In our years of working with young people, we have witnessed how helping out others helps (people) develop self-esteem, gain leadership skills, and acquire a sense of purpose and direction. It allows youth to learn respect for themselves and others while fulfilling their true potential. In case after case, we have seen self-doubt replaced with self-respect and watched apathy give way to action" (p. 122).

Many people find that they want to make a difference in society by choosing a career such as social work, law, or health care where they can directly help individuals who are dealing with social problems. Some social workers work with people who are disadvantaged or who are struggling with various challenges. Many students at Centennial College are studying to become social workers in order to help children and youth in the community. Other social workers will work on organizing communities around social justice issues.

Another way that people get involved is through local community organizations or political parties. Millions of Canadians are involved in various kinds of community groups, associations or political parties. Mothers Against Drunk Driving (MADD), a non-profit organization that works to stop drunk driving, was created in 1980 by Candy Lightner, after her 13 year old daughter Cari was struck and killed by a drunk driver. Lightner committed herself to working with other mothers who had lost children in

"If you don't know what you're passion is, realize that one reason for your existence is to find it. Real success means creating a life of meaning through service that fulfills your reason for being here."
~ Oprah Winfrey, television host

drunk driving accidents in an effort to raise awareness about the problem and to change laws so that penalties for drunk driving could be increased.

Courtesy of Shutterstock.

Courtesy of Shutterstock.

People can also get involved in social action work through their places of employment. Increasingly, corporations are not just looking at the financial bottom line but they are also concerned about the social and environmental bottom lines. The Hewitt Associates' 2010 Best Employers in Canada study found a number of linkages between corporate social responsibility and level of employee engagement. In fact, the study found a strong correlation between an employee's perception of the level of corporate social / environmental responsibility and their level of engagement. In addition, leaders of Canadian businesses indicated in the study that they believe corporate social responsibility is good for their reputation as well as employee engagement. These findings demonstrate the importance of social responsibility to businesses (Canadian Business for Social Responsibility, 2010).

SOCIAL ACTION AND YOU!

What are the social issues that you are passionate about? Maybe you lost a relative to cancer and you feel strongly that we need to reduce carcinogenic toxins in the environment. Perhaps you moved to Canada from a country where there was civil war and you believe strongly in peace and non-violence.

What are your motivations and passions?

_____

_____

_____

_____

What are some ways that you could take action?

_____

_____

_____

_____

_____

_____

_____

_____

_____

"Once social change begins it can not be reversed. You can not un-educate the person that has learned to read. You can not humiliate the person who feels pride. You can not oppress the people who are not afraid anymore."
~ Cesar Chavez, Mexican American farm worker and labour leader

A POEM

What is a Social Movement?
it goes on one at a time
it starts when you care
to act, it starts when you do
it again after they said no,
it starts when you say We
and know who you mean, and each
day you mean one more

~ Marge Piercy, The Low Road (2006)

Many people decide that they want to get involved in social change by volunteering in their communities. Almost 12.5 million Canadians, or 46% of the adult population over the age of 15 volunteered over 2.1 billion hours in 2007, (Imagine Canada, 2010) Canadians are also strong supporters of charities through financial donations - 23 million Canadians , 86% of the adult population, donated a total of $10 billion to charities and non-profit organizations in 2000 (Imagine Canada, 2010).

Here at Centennial College, we have the Institute for Global Citizenship. The Institute conducts research on global citizenship and social justice, and serves as a catalyst for social action. The programs and activities of the Institute include the Philosopher's Café, Global Citizenship Programs, Student Exchanges and programs to support new immigrants. These programs offer students an opportunity to

Courtesy of Shutterstock.

get involved in social action and events that are relevant to global citizenship as part of their day-to-day lives at school (Institute for Global Citizenship and Equity, 2010). There are also opportunities for students at Centennial to get involved in the community through volunteer work and student clubs.

> *"The world changes according to the way people see it, and if you can alter, even by a millimeter, the way people look at reality, then you can change the world."*
> ~ James Baldwin, writer and civil rights activist

How Can You Get Involved? Ways to Take Action

You could:

- ✓ gather four friends and initiate a food drive or plant a community garden at a local women's shelter
- ✓ write a letter to your local member of parliament (MP) about an issue that concerns you
- ✓ make a video about a social justice issue such as racism
- ✓ take the bus or your bike one day a week instead of using your car
- ✓ donate to an organization that makes loans to entrepreneurs in developing nations to grow their business and escape poverty
- ✓ take a stand against consumerism and boycott shopping for a day, a week or longer
- ✓ adopt a clean water project with a group of classmates or friends in an at-risk community
- ✓ research the challenges facing Aboriginal people in Canada and advocate for this group by beginning a petition that demands better living standards in Aboriginal communities
- ✓ support the work of a local charity by contacting them and asking if you can volunteer your time
- ✓ join an online social change community such as www.change.org or www.care2.com
- ✓ visit and talk to seniors at a local community centre
- ✓ build awareness of the dangers of Internet addiction in young males by researching the issue and handing out information sheets at the college or in the community
- ✓ participate in a protest rally against government policies on the rights of migrant workers
- ✓ write a song about a social injustice or inequality that you've observed
- ✓ apply to a program for Canadians to volunteer their skills in a country in the global south
- ✓ participate in a fundraising bike rally, run, or walk-a-thon to raise money for a charity
- ✓ volunteer once a week to tutor a newcomer child in English

So, as a global citizen, are you prepared to participate? Will you make a difference? Are you going to analyse and take action on an issue that you care about? Ask yourself these questions and challenge yourself to be engaged, to care about injustice and to do your part to change the world one action at a time!

Getting Inspired: A Word from Toronto's Local Heroes!

As you consider how you can take action read about a few local heroes who have made a difference.

Neethan Shan came to Canada as a 16 year old refugee from the civil war in Sri Lanka. Today, he is the Executive Director of the Coalition of Agencies Service South Asians, an elected School Board Trustee in York Region and has been a candidate for the Provincial Legislature. Neethan is particularly inspired by young people and has been a passionate advocate for youth and immigrant issues.

"I came to Canada from a war torn country. During my childhood, I had survived many close calls for my life. As someone who escaped death many times, I have developed a very strong appreciation for my life. When I think about tens of thousands of people who have perished in the war, I not only feel fortunate but also feel a social responsibility to address the very social injustice and inequities in the world that took their lives." ~ Neethan Shan

---

Farheen Khan is a young Muslim feminist from Mississauga who works with women survivors of sexual violence. She left her job in corporate Canada to become an activist against violence against women, in particular sexual violence, Islamophobia, and all other forms of oppression. She first became active as a student where she led a campaign to encourage the Canada Student Loans Program to develop an interest-free student loans program for Muslim students. This program was to accommodate Muslim students from having to use interest, which many believe compromises their religious values. Since then, Farheen has been involved in many organizations across the GTA. Her focus is stopping violence against women and ensuring that survivors "find a voice to speak". Her book titled "From Behind the Veil: A Hijabi's Journey to Happiness" speaks to her own experience of Islamophobia and racism post 9/11 and the impact of gendered violence that led her to the path of social activism she walks today.

"Social justice work is about finding your inner passion, something that's near and dear to your heart and being able to use your voice to express your vision of changing the status quo and ensuring that equal rights are being given to all. It's the passion to want change and the intention that you make, that will open the windows and doors you need to get to your journey of social activism. Surround yourself with people who think, feel and want change and work on actively engaging with others and sparking that inner desire within them as well. Social Activism can take many shapes and forms find out what you want, why and how, and then take action. Only you can make the change you want to, all you need to do is decide." ~ Farheen Khan

---

Karen Sun is the Executive Director of the Chinese Canadian National Council Toronto (CCNTO), an organization that promotes justice, equity and the civic participation of Chinese Canadians. Originally an environmental activist working on community tree planting and ravine clean-ups, she ended up becoming the head of CCNCTO, and now works against racism, and for the inclusion of Chinese Canadians and other newcomers in the full political life of Toronto and Canada.

"Much like the well worn environmental slogan, I would say "Think Global, Act Local". I am a strong non-believer in international development work. I think we should instead focus on our own local problems. Whatever solutions we develop should be shared openly with the world. Members of our communities who are also members of other communities around the world should be the ones to bring these ideas back home and adapt our solutions to their local context." ~ Karen Sun

Getting Engaged: Activities

A CASE FOR SOCIAL ACTION

In Ontario, women still earn on average only 71 cents for every dollar that men earn (Equal Pay Coalition, Date Unknown). This gender gap leaves many women in positions of poverty. According to the Equal Pay Coalition, "The pay gap affects women of all ages, races, and education levels. It affects women in all parts of the province, regardless of where they work in the economy, the size of their workplace or the precariousness of their work. The pay gap is even larger for racial minority women, Aboriginal women and women with disabilities" (Equal Pay Coalition, Date Unknown, equalpaycoalition.org).

• How does this make you feel?

• Does it make you want to change this situation?

• Which groups are not treated equally?

• Do you know of any individuals or communities that do not enjoy the same rights as the majority?

• What should be done about these issues?

In your opinion...

After thinking about these questions, what is your position?

_____

_____

_____

_____

_____

_____

_____

_____

_____

_____

_____

_____

_____

_____

_____

_____

_____

IDENTIFY THE ISSUE AND CREATE CHANGE

Look back through the chapter at the stories of individuals who are taking social action throughout this chapter What type of inequality or issue is each individual addressing? What is the level of social change? Complete the following table:

Name	Inequality or Issue	Level of Social Change

"You just need to be a flea against injustice. Enough committed fleas biting strategically can make even the biggest dog uncomfortable and transform even the biggest nation."
~ Marian Wright Edelman, founder of the Children's Defense Fund

BEGINNING SOCIAL ACTION

Before we can engage in social action we need to think critically about a problem that exists in our society to gain a deeper understanding of the best ways in which we can help to bring about change.

What questions do you have about society? What problems exist?

_____
_____
_____
_____
_____

Where do you stand on these issues?

_____
_____
_____
_____
_____

Analyze an issue using one of the frameworks from Chapter 3.

_____
_____
_____
_____
_____
_____
_____
_____
_____
_____
_____
_____
_____
_____
_____
_____
_____
_____
_____
_____
_____
_____

CREATING A PLAN OF ACTION

Step 1: Identify social issues that are important to you.

_____

_____

_____

_____

Step 2: Identify 3-5 social action goals in response to the social issue from Step 1.

_____

_____

_____

_____

_____

Step 3: Pick the social action goal that is most important and relevant to you.

Make this goal a SMART goal (i.e., Specific, Measurable, Attainable, Realistic, Time-bound)

_____

_____

_____

_____

_____

Step 4: Now that you have a SMART social action goal, identify 4-6 action steps that are required to achieve this goal. Provide details for each step.

_____

_____

_____

_____

_____

_____

_____

_____

_____

_____

Step 5: Take action!

Portfolio Sharing Session

Make a list of the activities, assignments and course work you have completed during this unit:

_____
_____
_____

Decide which artifact from the list above you would like to share with your classmates. Which of the things on this list had the most impact on you or provided the most learning?

_____
_____
_____

Reflect on why this item was so meaningful: Why did you choose that item of learning? What did it tell you about yourself? What have you learned or discovered that you hadn't thought of before? How does it relate to your life, your own experiences? How will it affect your actions in the future? What do you still feel you need to learn?

_____
_____
_____
_____
_____

Bring your portfolio to class, including your selected artifact and reflection, and be prepared to share them in a group and/or the class.
Listen carefully to the feedback of others. Write points about that feedback here:

_____
_____
_____

What insight does this feedback provide you with? How does it affect your thinking and what you might do in the future as you continue learning in this area?

_____
_____
_____

Listen attentively to others as they share their artifacts with you. Provide them with respectful and thoughtful feedback. Make some notes here about anything they share that has particular meaning for you:

_____
_____
_____

Developed by Gina Marshall, Stanley Doyle-Wood, Holly Baines, Julia Satov, Zabedia Nazim (2010) Centennial College, Toronto, ON.

Assignments

Social Action Assignment: Refer to pg. 239 in the text.

Chapter Summary

Definitions:

Activist: An individual who devotes their time, either paid or unpaid, to social change work.

Charity: Generosity and helpfulness especially towards the needy or suffering; aid given to those in need. Also, an institution engaged in relief of the poor (Merriam-Websters Dictionary).

Social Action: Individual or group behavior that involves interaction with other individuals or groups, especially organized action towards social reform (Dictionary.com).

Fair Trade: An alternative approach to conventional international trade. It is a trading partnership which aims at sustainable development for excluded and disadvantaged producers. It seeks to do this by providing better trading conditions, by awareness raising and by campaigning (Oxfam).

Grassroots: A term used to describe social activism at a local or community level.

Micro: Basic or small scale (Free Dictionary Online by Farlex).

Mid: Medium or middle scale.

Macro: Large scale (Free Dictionary Online by Farlex).

Social Movement: A group of people with a common ideology who try together to achieve common goals (Free Online Dictionary).

Social Justice: Refers to the idea of creating an egalitarian society or institution that is based on the principles of equality and solidarity, that understands and values human rights and recognizes the dignity of every human being (Wikipedia).

Xenophobia: A very strong fear or dislike of individuals who are different from the self or foreign.

Main Concepts:

- Understanding social action and its local or global impact.
- Differentiating between types of social action, ranging from grassroots to institutional.
- Identifying leaders of social action including both historical activists and current global activists.
- Understanding the difference between social justice and charity.
- Establishing the link between social justice and equity.
- Understanding the importance of personal social action and the many opportunities to make a difference.
- Setting goals for personal social action

Additional Resources

Centre for Social Justice www.socialjustice.org

> *Description:* "The Centre for Social Justice is an advocacy organization that seeks to strengthen the struggle for social justice" (source: www.socialjustice.org/about us).

How to change the world : Social entrepreneurs and the power of new ideas, by David Bornstein (Centennial College Libraries)

> *Description:* This book profiles nine champions of social change who developed innovative ways to address needs they saw around them in places as distinct as Bombay, India; Rio de Janeiro, Brazil; and inner-city Washington, D.C (source: amazon.ca).

Ontario Coalition for Social Justice www.ocsj.ca

> *Description:* "The Ontario Coalition for Social Justice is dedicated to: expanding the quality, accessibility, and universality of health care, education, and social services; advocating economic policies which protect the rights of workers and lead to fair employment at a liveable wage; and promoting the human rights of and respect for every person in this province, including women, immigrants and refugees, undocumented workers, and aboriginals" (source: www.ocsj.ca /aboutus).

Social Actions www.socialactions.com

> *Description:* The goal of this website is 'to make it easier for people to find and share opportunities to make a difference'. (source: www.socialactions.ca/about us).

Volunteering and Social Activism www.unv.org/fileadmin/img/wvw/Volunteerism-FINAL.pdf

> *Description:* This article, found on the United Nations Volunteering website, discusses the links between social activism and volunteerism.

References

Augustine. (Date Unknown). Social Action Quote. Retrieved on August 16, 2010 from http://www.famous-quotes.com/topic.php?tid=177

Baldwin, J. (Date Unknown) Social Action Quote. Retrieved on August 2, 2010 from http://www.bellaonline.org/articles/art12105.asp

Canadian Business for Social Responsibility. (2010). *A Closer Look at Responsible Business.* Retrieved on September 2, 2010 from http://www.cbsr.ca/resources/cbsr-publications.

Canadian Encyclopedia. (Date Unknown). The Women's Suffrage Movement. Retrieved on October 2, 2010 from http://www.thecanadianencyclopedia.com/PrinterFriendly.cfm?Params=J1ARTJ0008687

Canada Revenue Agency. (Date Unknown). *Information for Donors.* Retrieved from the world wide web on September 2, 2010 from http://www.cra-arc.gc.ca/chrts-gvng/dnrs/svngs/2-eng.html.

CBC News (2007). *Homelessness 'chronic' in Canada: study.* Retrieved on August 16, 2010 from http://www.cbc.ca/canada/story/2007/06/26/shelter.html.

Chavez, C. (Date Unknown) Social Action Quote. Retrieved on September 17, 2010 from http://thinkexist.com/quotation/once-social-change-begins-it-cannot-be-reversed/761489.html

Clarke, R., Czerny, M.S.J., & Swift, J. (2009) *Global Citizenship: From Social Analysis to Social Action.* Toronto: Pearson Publishers.

Collins, C., Rogers, P., & Garner, J. P. (2000). *Robin Hood Was Right.* New York, W. W. Norton & Company, Inc.

Corporate Knights. (Date Unknown) Social Action in the Business World. Retrieved on August 16, 2010 from http://www.corporateknights.ca.

Daubs, K. (2010). *Taking comfort in making kids 'snug as a bug.'* Toronto: Toronto Star. February 22.

Dictionary.com (Date Unknown) Definition for Social Action. Retrieved on September 25, 2010 from http://dictionary.reference.com/browse/social+action

Dictionary.com (Date Unknown) Definition for Social Movement. Retrieved on September 25, 2010 from http://dictionary.reference.com/browse/social+movement?fromAsk=true&o=100074

Degan, R., & Disman, M. (Date Unknown) *Cultural Competency Handbook.* Department of Public Health Sciences, Toronto: University of Toronto.

Dudley, William. (2009). *Global Citizenship: From Social Analysis to Social Action.* Toronto, Pearson Publishers.

Edelman, M. W. (Date Unknown). Social Action Quote. Retrieved on August 2, 2010 from http://thinkexist.com/quotation/you_just_need_to_be_a_flea_against_injustice/339110.html.

Equal Pay Coalition (Date Unknown). Ontario's 20th Anniversary Celebration. Retrieved on August 16, 2010 from http://equalpaycoalition.org/anniversary.php.

Farlex. (Date Unknown) Definition for Micro. Retrieved on September 20, 2010 from http://www.thefreedictionary.com/

Farlex. (Date Unknown) Definition for Macro. Retrieved on September 20, 2010 from http://www.thefreedictionary.com/

Fifteen - Mission. (Date Unknown) UK Chef Jamie Oliver. Retrieved on August 16, 2010 from http://www.fifteen.net/mission/Pages/default.aspx.

Goldman Prize. (Date Unknown). MC Mehta. Retrieved on September 24, 2010 from goldmanprize.org

Javed, N. (2010). *Not all cab licences equal, driver says.* Toronto: Toronto Star. January 25.

Institute for Global Citizenship & Equity. (2010). Retrieved on August 6, 2010 from http://www.centennialcollege.ca/citizenshipandequity.

Imagine Canada. (2010). *Highlights from the 2007 Canada Survey of Giving, Volunteering and Participating.* Retrieved on August 2, 2010 from http://www.givingandvolunteering.ca.

Kielburger, C., & Kielburger, M. (2004). *Me to We: Finding Meaning in a Material World.* Mississauga, John Wiley & Sons Canada, Ltd.

King, Martin Luther Jr. (Date Unknown). Retrieved on August 2, 2010 from http://en.wikipedia.org/wiki/Nellie_McClung.

Lepofsky, D. (2002). ODA Committee. Retrieved on August 2, 2010 from http://www.odacommittee.net/20years-charter.html

Khan, F. (2010) A Word from Toronto's Local Heroes. Toronto: Interview.

Mead, M. (Date Unknown) Social Action Quote. Retrieved on August 2, 2010 from http://en.wikiquote.org/wiki/Margaret_Mead.

Mclung, N. (Date Unknown). Retrieved on August 2, 2010 from http://en.wikipedia.org/wiki/Nellie_McClung

MC Mehta Environmental Foundation. (Date Unknown) MC Mehta. Retrieved on September 24, 2010 from mcmef.org

Merriam-Webster. (Date Unknown) Definition for Charity. Retrieved on September 25, 2010 from http://www.merriam-webster.com/

Mohandas, K. G. (Date Unknown). Retrieved on August 2, 2010 from http://en.wikipedia.org/wiki/Nellie_McClung.

Morrison, T. (Date Unknown) Social Action Quote. Retrieved on September 26, 2010 from http://thinkexist.com/quotation/if_there-s_a_book_you_really_want_to_read_but_it/164827.html.

Mothers Against Drunk Driving (2010). History. Retrieved on August 2, 2010 from http://www.madd.org/About-us/About-us/History.aspx.

Ontario Ministry of Training, Colleges and Universities. (Date Unknown) OSAP Basics: What is OSAP? Retrieved fon September 2, 2010 from https://osap.gov.on.ca/OSAPPortal/en/OSAPBasics.

Oxfam. (Date Unknown) Definition for Fair Trade. Retrieved on September 25, 2010 from http://www.oxfam.ca/

Piercy, M. (2006) The Low Road. Middlemarsh Inc. Retrieved on August 18, 2010 from http://www.margepiercy.com/sampling/The_Low_Road.htm

Porter, C. (2010). Social entrepreneur needs help to develop our dreams. Toronto: Toronto Star. January 19.

Quotations Page, The. (Date Unknown). Chinese Proverb. Retrieved on September 26, 2010 from http://www.quotationspage.com/search.php3?homesearch=give+a+man+a+fish.

Shan, N. (2010) A Word from Toronto's Local Heroes. Toronto: Interview.

Sherrils, A. (Date Unknown). Social Action Quote. In Mack, T. & PicowerB. (2010) *Planning to Change the World: A Plan Book for Social Justice Teachers.* New York Collective of Radical Educators and the Education for Liberation Network: NY, p. 73.

Statistics Canada. (2003). *National Survey of Non-profit and Voluntary Organizations.* Ottawa, ON: Statistics Canada.

Sun, K. (2010) A Word from Toronto's Local Heroes. Toronto: Interview.

Tubman, H. (Date Unknown) Social Action Quote. In Mack, T. & Picower, B. (2010) In *Planning to Change the World: A Plan Book for Social Justice Teachers.* New York Collective of Radical Educators and the Education for Liberation Network: NY, p. 79.

Westhead, R. (2010). *Battling for India's Environment.* Toronto: Toronto Star. February 6.

Winfrey, O. (Date Unknown) Social Action Quote. Source Unknown.

Wikipedia. (2010). LGBT Rights by Country or Territory. Retrieved on September 2, 2010 from http://en.wikipedia.org/wiki/LGBT_rights_by_country_or_territory.

Notes

CHAPTER 8

Global Citizenship

Courtesy of Shutterstock.

CHAPTER OBJECTIVES:

- Understanding global citizenship

- Looking at Centennial College's definition of global citizenship

- Discussing different aspects of global citizenship

- Reflecting on one's personal responsibilities as a global citizen

Renee M. Sgroi

Introduction

As we saw in chapter one, Global Citizenship is an approach to teaching and learning that looks at how we can become responsible citizens at a global level. When you started this course, you probably had some sense of what it means to be a global citizen. You may have even been involved in projects aimed at bettering the lives of others in your local community, country of origin, or elsewhere in the world. This chapter aims to deepen your understanding of global citizenship by providing you with some background into the concept, alternative understandings of what global citizenship may mean, and a place to think about and reflect upon your own responsibilities as a global citizen.

> *"These are the times to grow our souls. Each of us is called upon to embrace the conviction that despite the powers and principalities bent on commodifying all our human relationships, we have the power within us to create the world anew."*
> ~Grace Lee Boggs, author and feminist

Before Global Citizenship, Globalization

The past twenty to thirty years have seen dramatic changes around the world. Shifts in economies, manufacturing, workers, political powers, technologies, and cultural influences have all had an impact on what it means to be a resident of this planet. Economists, global leaders, politicians, educators, and even the average person will make reference to these changes by using the term **globalization**. Although the term gets used widely, in this chapter, we define globalization by stating that it is an economic process with political, social, and cultural effects. Beginning in the 1970s, new economic policies began to take shape around the world.

These policies pushed for less government control over how economies would run. Governments gave up some of their powers especially with regards to business. As a result, corporations and businesses gained more power, and began to run without government interference.

Globalization: Refers to an economic process of political, social, and cultural integrations across the entire planet.

The result of these economic policies was felt in both local and global contexts. A Canadian example will help to explain. Beginning in the mid-1980s, Canada and the U.S. were pushing towards having fewer trade restrictions between our two countries. The negotiations led to trade agreements between Canada and the United States, and later with Mexico in the North American Free Trade Agreement (otherwise referred to as "NAFTA"). Similarly, European countries established the European Union and one currency, the "Euro", to reduce trade and economic barriers between European countries. Regulatory laws now encompass every facet of trade and economic relations. These laws deal with everything from access to resources, to technology, to intellectual property rights, which are now globally imposed, especially through global bodies such as the World Trade Organization (WTO).

The impact of these global changes in economics is that two levels of society were established. Developed countries benefited from these economic changes, while many other countries found themselves worse off because of trade regulations imposed by the WTO. In other words, many people would argue that as a result of globalization and its economic policies, the rich continue to get richer, while the poor only get poorer.

Photo by Jared Purdy.

Globalization also has political and social consequences. Decisions made by politicians regarding the control of natural resources, the structure and shape of economies, access to global markets, and so forth relate to issues of power. Who dominates the world's supply of food? Who decides how much oil should be drilled in a particular region? Who then decides how oil should be priced? And which countries should oil be shipped to? Each of these questions are political in nature, because they affect whether or not countries have access to resources, and often, these decisions are based on relations of power.

Courtesy of Shutterstock.

Social changes, especially with regards to technology, have also had an impact on how the world works. The technological changes brought about by microcomputers and the Internet age (work that previously might have taken days, weeks, or months to complete) can now be accomplished in the span of an hour or several hours. More importantly, that work can now be transmitted across time and space. In the past, workers had to be physically present to accomplish their work. Now, people take advantage of flexible hours, and might work Tuesday to Saturday, instead of the traditional Monday to Friday.

Or, people don't even have to go in to work anymore. They simply work from the comfort of their own homes. Workers can even be stationed in different countries. Think of the last time you went online or phoned for technical assistance with your computer, internet connection or other device. Have you ever asked the person you were speaking to where he or she was based? Chances are that the person providing you with support was based in another province, or more likely, another country. Technology has provided us with great freedoms such that we are no longer "tied to our desks".

Did you or your family come to Canada from another country? If so, why? If not, do you know anyone who has immigrated to Canada? Why did they immigrate?

_____
_____
_____
_____
_____

What was the experience like? Or, do you know what this experience has been like for them?

_____
_____
_____
_____
_____
_____

For the most part, people who discuss issues of globalization argue that it has had a negative effect on the world. "On the one hand there is increasing poverty in societies, ... low standards of living, disease, forced migration and human rights violations... On the other hand, there are many environmental repercussions such as the greenhouse effect, climate-change, pollution and the exhaustion of natural resources" (Global Education Guidelines Working Group, p. 15). Similarly, although the cultural mixing we see in a place such as Toronto is considered a positive thing, one of the outcomes for many people as a result of globalization is that they have lost their traditional knowledge, cultures, or customs. This is not because of cultural mixing. Instead, it is because people have watched as imposed economic policies have affected their traditional ways of doing business, or of existing within their communities. For instance, while people no longer see themselves simply as citizens of the place in which they were born, and instead might see themselves as citizens of the world, other people have had little choice but to migrate to another country for employment. Because of changing economic policies, millions of people around the world have been forced to leave their families at home, and travel to another country for work. Generally, the host country does not give workers the same rights as it gives its citizens, and so these workers labour, often under exploitative laws. Yet people leave so they can send money home to their families. After a number of months, these workers will return home for a short period, only to return back to the host country for another work contract. For example, did you know that much of the local produce we find in Ontario is picked by Mexican migrant workers?

And yet, globalization nevertheless allows for " the widening of peoples' horizons, access to knowledge and the products of science and technology, multiculturalism and intercultural views, an increase in opportunities, personal and social development and possibilities of sharing ideas and joint action towards solutions to common problems" (Global Education Guidelines Working Group, p. 15).

While you may debate the benefits or losses that have resulted from globalization, a new field of research and study has emerged to help us sort through the questions. Many people have started to teach students about global citizenship as a way to address the changes brought about by globalization, and to educate students about what can be done to make the world a better place. But what is global citizenship? And how can we make the world a better place?

Stop and Reflect

Can the economic policies and processes that have had such a huge effect on the world, also have positive consequences? What do you think?

Courtesy of Shutterstock.

Citizenship

To answer these questions, we should first try and define **citizenship**. What does it mean to be a citizen of a particular country? Generally speaking, we might say that a citizen is someone who resides in a country and is legally entitled to vote, hold property, work, go to school, drive a car, and participate in any and all other rights given to citizens of that nation. Yet it can be argued that in some countries, citizens are not provided with equal rights based on their class, race, culture, religion, and so forth. In other words, a citizen is someone who, more or less, can participate in the activities and lifestyle of a given country. Evans and Reynolds (2004) define citizenship as: "1) A sense of membership or identity with some wider community, from the local to the global; 2) A set of rights and freedoms, such as freedom of thought or the right to vote; 3) A corresponding set of duties or responsibilities, such as an obligation to respect the rights of others or a duty to obey the law; and 4) A set of virtues and capacities that enable a citizen to effectively engage in and reflect upon questions and concerns of civic interest" (p. 5).

But questions generally arise when we think about who is entitled to vote, or work, or hold property, for we must also consider the relevance of citizenship as it relates to access to adequate healthcare, sanitation services, clean water, education, transportation, safety, and security. Should all people around the world have access to these same, basic

Citizenship: A concept that implies membership or identity in a wider community along with a set of rights and responsibilities (Reynolds, 2004).

services and rights? Do these rights and responsibilities apply to all people in all places? At all times? Consider, for instance, that women were denied the right to vote in Canada until 1918, and even then, many women, including Québecois and Aboriginals were denied the vote until much later. Did Canadian citizenship apply equally to these people, even though they were born in Canada?

As you can see from these examples, citizenship therefore doesn't necessarily apply to all people at all times, even though they may have been born or reside in the same country. The topic of citizenship therefore raises equally important questions about human rights, because it touches on the forms of power, the types of rules, and the people in charge who decide whether or not certain groups of people have access to rights and privileges that are denied to others. And, if we begin to discuss human rights, then we enter into a discussion about equity, about social justice, about what is fair (or not, as the case may be) for all people living within a political state. Citizenship thus encompasses more than just questions of who has the right to drive, or own property within a given political state; it deals also with human rights, equality, access to basic resources, health care, safety, and so forth.

Social justice is a teaching approach and theory that aims to better the lives of students and people everywhere. Core principles of social justice are the fundamental beliefs in each person's right to dignity, to respect, to earn an education in a safe and productive environment, and to live in a world where access to resources is equitably shared and ethically sustained.

Photo by Alice Kieltyka

Going back to our discussion of globalization, let us now consider citizenship as it relates to human rights in a global context. What would this look like? And what issues would we begin to question? Learning about global citizenship in an educational setting helps us "move towards a better understanding of the current issues of the world" Global Education Guidelines Working Group, p. 15).

EVENTS THAT CONTRIBUTED TO SOCIAL CHANGE

Event: The Universal Declaration of Human Rights is Approved

WHEN: 1948
WHERE: Paris, France
WHAT: A defining moment for human rights around the world.

Compiled by Sarah Duffy

After World War II, the world was changing. The devastation of the war had created a desire for change, a desire to protect human rights. Countries from around the globe came together to create a universal document that captured the human rights of all people, from all nations. This document, the **Universal Declaration of Human Rights**, was unanimously approved by the United Nations General Assembly on December 10, 1948. It included 30 articles, describing the fundamental rights and freedoms of all individuals and it had a significant impact on the world. "The adoption of the Declaration was immediately hailed as a triumph, uniting very diverse and even conflicting political regimes, religious systems and cultural traditions." ("A United Nations Priority").

A United Nations Priority. (Date Unknown). Retrieved from http://www.un.org/rights/HRToday/declar.htm.

"All human beings, whatever their cultural or historical background, suffer when they are intimidated, imprisoned or tortured . . . We must, therefore, insist on a global consensus, not only on the need to respect human rights worldwide, but also on the definition of these rights . . . for it is the inherent nature of all human beings to yearn for freedom, equality and dignity, and they have an equal right to achieve that."
~ 14th Dalai Lama

Stop and Reflect

Make a list of issues, topics, ideas, or responses to the question:

"What rights and privileges should all global citizens have access to?"

_____
_____
_____
_____
_____
_____
_____
_____

What would you include in your list?

_____
_____
_____
_____
_____

What issues are of global importance?

_____
_____
_____
_____
_____
_____
_____
_____
_____
_____
_____

"To me success means effectiveness in the world, that I am able to carry my ideas and values into the world - that I am able to change it in positive ways."
~ Maxine Hong Kingston, author

Centennial College's Definition of Global Citizenship

Historically, the concept of global citizenship in education stemmed from people's interests in internationalizing student education. What is internationalizing? It is a way of educating students by giving them international learning experiences. For instance, students at Centennial have been fortunate to travel to Dominica, Turkey, and elsewhere in order to gain experience of other cultures, other people, and other forms of knowledge. "According to Shiel & McKenzie (2008), the

Courtesy of Shutterstock.

editors of a recent publication, *The Global University: the role of senior managers,* post-secondary institutions are using internationalization as a 'strategic aim' to develop 'active global citizens' (p.6)" (qtd. in Shultz and Jorgensen, 2008, p. 7). This suggests that universities, and colleges as well, are interested in teaching students to be prepared for the global workforce, and to have the skills necessary to compete with others globally. Indeed, Shultz and Jorgensen point to the work of Lapayese (2003) who suggests that our globalized world has resulted in a situation where "education has been called upon to prepare people for multiple and evolving forms of activity as citizens" (p. 5). In a sense, then, global citizenship developed out of a response to changing economic, social, political, and technological forces that are part of globalization, combined with a recognition of the value of educating students in an international context in order to raise students' awareness of the issues and problems facing the world.

> *"Until the great mass of the people shall be filled with the sense of responsibility for each other's welfare, social justice can never be attained."*
> ~ Helen Keller, author, political activist, and first deaf-blind person to earn a university degree

Yet those involved in the practice of teaching global citizenship would argue that the core ideas that make up this approach to education stem more from an awareness of our roles and responsibilities towards our fellow human beings and our planet, as opposed to a need to give students international learning experiences. From this perspective, global citizenship becomes a complex, and by no means uncontested approach to educating students.

Courtesy of Shutterstock.

Here at Centennial College, we see global citizenship as a concept based on the search for equity and social justice. As defined by the College's Institute for Global Citizenship and Equity, "To be a citizen in the global sense means recognizing that we must all be aware of our use of the world's resources and find ways to live on the earth in a sustainable way. When we see others are treated without justice, we know that we are responsible for trying to ensure that people are treated justly and must have equitable opportunities as fellow citizens of this world. We must think critically about what we see, hear and say, and make sure that our actions bring about positive changes" (http://www.centennialcollege.ca/citizenshipandequity/concepts).

> **Institute for Global Citizenship and Equity: Centennial College**
>
> "To be a citizen in the global sense means recognizing that we must all be aware of our use of the world's resources and find ways to live on the earth in a sustainable way. When we see others are treated without justice, we know that we are responsible for trying to ensure that people are treated justly and must have equitable opportunities as fellow citizens of this world. We must think critically about what we see, hear and say, and make sure that our actions bring about positive changes."

What does this mean? Our College's vision for global citizenship aims to develop greater social, economic, political, cultural, and environmental awareness. Take plastic water bottles, for instance. Plastic bottles do not decompose, and therefore can remain intact in landfills for hundreds of years. What does this do to our environment? What about the process of *creating* those plastic water bottles? What materials go into their production? What impact do they have on the atmosphere, or the surrounding environment? What if toxic chemicals from the plastic water bottle processing plant leaked into the water supply nearby? More importantly, think about how necessary it is to have plastic water bottles. Do we really need them? Haven't people survived for thousands of years without such an invention? As Shultz and Jorgensen (2008) write, "Linking local and global issues and perspectives is core to global citizenship education". Part of global citizenship then is to consider how our actions, at a local level, impact on issues and people at a global level, and vice versa. The world is interconnected, and global citizenship examines those interconnections in order to better understand how we might make a more just world. How equitable is it, for instance, for certain countries to go on creating water bottles that will harm the environment? Is this responsible to all the people who share our planet?

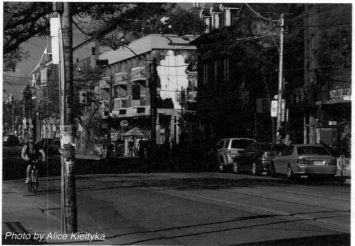
Photo by Alice Kieltyka

CONSCIOUS ABOUT WASTE

Can you think of other examples of resources that we are wasting? What are they?

_____
_____
_____
_____
_____
_____
_____

How are they being wasted?

_____
_____
_____
_____

What can we do to stop it?

_____
_____
_____
_____
_____
_____
_____
_____

Courtesy of Shutterstock.

Centennial College's definition of global citizenship thus takes into account the need to help others. How can we help others in ways that treat people with respect and dignity? How can we create situations that will make lasting change in people's lives? And what about the need to help people as a group, and not at an individual level? Global citizenship sees equity and social justice at a social, or collective level, rather than simply at an individual level. What does this mean? Imagine you have the opportunity to help one homeless person. Now imagine you have the opportunity to change economic, political, and social factors so that the root causes of homelessness could be addressed. Which option would you choose? If you chose the second option, would you be working alone? Or with others? And if you chose the first option, you would certainly have done something worthwhile in helping another human being. Yet, how much more could you accomplish if you were to team up with others and help even more individuals? In this sense, global citizenship advocates for collective action.

Courtesy of Shutterstock.

Understanding and respecting diversity is another significant aspect of global citizenship. Within this framework, we see ourselves as citizens of the world. It becomes important to recognize that each of us possesses diverse identities, knowledge, experiences, cultural practices and beliefs, and that in order to benefit from the dialogue we can potentially have with one another, we must create spaces for understanding and respecting diversity. As you have seen in other chapters, diversity can take many forms, and includes ethnic, racial, gendered, classed, sexual, abled, religious, cultural, and linguistic diversity. By recognizing that we are all different, and that each of us is able to make valuable contributions to the world, we see that diversity enriches our knowledge and experience.

Global citizenship also stresses the importance of learning about "how the world works economically, politically, socially, culturally, technologically and environmentally"(Oxfam, Date Unknown). It is critical that we see how we connect with each other and with others and that we understand the ways in which social and institutional structures intertwine to shape the kinds of behaviours, activities, knowledge, and practices that shape our world. The chapter on social analysis explained how social and institutional structures function to (inadvertently or not) create social problems in the world. To be a global citizen thus requires a solid understanding of political, economic, and social structures so that our understanding of social problems can move from simply recognizing and feeling bad about social problems, to being able to identify and critically analyse what has created those problems. This knowledge base allows us to realize that very little in the world occurs without the intersection of economics, power, politics, and the social demands and concerns of the people involved. It also enables us to begin the work of social analysis, and social action. Armed with the knowledge of these interconnecting processes, we can begin to get at the root of social problems and find creative ways to develop solutions for social change.

Another aspect of global citizenship focuses on understanding our place in the world. How can we participate as global citizens if we are not fully aware of ourselves? In the chapter on identity, you had an opportunity to think critically about how identities are formed, how you see your own identity, and the factors and influences you believe have helped to shape who you are today. In order to accomplish this understanding, you probably reflected on your sense of self. Reflection is a part of global citizenship in that it allows us to take stock of what we have done, analyse the gaps in our knowledge, think about what we know and what we do not know, and then develop a plan to move forward to create change. This change can happen within us, over time, or it can be through the social change that you read about in chapter 7 or through the portfolio work that you read about in chapter 2.

> "Don't be a marshmellow. Walk the street with us into history. Get off the sidewalk. Stop being vegetables. Work for justice. Viva the boycott!"
> ~ Dolores Huerta, labor activist

Reflection is also significant because it helps us to understand what our responsibilities are in the world, and how we can take charge of those responsibilities. Think about the example above where we discussed plastic water bottles. If we know what the environmental effects are on the earth as a result of water bottle production and collection in waste facilities, what is our social and individual responsibility with regards to our use of plastic water bottles? Should we buy them? Should we ask stores to discontinue selling them? Should we advocate for more public water fountains in public areas such as parks or community centres? What are our responsibilities around this issue?

What Are My Responsibilities as a Global Citizen?

Responsibility is thus a key aspect of global citizenship. From this perspective, we must begin to see ourselves as individuals rooted in a local context, but interconnected with the entire world. It is not good enough to stand back and watch while others suffer, even if it is halfway around the world. Global citizenship recognizes that we have a responsibility to our fellow human beings. This responsibility requires us to become involved in helping others who are in need, but it also requires that we are aware of our own actions, beliefs and behaviours. We must recognize our own practices and ways of being so that we can live in a way that respects diversity, honours our environment and the natural resources available to us, and creates spaces for social change and social justice.

MY RESPONSIBILITIES AS A GLOBAL CITIZEN

What are your responsibilities as a global citizen? What do you think?

_____

_____

_____

_____

_____

_____

In what ways can you make positive change in the world?

_____

_____

_____

_____

_____

_____

_____

_____

_____

AGENTS OF SOCIAL CHANGE: GLOBAL CITIZENS IN ACTION

Activist: Shirin Ebadi

Born: June 21, 1947
Activist for Women's, Children's, and Refugee Rights, Nobel Peace Prize Winner
Iran

Compiled by Sarah Duffy

Shirin Ebadi was born June 21 1947 and is an Iranian lawyer, a former judge and human rights activist and founder of Centre for the Defence of Human Rights in Iran. Ebadi was a student in the law department of the University of Tehran in 1965. In 1975, she became the first woman to preside over a legislative court in Iran.

After the Iranian revolution in 1979, however, Ebadi was demoted to a secretarial position and subsequently, she applied for early retirement. After trying for a number of years, she then received her lawyer's license in 1993. In the years between her demotion and practicing law, she used her time to write books and articles and became well known in Iran.

In her role as a lawyer, Ebadi is known for representing individuals who are considered dissident figures. She is also a campaigner for the status of women and children. Other examples of Ebadi's social activities include (Shirin Ebadi, n.d.):

- Leading several research projects for the UNICEF office in Tehran.

- Cofounding the Association for Support of Children's Rights in1995.

- Providing various stages of free tuition in children's rights and human rights.

- Cofounding the Human Rights Defence Centre

- Delivering lectures to university and academic conferences and seminars on human rights in Iran, France, Belgium, Sweden, Switzerland, Britain and America.

- Representing several journalists or their families, accused or sentenced in relation to freedom of expression.

- Proposing to the Islamic Consultative Assembly to ratify a law on prohibiting violence against children; resulting in ratification of the law.

Ebadi was awarded the Nobel Peace Price on October 10, 2003 for her efforts in democracy and human rights, particularly for women and children.

Ebadi, Shirin. (Date Unknown). *The Nobel Peace Prize, 2003 – Autobiography.* Retrieved from http://nobelprize.org/nobel prizes.

Shirin Ebadi. (Date Unknown). Retrieved from http://en.wikipedia.org/wiki/Shirin_Ebadi.

Being a global citizen is no easy task; however, in working together to produce social change, and by becoming aware of our locations and responsibilities as global citizens, we can make a difference in the world. As the Global Citizenship Community of Practice, at the Centre for Teaching and Academic Growth at the University of British Columbia (2004) has stated:

> [A] global citizen is someone who feels a duty to respect the Earth, the global community of fellow human beings and all other living creatures. ... Global citizens are individuals who are willing and enabled to take action to make the world a fairer place for ourselves and other living creatures. (p. 7)

Photo by Alice Kieltyka

The point of being a global citizen then is to feel that duty, to recognize our responsibilities, and to attempt to make a difference. In your work and in your life, what changes can you make to transform the lives of others and make the world a better place? What will you do to become a global citizen?

> *"What I treasure most in life is being able to dream. During my most difficult moments and complex situations I have been able to dream of a more beautiful future."*
>
> ~ Rigoberta Menchu Tum, Guatemala Mayan human rights activist

Getting Engaged: Activities

Global Citizenship Revisited

In chapter 1 you had an opportunity to think about what global citizenship means to you. Having almost completed this course has the concept of global citizenship changed for you? If so, how?

_____
_____
_____
_____
_____
_____
_____
_____
_____

What does global citizenship mean to you?

_____
_____
_____
_____
_____
_____
_____
_____
_____

How is global citizenship reflected in your life today?

_____
_____
_____
_____
_____
_____
_____
_____
_____

How can global citizenship be reflected in your future career?

_____
_____
_____
_____
_____
_____
_____
_____

GLOBAL CITIZENSHIP, YOU, AND THE WORLD

Why should you care about your role as a citizen of the world? Reflect on this question and discuss it with a partner or in a small group.

_____
_____
_____
_____
_____
_____
_____
_____
_____
_____
_____
_____
_____
_____
_____
_____

Retrieved from Arcaro, T. & Haskell, R. (2010). Understanding the Global Experience: Becoming a Responsible World Citizen. Allyn and Bacon: Boston, MA., p. 5.

REVISITING MY GOALS

In chapter 1 you were asked to set goals for the semester and you were also asked to indicate what you hoped to get from this course. Did you meet these goals and expectations? Why or why not?

_____
_____
_____
_____
_____

What other questions do you have? What would you like to learn more about?

_____
_____
_____
_____
_____
_____

Assignments

Post Reflection: Refer to pg. 253 in the text.

Post Reflection Rubric: Refer to pg. 254 in the text.

Chapter Summary

Definitions:

Citizenship: A concept that implies membership or identity in a wider community along with a set of rights and responsibilities (Reynolds, 2004).

Globalization: Refers to an economic process of political, social, and cultural integrations across the entire planet.

Main Concepts:

• Evaluating the impact of globalization and its link to global citizenship
• Comparing national citizenship to global citizenship
• Discovering Centennial College's perspective on global citizenship
• Reflecting on individual responsibilities as global citizens

Additional Resources

Global citizenship and social movements [electronic resource] : creating transcultural webs of meaning for the new millennium, by Janet McIntyre-Mills

Description: "In this book, Janet McIntyre-Mills addresses the need for transcultural thinking tools, to not only mend problems in the global environment but also to understand the essential nature of the problems. Thinking tools comprise the analytical concepts which organize, disorganize, pattern and question thoughts about the social and natural world." (Informaworld (n.d.). Retrieved from http://prod.informaworld.com.)

Prosperity for all: consumer activism in an era of globalization, by Matthew Hilton (Centennial College Libraries)

Description: This book "traces the history of the consumer movement, focusing on how its agenda has changed and how, in the process, it has neglected two critical issues, over-consumption by some groups and under-consumption by others... The powerful narrative makes insightful links to broader social and global issues." (Veseth, M. (September 2009). Retrieved from http://www.cornellpress.cornell.edu.)

Rethinking globalization: teaching for justice in an unjust world, by Peterson, Bob (Centennial College Libraries)

Description: This book, which is designed as a teaching resource, provides numerous articles and activities related to globalization, encouraging students to think critically about globalization and its impact.

References

Arcaro, T. & Haskell, R. (2010). Understanding the Global Experience: Becoming a Responsible World Citizen. Allyn and Bacon: Boston, MA., p. 5.

Boggs, G.L. (Date Unknown) Citizenship Quote. Retrieved on September 24, 2010 from http://boggsblog.org/2009/04/15/quotable-grow-our-souls/

Ebadi, S. (Date Unknown). *The Nobel Peace Prize, 2003 – Autobiography.* Retrieved on September 26, 2010 from http://nobelprize.org/nobel_prizes.

Ebadi, S. (Date Unknown). Retrieved on September 26, 2010 from http://en.wikipedia.org/wiki/Shirin_Ebadi.

Evans, M. and C. Reynolds (2004). "Education for Global Citizenship in a Changing World: Perspectives and Classroom Practices". (pp. 1-13). Educating for Global Citizenship in a Changing World. Toronto: OISE/UT.

Global Citizenship Community of Practice, Centre for Teaching and Academic Growth. (2004). Road to Global Citizenship: An educator's toolbook. Vancouver: University of British Columbia.

Global Education Guidelines Working Group (2008). Global Education Guidelines: A Handbook for Educators to Understand and Implement Global Education. Lisbon: North-South Centre of the Council of Europe.

Huerta, D. (Date Unknown) Citizenship Quote. Retrieved on October 4, 2010 from http://thinkexist.com/ quotes/dolores_huerta/

Keller, H. (Date Unknown) Citizenship Quote. Retrieved on October 4, 2010 from http://thinkexist.com/ quotation/until_the_great_mass_of_the_people_shall_be/209134.html

Key Concepts and Definitions. Institute for Global Citizenship and Equity. Centennial College. (Date Unknown) (Retrieved September 8, 2010) http://www.centennialcollege.ca/citizenshipandequity/concepts

Kingston, M.H. (Date Unknown) Citizenship Quote. Retrieved on October 4, 2010 from http:// thinkexist.com/quotation/to-me-success-means-effectiveness-in-the-world/364812.html

Lama, D. (Date Unknown) Citizenship Quote. Retrieved on October 4, 2010 from http:// www.betterworld.net/quotes/humanrights-quotes.htm

Oxfam. (Date Unknown) Retrieved on August 4, 2010 from http://www.oxfam.ca/

Scholte, J.A. (2004). Globalization studies past and future: A dialogue of diversity. Centre for the Study of Globalization and Regionalization Working Paper No. 135/04, University of Warwick.

Shultz, L. and S. Jorgensen. (2008). "Global citizenship education in post-secondary institutions: A review of the literature." Retrieved October 5, 2009, from http://www.uofaweb.ualberta.ca/uai_globaleducation/nav04.cfm?nav04=91625&nav03=9160 6&nav02=75648&nav01=71443

United Nations Priority. (Date Unknown) Retrieved on September 26, 2010 from http://www.un.org/ rights/HRToday/declar.htm.

Notes

CHAPTER 9

Communication

Courtesy of Shutterstock.

CHAPTER OBJECTIVES:

- Writing tips

- Research

- Report writing

- Plagiarism

- References

- Critical thinking

- Presentation preparation and delivery

Compiled by Sarah Duffy

Introduction

In this chapter you will learn the key communication components that are part of GNED 500, Global Citizenship & Equity. Each section will provide tips that you can apply in the course. Your communication skills will develop throughout the course as you participate in class activities and work through the various course assignments. A number of the sections in this chapter focus on written communication; however, there is also a section on presentation preparation and delivery. The material in this chapter is intended to be directional and applicable to GNED 500. However, for each of the topics in this chapter, you can read more by accessing additional readings online or in references materials available at the Centennial College library. The topics that are covered in this chapter are: writing tips, research and report writing, plagiarism, citations and references, and presentation preparation and delivery.

Writing Tips

In this course, your assignments will include reports, reflections and journals. When you complete these assignments, clear, concise and effective writing will help to communicate your key messages. Before beginning your assignments, please review the following writing tips for writing paragraphs, writing sentences, punctuation and formatting.

> *"The role of a writer is not to say what we all can say, but what we are unable to say."*
> ~Anais Nin

Tip 1: Writing and Editing Paragraphs

Develop paragraphs	In revising, focus on each paragraph one at a time. For each one, ask yourself what your reader will notice and remember. • Is the main point fully developed? • Does the paragraph include examples? • Are key ideas emphasized in vivid sentences?
Pay attention to paragraph length	Evaluate your paragraphs from a reader's perspective, with your purpose and format in mind. • Divide paragraphs if you find long stretches of text without breaks. • If you find too many short paragraphs, develop or combine them.
Link within and across paragraphs	Be aware of transitions in your writing. Ask yourself why one main idea leads into the next. The answer to these questions can become your transition. • What step or shift takes place between paragraphs? • How does this step or shift fit into the overall development of the piece?
Start fast	Grab your reader's attention quickly by perfecting your title and opening paragraph. Be sure you provide strong reasons to keep reading. • Be sure your title is specific enough to indicate both your topic and approach. • Cut out any empty phrases and sentences that clutter up your opening paragraph.
Conclude with strength	• Be sure that your ending paragraph is more than a summary of your main points. • Use a strong concluding image or question to leave your readers with something to remember and think about.

Taken from *Writing: A Journey,* Canadian Edition, by Lester Faigley and Melanie Rubens

Tip 2: Writing Sentences

Pay attention to verbs	Circle every *is, are, was,* and *were.* Think about the action. Does the verb express the action? Can you think of a better verb?
Stay active	Ask who or what is doing the action. If the doer is not the subject, consider rewriting so the doer is the subject.
Find characters	Use characters as the subjects of sentences.
Write concise sentences	Eliminate wordy phrases, redundant modifiers, and empty intensifiers from your sentences.
Write ethical sentences	Avoid stereotypes and biased language by using inclusive and accurate language instead.
Match structure with ideas	Match grammatical elements to provide strong parallelism in sentences with parallel ideas or lists.

Taken from *Writing: A Journey,* Canadian Edition, by Lester Faigley and Melanie Rubens

Tip 3: Punctuation and Conventions

Commas	• Place commas after introductory elements and between main clauses joined by *and, but, or, nor, yet, so,* and *for.* • Use commas with nonrestrictive modifiers, coordinate adjectives, and items in a series. • Use a comma after an introductory clause or a long introductory phrase but not to set off a *because* clause at the end.
Semicolons and colons	• Pay close attention to semicolons and colons that join main clauses.
Hyphens, dashes, and parentheses	• Know the difference in how hyphens and dashes are used, and don't use dashes as periods.
Quotation marks	• Check that all direct quotations are within quotations marks and that periods and commas are inside the closing quotation mark.
Other punctuation	• Check all periods, question marks, exclamation points, and ellipses.
Print conventions	• Check all capitalization, italics, abbreviations, and numbers.

Taken from *Writing: A Journey,* Canadian Edition, by Lester Faigley and Melanie Rubens

Tip 4: Headings

Headings

Make Headings Descriptive

Each section and subsection of a report should have a heading. Try to make headings "high information"—as descriptive and specific as possible—especially in your discussion of findings. They should tell the story of the report so that a reader glancing through it will recognize the important points. In fact, descriptive headings often reflect key points. Notice the difference between the following sets of headings for a short report comparing brands of office carpeting:

> Low-information headings:
> a) Durability
> b) Cost
> c) Colour choice
>
> High-information descriptive headings:
> a) Brand X is most durable
> b) Brand Z is least expensive
> c) Brands X and Y have preferred colours

It's not always possible to make every heading reflect a key point. Occasionally a heading that simply tells the nature of the content will serve well. For example, if you must have a separate section explaining how you conducted your research, it may be appropriate to call it simply "Method." On the whole, though, the more descriptive the headings, the easier the report will be to read and remember. Descriptive headings are a decided advantage.

Keep Headings Short

Although complete sentences are often useful for headings, keep them short.

> ✗ In the future, laptops will show a substantial decrease in price
> ✓ Laptop prices will drop

Taken from *Impact! A Guide to Business Communication*, Seventh Edition, by Margot Northey and Joan McKibbin

Tip 4: Headings Continued

Make Headings Parallel

Since headings act as signposts, they should all be written in the same grammatical form. The following headings are not parallel because they switch from one type of grammatical structure to another:

✗ • Location
   • Ordering supplies
   • Hiring staff

The correct parallel structure is

✓ • Location
   • Supplies
   • Staff

or, if more information is required

✓ • Five-year lease has been signed
   • Supplies for first quarter have arrived
   • Staffing has been finalized

Research and Report Writing

One or more of the assignments you complete for the course GNED500: Global Citizenship: From Social Analysis to Social Action involve research. An effective approach to research will ensure that you are able to find appropriate and informative sources for your research report. In addition, if you do your research with a well-organised approach, you will work more efficiently. The following research tips can be found on the Centennial College library website (Centennial College, 2010), with links to various Centennial College and online resources. You can access this website from the college or remotely at the following url: http://library.centennialcollege.ca/.

As you read through these research tips, make notes in the space provided about how you can apply the tips to your assignment.

Courtesy of Shutterstock.

Report Writing Tips

This section provides you with some tips for writing a report and is also available on the Centennial College library website (Centennial College, 2010).

- Write "on topic": Make sure you are clear about what your instructor wants. Ask your instructor for clarification if in doubt.

- Make an outline: draft the introduction, the main body, and the conclusion. Refer to it constantly as you write. Adjust it if necessary as you go.

- Be "up front" about your views: in many cases your assignment involves a presentation of your views after you have done some research. Your views (also called an "argument") are usually expressed in your introduction: you tell the reader where you stand on your topic.

- Be "compelling": your job is to convince your readers of your point of view. Make statements that support your view, and back them up with the research you have done to argue your points.

Courtesy of Shutterstock.

- Conclude: at the end, you remind the reader of your argument (as stated in your introduction) and summarize how your discussion supports it. A really good conclusion often adds "a little something new" - a brief reference to another perspective, a recommendation for more research into some aspect of the topic, etc.

Plagiarism

Courtesy of Shutterstock.

Plagiarism is an important concept for all college students to understand. It applies to assignments that require research or representation of someone else's work. In this course, you will be required to conduct research for one or more of your assignments; in addition, you may be required to represent or discuss ideas from this textbook or other relevant material in your assignments. In all of these cases, it's critical that you avoid plagiarism. The following section will provide you with an understanding of plagiarism and the steps you can take to make sure that you do not plagiarize.

What is Plagiarism? School of Advancement Plagiarism Guidelines (2009):

- The definition of plagiarism is "to present another person's ideas, writing, artistic work, drawings, images or data etc. as one's own. This includes:

- Copying another person's work (including information found on the Internet and unpublished materials) without appropriate referencing. Examples of appropriate referencing include APA or MLA documentation styles, or any other preferred documentation styles as indicated by the College course instructor.

- Any use of the work of others, whether published, unpublished or posted electronically, attributed or anonymous, must include proper acknowledgement.

- Presenting someone else's work, opinions, or theories as if they are one's own.

- Presenting another's substantial compositional changes to an assignment as one's own.

- Working collaboratively with others without the permission of the instructor on an assignment, and then submitting the finished product as if it were created solely by the submitting individual

- Submitting the same work, in whole or in part, for credit in two or more courses, or in the same course more than once, without the prior written permission of the instructor.

How Do I Avoid Plagiarism? (Centennial College Library, 2010):

- When you present your work show that you have:

- Explored relevant sources (done the research)

- Understood what you have studied

- Developed views of your own, based on your studies

So how do you refer to the ideas of others in your work in a way that shows that you know your stuff without making it look as if you are presenting others' ideas as your own?

When you use the exact words of another person, place those words in quotation marks and provide a citation that identifies precisely the source. For example:

> *Albert Einstein has said: "Laws alone can not secure freedom of expression; in order that every man present his views without penalty there must be spirit of tolerance in the entire population". (1949, p. 20)*

When you use the idea of another person, clearly indicate that the idea is his/hers (not yours). Sometimes the source of an idea is unclear - some ideas, for example, you may see as being common knowledge. When in doubt, cite the source where you saw or heard the idea expressed. In this way you are protecting yourself from the charge of plagiarism. For example:

Legislation by itself cannot ensure freedom of speech. (Einstein, 1948, p. 20)

Cite Your Sources

Your instructor may ask you to use a standard style to document the sources in your work. There are many styles to choose from. The most popular documentation styles at Centennial College are:

• APA Style (American Psychological Association)

• MLA Style (Modern Languages Association)

Use the style your instructor recommends to document your work.

Did You Know?

Centennial College has a policy on plagiarism. The title is Academic Honesty and Plagiarism Policy. Please review it and ask your instructor if you have any questions or concerns. You can find the policy on the Centennial College website.

Plagiarism is forbidden in academic institutions, and those who are caught plagiarizing are dealt severe penalties.

How Do I Use Material Gathered from Sources?

How to Use Material Gathered from Sources

Once you find information that you want to use, you need to figure out how best to present it in your paper or report. You have several options, and your decisions should be based on making the most effective use of the material for your purposes. Essentially, you can integrate material into your paper in three ways—through summary, paraphrase, or quotation.

Taken from *What Every Student Should Know About Avoiding Plagiarism*, by Linda Stern

How Do I Use Material Gathered from Sources? Continued

Summary

A **summary** is a brief restatement in your own words of the main ideas in a source. Summary is used to convey the general meaning of the ideas in a source, without specific details or examples that may appear in the original. You can summarize a paragraph, but summaries are mostly used for long items—a chapter, an Internet document, or even an entire book. A summary is always much shorter than the work it treats. For example, a summary of an entire book can take just 50 to 100 words.

Write a summary when (1) the information is important enough to be included, but not important enough to be treated at length; (2) the relevant material is too long to be quoted fully; or (3) you want to give the essence of the material without the corroborating details. In summarizing, you need to revise again and again to condense your writing as much as possible. Be objective, but if the original has a particular tone—ironic or critical, say—give an indication of the tone in your summary.

Taken from *What Every Student Should Know About Avoiding Plagiarism*, by Linda Stern

Paraphrase

A **paraphrase** is a restatement in your own words, and using your own sentence structure, of specific ideas or information from a source. Paraphrase is useful when you want to capture certain ideas or details from a source but do not need or want to quote the source's actual words. A paraphrase can be about as long as the original passage.

Use a paraphrase when (1) you don't want to interrupt the flow of your writing with another person's writing; (2) you want to avoid using a long quotation or a long string of quotations; or (3) you want to interpret or explain the material as you include it.

Taken from *What Every Student Should Know About Avoiding Plagiarism*, by Linda Stern

If you remember that the chief purpose of a paraphrase is *to maintain your own writing style* throughout your paper, you'll avoid falling into a trap that many inexperienced writers succumb to—that is, using the original passage, but changing just a few phrases here and there. The most effective way to write a paraphrase is to read the original passage, put the passage aside, and then compose your own restatement of the material in the passage. If you want to repeat particular words or phrases from the original, put those items in quotation marks.

Taken from *What Every Student Should Know About Avoiding Plagiarism,* by Linda Stern

Courtesy of Shutterstock.

Quotation

A **quotation** reproduces an actual part of a source, word for word, to support a statement or idea, to provide an example, to advance an argument, or to add interest or color to a discussion. The length of a quotation can range from a word or phrase to several paragraphs. In general, quote the least amount possible that gets your point across to the reader. Quoting many long passages from source material can make your paper seem choppy and can give the impression that you have no thoughts of your own.

Use quotations if (1) the original writing is especially powerful, descriptive, clear, or revealing; (2) the original contains language you are analyzing or commenting on; (3) the original provides authenticity or bolsters the credibility of your paper; or (4) the original material is difficult to summarize or paraphrase adequately.

Taken from *What Every Student Should Know About Avoiding Plagiarism,* by Linda Stern

Practicing Summarizing, Paraphrasing, and Quoting

Read the following paragraph and then: a) write a summary of it; b) write a paraphrase of it; c) incorporate a direct quotation from it into a sentence.

A BROADER VIEW OF POLITICS

Various environmental groups have sought to end the clear-cutting practices of forest companies in British Columbia. Having had limited success in persuading the B.C. government to pass stricter logging regulations, they turned to other methods to achieve their objective. Europeans were encouraged to participate in a boycott of products made with B.C. lumber, and pressure was put on retail businesses such as Home Depot only to sell lumber produced in an environmentally friendly manner. These activities had considerable success, and a number of B.C. forest companies began to change their logging practices.

In many ways, these activities by environmental groups are similar to what we normally consider as political. People were mobilized to try to achieve an objective that was viewed as being in the public interest. Rather than influencing government to adopt a policy that might change the actions of logging companies, environmental groups were able to directly pressure some of the companies to change their actions to deal with a public problem. The activities of environmental groups might therefore be considered political, even though the groups decided to try to affect the decisions of private businesses rather than the decisions of government.

Taken from *Politics, Power, and the Common Good: An Introduction to Political Science*, Second Edition, by Eric Mintz, David Close, and Osvaldo Croci

Summary:

Paraphrase:

Direct Quote:

Citations and References

To avoid plagiarism it is very important to include citations and references in any of your assignments, when appropriate. It's also important to format your citations and references correctly. The two styles of documentation used most frequently are the American Psychological Association (APA) style and the Modern Languages Association (MLA). The APA style is followed in the social sciences and education, and the MLA style is followed for the humanities and fine arts. For this course, you will be asked to use APA style citations and referencing.

In Text Citations in APA

1. Author named in your text	Business Professor Rosabeth Moss Kanter (2002) claims "men and women employed in similar jobs in an organization will react in similar ways to their job conditions" (p. 202).
2. Author not named in your text	Women in Canada have a longer life expectancy than men (Statistics Canada, 2006, p. 12). Female children born in 2001 could expect to live an average of 82 years. Male children born the same year were expected to live just 77 years.
3. Work by a single author	(Moss Kanter, 2002, p. 202)
4. Work by two authors	Notice that APA uses an ampersand (&) with multiple authors' names rather than *and*. (Suzuki & Irabu, 2002, p. 404).
5. Work by three to five authors	The authors' last names follow the order of the title page. The first in-text citation includes all the authors' names. (Francisco, Vaughn, & Romano, 2001, p. 7) Subsequent references can use the last name of the first author and *et al.* (Francisco et al., 2001, p. 49)
6. Work by six or more authors	Use the first author's last name and *et al.* for all in-text references. (Swallit et al., 2004, p. 49)
7. Work by a group or organization	If the group author is in the text, place the date and page number in parentheses. The National Organization for Women (2001) observed that this "generational shift in attitudes towards marriage and childrearing" will have profound consequences (p. 325).

Taken from *Writing: A Journey,* Canadian Edition, by Lester Faigley and Melanie Rubens

In Text Citations in APA Continued

8. Work by an unknown author	Use a shortened version of the title (or the full title if it is short) in place of the author's name. Capitalize all key words in the title. If it is an article title, place it in quotation marks. ("Derailing the Peace Process," 2003, p. 44)
9. Quotations 40 words or longer	Indent long quotations 1.25 cm and omit quotation marks. Note that the period appears before the parentheses in an indented "block" quote. Orlean (2001) has attempted to explain the popularity of the painter Thomas Kinkade: People like to own things they think are valuable. . . . The high price of limited editions is part of their appeal; it implies that they are choice and exclusive, and that only a certain class of people will be able to afford them. (p. 128)
10. Two works by one author with the same copyright date	Assign the dates letters (a, b, etc.) according to their alphabetical arrangement in the references list. The majority of books written about coauthorship focus on partners of the same sex (Laird, 2001a, p. 351).
11. Two or more sources within the same sentence	Place each citation directly after the statement it supports. Some surveys report an increase in homelessness rates (Alford, 2004) while others chart a slight decrease (Rice, 2003a) . . . If you need to cite two or more works within the same parentheses, list them in the order they appear in the references list and separate them with a semicolon. (Alford, 2004; Rice, 2003a)
12. Work quoted in another source	Name the work and give a citation for the secondary source. Saunders and Kellman's study (as cited in McAtee, Luhan, Stiles, & Buell, 1994) . . .

Taken from *Writing: A Journey,* Canadian Edition, by Lester Faigley and Melanie Rubens

Books in APA Style Reference List

Sample references for books

Book by one author

The author's last name comes first, followed by a comma and the author's initials.

Ball, E. (2000). *Slaves in the family*. New York, NY: Ballantine Books.

If an editor, put the abbreviation *Ed.* in parentheses after the name.

Kavanagh, P. (Ed.). (1969). *Lapped furrows*. New York, NY: Hand Press.

Book by two authors

Join two authors' names with a comma and ampersand.

Hardt, M., & Negri, A. (2000). *Empire*. Cambridge, MA: Harvard University Press.

If editors, use (*Eds.*) after the names.

McClelland, D., & Eismann, K. (Eds.).

Book by three or more authors

Write out all of the authors' names up to seven. For works with eight or more authors, write out the first six names, add an ellipsis mark (. . .), and give the last author's name.

Konishi, C., Hymel, S., Zumbo, B. D., Li, Z., Taki, M., Slee, P., . . . Kwak, K.

Chapter in an edited collection

Add the word *In* after the selection title and before the names of the editor(s).

Howard, A. (1997). Labor, history, and sweatshops in the new global economy. In A. Ross (Ed.), *No sweat: Fashion, free trade, and the rights of garment workers* (pp. 151–172). New York, NY: Verso.

Government document

Advisory Committee on Radiological Protection. (2001). *Guidelines on hospital emergency plans*. Ottawa, ON: Canadian Nuclear Safety Commission.

Taken from *Writing: A Journey*, Canadian Edition, by Lester Faigley and Melanie Rubens

Periodicals in APA Style Reference List

Sample references for print periodical sources

Article by one author	Kellogg, R. T. (2001). Competition for working memory among writing processes. *American Journal of Psychology, 114,* 175–192.
Article by multiple authors	Write out all of the authors' names, up to seven authors. For eight or more authors, write out the first six names, insert an ellipsis mark, and finish with the final author's name. Blades, J., & Rowe-Finkbeiner, K. (2006). The motherhood manifesto. *The Nation, 282*(20), 11–16.
Article by a group or organization	National Organization for Women. (2002). Where to find feminists in Austin. *The NOW guide for Austin women.* Austin, TX: Chapter Press.
Article in a journal with continuous pagination	Include only the volume number and the year, not the issue number. Engen, R., & Steen, S. (2000). The power to punish: Discretion and sentencing reform in the war on drugs. *American Journal of Sociology, 105,* 1357–1395.
Article in a journal paginated by issue	List the issue number in parentheses (not italicized) after the volume number. For a popular magazine that does not commonly use volume numbers, use the season or date of publication. McGinn, D. (2006, June 5). Marriage by the numbers. *Newsweek,* 40–48.
Monthly publications	Barlow, J. P. (1998, January). Africa rising: Everything you know about Africa is wrong. *Wired,* 142–158.
Newspaper article	Hagenbaugh, B. (2005, April 25). Grads welcome an uptick in hiring. *USA Today,* p. A1.

Courtesy of Shutterstock.

Taken from *Writing: A Journey,* Canadian Edition, by Lester Faigley and Melanie Rubens

Electronic Resources in APA Style Reference List Continued

Title of Web page

Author's name

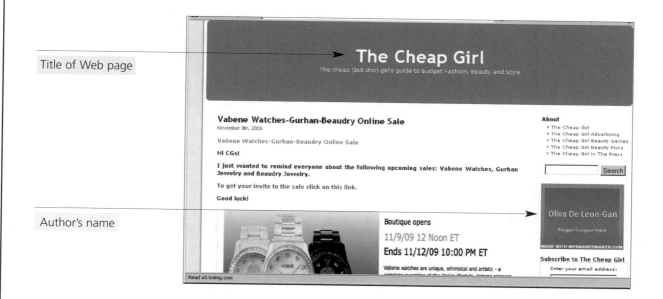

Websites are often made up of many separate pages or articles. Each page or article on a website may or may not have a title. If you are citing a page or article that has a title, treat the title like an article in a periodical. No retrieval date is needed unless the material may change over time.

Fidler, D. P. (2004, April). *World Health Organization's international health regulations.* Retrieved from the American Society of International Law website: http://www.asil.org/insights/ insigh132.htm

When no author is given, begin the citation with the title of the document first. Use (n.d.) If a publication date is not given.

Webcasting for rookies. (n.d.). Retrieved http://www.tvworldwide/globe_show/iwa/040305

If there is no title for the website, list it by author or creator. If it is an informally published or self-archived work, cite it as follows:

McDermott, John. (n.d.). *John McDermott tenor.* Retrieved from http://wwwjohnmcdermott.com/ ?m=3

Electronic Resources in APA Style Reference List Continued

Sample references for electronic sources

Journal article with Digital Object Identifier (DOI)	Some electronic content is assigned a unique number called a Digital Object Identifier (DOI). If a DOI is provided for an article, include it after the page number(s) of the article as **doi:doi number** (no spaces, and no period after it).
	Baruch, J. J. (2008). Combating global warming while enhancing the future. *Technology in Society, 30*(2), 111–121. doi: 10 .1016/j.techsoc.2007.12.008
Online journal article without Digital Object Identifier.	If no DOI number is assigned and the article was retrieved online, give the URL of the journal home page, even if the article was retrieved from a database.
	Elliot, A. (2003). Government faces pressure to tackle obesity. *British Medical Journal, 327*(7424), 1125. Retrieved from http://www.bmj.com
Online newspaper article	Mitchell, A. (2007, August 16). A precautionary charge. *The Globe and Mail*, p. A14. Retrieved from http://theglobeandmail.com
Online magazine article	Nicklen, P. (2007, June). Vanishing sea ice: Life at the edge. *National Geographic, 211*, 32–55. Retrieved from http://ngm.nationalgeographic.com/2007/06/vanishing-sea-ice/sea-ice-text.html
Article or document from an online reference work	Lennox, J. (2010). Darwinism. In E. N. Zalta (Ed.), *The Stanford encyclopedia of philosophy* (Spring 2010 ed.) Retrieved from http://plato.stanford.edu/archive/spr2010/entries/darwinism
Online book (ebook)	Immon, W. H., Imhoff, C., & Sousa, R. (2001). *Corporate information factory*. New York, NY: Wiley. Retrieved from http://www.ebooks.com/ebooks/book_display.asp?IID=117479

Other sources in APA-style references list

Television broadcast	Miller, W. (Producer/Director). (2006, January 4). *Encounters with Jack: Life and times of Jack Turner* [Television broadcast]. Toronto: CBC.
Videos and DVDs	Kaurismaki, A. (Director). (1999). *Leningrad cowboys go America* [Motion picture]. United States: MGM.
Presentation slides (PowerPoint)	Kunka, J. L. (n.d.). *Conquering the comma* [PowerPoint slides]. Retrieved from Purdue University Writing Lab website: http://owl.english.purdue.edu/Workshops/pp/index.html# presentations

Did You Know?

Microsoft Word 2007 includes a tool to help you prepare the citations and references for your paper. Look under the "References" tab.

Presentations: Preparation and Delivery

The final assignment for this course includes an oral presentation. For some students, this may be the first time that you have prepared a presentation for a class at Centennial College. For other students, you may have prepared several presentations previously and feel very comfortable in delivering presentations. Regardless of your experience, this section provides you with comprehensive tips to help you prepare and deliver the best presentation possible.

Courtesy of Shutterstock.

Delivering Presentations

The best speakers draw their inspiration from their audience, and they maintain contact with their audience, communicating with body language and presentation style in addition to the content. Audience members leave feeling like they've had a conversation with the speaker even if they have been silent through the presentation.

Plan a presentation

A successful presentation, like successful writing, requires careful planning. Look closely at what you are being asked to present and how long you will have. Decide early on what kind of presentation you will give and what visuals you will incorporate.

Select your topic

Choosing and researching a topic for a presentation is similar to choosing and researching a topic for a written assignment. Ask these questions:

- Will you enjoy speaking on this topic?
- Does the topic fit the assignment?
- Do you know enough to speak on this topic?
- If you do not know enough, are you willing to do research to learn more about the topic?

Remember that if your presentation requires you to do any research, then you will need to develop a written bibliography as you would for a research assignment. You will need to document the sources of your information and provide those sources in your presentation.

Taken from *Writing: A Journey*, Canadian Edition, by Lester Faigley and Melanie Rubens

Think about your audience

Unlike writing, when you give a speech you have your audience directly before you. They will give you concrete feedback during your presentation by smiling or frowning, by paying attention or losing interest, by asking questions or sitting passively. Ask these questions:

- Will your audience likely be interested in your topic?
- Are there ways you can get them more interested?

- What is your audience likely to know or believe about your topic?
- What does your audience probably not know about your topic?
- What key terms will you have to define or explain?
- Where is your audience most likely to disagree with you?
- What questions are they likely to ask?

Organize your presentation

Make a list of your key points	Think of the best way to order your key points.
Plan your introduction	You have to get the audience's attention, introduce your topic, convince the audience that it is important to them, present your thesis, and give your audience either an overview of your presentation or a sense of your direction.
Plan your conclusion	End on a strong note. Simply summarizing is a dull way to close. Think of an example or an idea that your audience can take away with them.

Design effective visuals

Visual elements can both support and reinforce your major points. They give you another means of reaching your audience and keeping them stimulated. Visuals should communicate content and not just be eye candy. Some of the easier visuals to create are outlines, statistical charts, flow charts, photographs, and maps.

At a minimum, consider putting an outline of your talk on a transparency or on a PowerPoint slide. An outline allows an audience to keep track of where you are in your talk and when you are moving to your next point.

Create visuals

Follow these guidelines to create better visuals.

Keep the text short	You don't want your audience straining to read long passages on the screen and neglecting what you have to say. Except for quotations, use short words and phrases on transparencies and slides.

Taken from *Writing: A Journey*, Canadian Edition, by Lester Faigley and Melanie Rubens

Always proofread	Typos and misspelled words make you look careless and can distract the audience from your point.
Use dark text on a white or light-coloured background	Light text on a dark background is hard to read.
Use graphics that reproduce well	Some graphics do not show up well on the screen, often because there isn't enough contrast.
Plan your timing when using visuals	Usually you can leave a slide on the screen for one to two minutes, which allows your audience time to read the slide and connect its points to what you are saying.

Know the advantages and disadvantages of presentation software

Presentation software allows you to combine text, images, sounds, animations, and even video clips on *computer-generated* slides, which can be projected onto a large screen. Presentation software, such as Microsoft PowerPoint, allows you to import charts and other graphics that you have created in other programs, and it gives you several options for presentation, including printed handouts and Web pages.

The major drawback of presentation software is perhaps that it is too easy to use. An attractive presentation can be empty of content. You can quickly get carried away with all the special effects possible—such as fade-ins, fade-outs, and sound effects. Presentations with many special effects often come off as heavy on style and light on substance. They also can be time-consuming to produce.

Give a memorable presentation

What makes an effective presentation?

Usually more effective	Usually less effective
Talk	Read
Stand	Sit
Make eye contact	Look down
Move around	Stand still
Speak loudly	Mumble

Taken from *Writing: A Journey,* Canadian Edition, by Lester Faigley and Melanie Rubens

Use visual elements	Lack visual elements
Focus on main points	Get lost in details
Give an overview of what you are going to say in the introduction	Start your talk without indicating where you are headed
Give a conclusion that summarizes your main points and ends with a key idea or example	Stop abruptly
Finish on time	Run overtime

Taken from *Writing: A Journey,* Canadian Edition, by Lester Faigley and Melanie Rubens

Stop and Reflect

Imagine sitting in the audience for your own presentation.

If you were sitting in the audience, what would keep you interested in a presentation?

_____
_____
_____
_____

What would help you follow the presentation?

_____
_____
_____
_____

How would the speaker engage you?

_____
_____
_____
_____

Chapter Summary

Main Concepts:

- Four writing tips: writing and editing paragraphs, writing sentences, punctuation and conventions
- Introduction to research and report writing
- Overview of referencing
- School of Advancement plagiarism guidelines
- Tips to avoid plagiarism
- Tips for presentation delivery

Additional Resources

Resources - Plagiarism

University of Hong Kong - Plagiarism & How to Avoid it (English Centre, David Gardner) - http://www4.caes.hku.hk/plagiarism/introduction.htm
McGill University - Student Guide to Avoid Plagiarism - http://www.mcgill.ca/students/srr/honest/
University of Toronto - How Not to Plagiarize - http://www.writing.utoronto.ca/advice/using-sources/how-not-to-plagiarize

What every student should know about preparing effective oral presentations by Martin R. Cox (Centennial College Libraries)

Description: "This brief guide provides brief and helpful insight into preparing an effective presentation, including how to overcome your nervousness." (Product Description (n.d.). Retrieved from http://www.amazon.ca/Student-Should-Preparing-Effective-Presentations/dp/0205505457).

Research and Citation http://owl.english.purdue.edu/owl/section/2/

Description: This website provides an overview and tips for approaching research and doing citation.

References

Centennial College. (2010). *Avoid Plagiarism*. Retrieved September 11, 2010, from Centennial College Library: http://library.centennialcollege.ca/library/researchhelp/avoidplagiarism.

Faigley, L., & Rubens, M. (2011). *Writing: A Journey*. Toronto, Ontario: Pearson Canada Inc.

McKibbin, M. N. (2008). *Impact: A Guide to Business Communication*. In Think, Engage, Respond: Communicating for Citizenship. Toronto, Ontario: Pearson Custom Publishing.

Nin, A. (Date Unknown). Writing Quote. Retrieved on October 7, 2010 from http://www.quotegarden.com/writing.html

School of Advancement Plagiarism Guide. (2009). Scarborough, Ontario: Centennial College, School of Advancement.

Stern, L. (2009). *What Every Student Should Know About ... Avoiding Plagiarism*. New York, NY: Pearson Publishing Inc.

Think, Engage, Respond – Communicating for Citizenship (2nd ed.).(2007).Toronto, Ontario: Pearson Custom Publishing.

Notes

Assignments

In GNED500, Global Citizenship: From Social Analysis to Social Action you will engage in a variety of assignments to further your understanding of the course content. In this section you will find an overview of each assignment as well as a rubric outlining the expectations in detail.

You will be expected to complete the following:

- Portfolio Sharing
- Identity and Values Assignment
- Social Action Project (Consists of the Social Analysis Assignment and the Social Action Plan)
- Global Citizenship Post-Reflection

Portfolio Sharing

Purpose:

- To encourage students to engage in reflective practice and relate concepts of the course to their personal and professional development

- To reflect on the course content covered and/or submitted in class

- Students will engage in a formative learning process where they are able to assess their own learning

Expectations:

- Develop a portfolio

- Demonstrate an understanding of the core course concepts in group discussions

- Demonstrate student's personal growth through the course

- Provide relevant examples

- Ability to articulate ideas to the group

Format:

- Faculty will choose the group

- Group members will provide feedback

- Students will share their work in groups of 3-4

- Students will showcase and discuss the artifact(s) they have included in their portfolio with the group

- Each student in a group will have 3 minutes to present his/her portfolio to the other members of the group

- **Instructions:**

- Identify and explain 2-3 concepts that have relevance and significance to your learning experience

- Connect artifact(s) to personal, academic and/or professional life

- Provide relevant examples used in your artifact(s)

- Relate artifact(s) to your role and responsibilities as a global citizen

- Identify area(s) of further learning

Portfolio Sharing Peer Assessment

Outcome Assessed	Emerging Level I		Developing Level II		Competent Level III		Strong Level IV		Outstanding Level V		Mark
	1	2	3	4	5	6	7	8	9	10	
Communication Skills	No clarity in presentation or sequential flow of ideas		There is little clarity in presentation. Minimal logical sequencing of ideas.		Presentation is mostly coherent and expresses ideas in a logical sequence.		Presentation is coherent and effectively expresses ideas in a logical sequence.		Presentation is fluid and easy to understand. Ideas are cohesive.		/10
Preparation	Did not bring a portfolio and artifact(s) Was not prepared to present.		Portfolio not very adequate and does not demonstrate good preparation – missing critical elements of the portfolio that reflect core concepts		Brought portfolio and/or artifact to class. Presentation was average		Brought portfolio and/or artifact to class. Presentation was above average		Brought full portfolio including artifact to class. Was thoughtfully prepared to present.		/25
Personal Growth and Relevant Examples	Cannot identify what has been learned. Retells the activity/artifact		Identifies some areas of growth and learning. Connects the artifact to previous learning and experiences		Identifies areas of growth and learning. Connects the artifact to previous learning and experiences		Effectively identifies areas of growth and learning. Connects the artifact to previous learning and experiences		Effectively identifies areas of growth – what they have learned or gained. Identifies areas for future growth and learning and possibly future actions.		/25
Self Reflection and Personal Position	There is no self-reflection and connection to personal experiences.		There is little self-reflection and minimal connection to personal experiences.		There is some self-reflection but lacks depth. Generally relates personal experiences to the concepts of the course.		There is self-reflection, Generally relates personal experiences to the concepts of the course.		There is self-reflection from multiple perspectives (self and others) In depth discussion of personal experiences as they relate to the concepts of the course.		/20
Assignment Expectations	Presentation not developed and does not demonstrate any evidence of preparation		Presentation not adequately developed; too brief		Does not adhere to time limit but somewhat developed		Adheres to time limit but somewhat developed		Adheres to 5 minute limit; presentation adequately developed		/20

Social Action Project

The aim of this project is to develop an understanding of social analysis and social action through an in-depth investigation of a social problem that impacts communities locally and/or globally. For the purpose of this assignment, students should work in groups of 3-4.

Grade Value of Assignment

The Social Action Project grade breakdown is as follows:
- Social Analysis Proposal (Part A): 15%
- Social Action Plan (Part B): 15%
- Social Action Project Presentation (Part C): 10%

Topic Selection

Topics can be selected through the following:

- A list of topics provided by the instructor
- A topic/issue that impacts your field of study/ professional designation
- If you are in a group with multi-program/ professional designations, the group should creatively combine fields of study in the issue/topic selection (i.e. Child and Youth Worker & Hospitality and Tourism – Children and Sex Tourism or Architecture, Environment & Business – Sustainable Housing)

Social Analysis Proposal – Part A:

Each group will be required to submit a social action proposal. Proposals should contain the following components:

- **Length**
  - 3 to 5 pages not including cover paper or bibliography, double spaced, 12 point font
- **Introduction**
  - Naming and defining the social problem
  - Connect the social problem to the course (How does it fit in?)
  - Locate yourselves individually (Why did you chose this social problem to focus on?)
- **Research**
  - Students should collect information using, books, journals, articles, websites, documentaries, pamphlets, organizations etc (See *Communication Chapter 9* for writing conventions, referencing, research, and plagiarism)
  - All research must be cited throughout the assignment – In text citation as well as a bibliography at the end of the document
- **Social Analysis**
  - Social analysis using one of the three frameworks taught in class
  - Using the information gathered from research, students should provide 2 to 3 paragraphs on each level of social analysis to effectively analyze the problem

Social Action Plan – Part B

Once the proposal is completed, your group will submit a plan of action to address the social problem you have selected. Each social action plan should contain the following components:

- **Introduction**

- **Basic Research**
  - Research current examples for social action being implemented by individuals, communities, government, agencies etc.

- **Recommendations for Social Action**
  - Based on the social analysis, feedback from the instructor, and research on current action, your group will develop a set of recommendations for social action related to your specific social problem
  - Recommendations must be appropriate and be within the scope of your group's ability
  - Your group should select the best appropriate action to develop a step by step plan

- **Action Plan**
  - Step by step plan to demonstrate what action your group is suggesting and how the action would be carried out

- **Conclusion**
  - Each group member should provide an individual reflection discussing the actions needed

Social Action Plan Presentation – Part C

Each group will be required to present their issue and social action plan to the class. Each presentation should contain:

- A description and analysis of the social issue/problem of focus
- A brief outline of the group's step by step plan of action
- A summary of current social action initiatives or organizations that seek to address the issue
- Use of visual aids at various points in the presentation (i.e. YouTube, powerpoint)
- Use of interactive techniques throughout the presentation
  - Creative questioning
  - Interactive activities

Social Analysis Proposal (Part A) Rubric

Outcome Assessed	Emerging Level I		Developing Level II		Competent Level III		Strong Level IV		Outstanding Level V		Mark
	1	2	3	4	5	6	7	8	9	10	
Language Conventions	There is little or no clarity. Meaning is distorted-because the product/ project has many grammatical and formatting errors.		Topic is unclear and there are many grammatical and formatting errors, which affect meaning.		Product/ project lacks punctuation. Has frequent grammatical and formatting errors; however, these do not interfere with meaning.		Product/ project is clear with few spelling, grammatical and formatting errors. Information is clearly and meaningfully organized.		Project / product is clear, has no grammatical errors; is logically organized and well structured.		/10
Identify the Social Problem	Does not clearly identify problem or issue. Chosen problem or issue is not directly related to course topics and material. Fails to establish a rationale on the importance of the issue from a global and/ or local standpoint.		Demonstrates limited ability to identify problem or issue. Chosen problem or issue is vaguely related to course topics and material. Loosely establishes a rationale on the importance of the issue from a global and/ or local standpoint.		Demonstrates some ability to identify problem or issue. Chosen problem or issue is moderately related to course topics and material. Establishes some basis of a rationale on the importance of the issue from a global and/or local standpoint.		Follows most instructions to identify problem or issue. Chosen problem or issue is related to course topics and material. Establishes a clear rationale on the importance of the issue from a global and/or local standpoint with limited detail.		Thoroughly identifies problem or issue. Chosen problem or issue is directly related to course topics and material. Establishes a clear and detailed rationale on the importance of the issue from a global and/or local standpoint.		/20
Basic Research Information	Does not identify, collect and reference relevant material to provide basic information and details on topic/issue of the project. (Material must be clearly connected to the topic/ issue to provide enough background for social analysis).		Demonstrates limited ability to identify, collect and reference relevant material to provide basic information and details on topic/ issue of the project. (Material must be clearly connected to the topic/issue to provide enough background for social analysis).		Demonstrates some ability to identify, collect and reference relevant material to provide basic information and details on topic/issue of the project. (Material must be clearly connected to the topic/issue to provide enough background for social analysis).		Follows most instructions to identify, collect and reference relevant material to provide basic information and details on topic/issue of the project. (Material must be clearly connected to the topic/issue to provide enough background for social analysis).		Demonstrates an excellent ability to identify, collect and reference relevant material to provide basic information and details on topic/issue of the project. (Material must be clearly connected to the topic/issue to provide enough background for social analysis)		/20

Social Analysis Proposal Rubric Continued

Outcome Assessed	Emerging Level I (1, 2)	Developing Level II (3, 4)	Competent Level III (5, 6)	Strong Level IV (7, 8)	Outstanding Level V (9, 10)	Mark
Social Analysis	Does not complete social analysis of topic/issue using researched material and one of three frameworks provided in class.	Demonstrates limited ability to complete social analysis of topic/issue using researched material and one of three frameworks provided in class.	Demonstrates some ability to complete social analysis of topic/issue using researched material and one of three frameworks provided in class .	Follows most instructions to complete social analysis of topic/issue using researched material and one of three frameworks provided in class with detail.	Demonstrates an excellent ability to complete social analysis of topic/issue using researched material and one of three frameworks provided in class with extensive detail.	/40
Group Organization	Does not indicate group member's roles and responsibilities. No group rules or/and expectations established.	Vaguely indicates group member's roles and responsibilities. Loosely establishes group rules or/and expectations.	Provides some detail on group member's roles and responsibilities. Some group rules or/and expectations established.	Indicates most group member's roles and responsibilities. Group rules or/and expectations established.	Thoroughly indicates group member's roles and responsibilities. Group rules or/and expectations established in extensive detail.	/10

Social Action Plan (Part B) Rubric

Outcome Assessed	Emerging Level I (1, 2)	Developing Level II (3, 4)	Competent Level III (5, 6)	Strong Level IV (7, 8)	Outstanding Level V (9, 10)	Mark
Language Conventions	There is little or no clarity. Meaning is distorted because the product/ project has many grammatical and formatting errors.	Topic is unclear and there are many grammatical and formatting errors, which affect meaning.	Product/ project lacks punctuation. Has frequent grammatical and formatting errors; however, these do not interfere with meaning.	Product/ project is clear with few spelling, grammatical and formatting errors. Information is clearly and meaningfully organized.	Project / product is clear, has no grammatical errors; is logically organized and well structured.	/10
Use of Feedback and Course Material	Does not make use of course material, original proposal and feedback to develop a social action plan.	Demonstrates limited use of course material, original proposal and instructor feedback to develop a social action plan.	Demonstrates some use of course material, original proposal and instructor feedback to develop social action plan.	Follows most instructions to use course material, original proposal and instructor feedback to develop social action plan.	Demonstrates excellent use of course material, original proposal and instructor feedback to develop social action plan.	/20
Social Action Plan Process	Does not document and/or follow steps in developing appropriate social action plan based information provided in class.	Loosely documents and/or follows steps in developing appropriate social action plan based information provided in class.	Demonstrates some ability to document and/ or follow steps in developing appropriate social action plan based information provided in class.	Follows most instructions to document and/or follow steps in developing appropriate social action plan based information provided in class with detail.	Fully documents and/or follows steps in developing appropriate social action plan with detail based information provided in class.	/20
Basic Research on Social Action	Does not identify and collect relevant material to provide basic information and details on current social action projects/plans being implemented to address topic/issue of the project.	Demonstrates limited ability to identify and collect relevant material to provide basic information and details on current social action projects/plans being implemented to address topic/issue of the project.	Demonstrates some ability to identify and collect relevant material to provide basic information and details on current social action projects/plans being implemented to address topic/issue of the project.	Follows most instructions to identify and collect relevant material to provide basic information and details on current social action projects/plans being implemented to address topic/issue of the project.	Thoroughly identifies and collects relevant material to provide basic information and details on current social action projects/plans being implemented to address topic/issue of the project.	/20
Recommendations For Social Action	Does not connect social analysis of issue and create realistic and practical solutions for change.	Demonstrates limited ability to connect social analysis of issue and create realistic and practical solutions for change.	Demonstrates some ability to connect social analysis of issue and create realistic and practical solutions for change.	Follows most instructions to connect social analysis of issue and create realistic and practical solutions for change.	Follows all instructions to connect social analysis of issue and create realistic and practical solutions for change.	/30

Social Action Presentation (Part C) Rubric

Outcome Assessed	Emerging Level I		Developing Level II		Competent Level III		Strong Level IV		Outstanding Level V		Mark
	1	2	3	4	5	6	7	8	9	10	
Social Problem Explanation and Analysis	Does not demonstrate ability to accurately and clearly explain topic/issue with relevant supporting detail and evidence. Fails to incorporate several perspectives in discussion.		Demonstrates limited ability to accurately and clearly explain topic/issue with relevant supporting detail and evidence. Loosely incorporates several perspectives in discussion.		Demonstrates some ability to accurately and clearly explain topic/issue with relevant supporting detail and evidence. Moderately incorporates several perspectives in discussion.		Follows most instructions to accurately and clearly explains topic/issue with relevant supporting detail and evidence. Successfully incorporates several perspectives in discussion.		Demonstrates an excellent ability to accurately and clearly explain topic/issue with relevant supporting detail and evidence. Thoroughly incorporates several perspectives in discussion.		/30
Preparation and Delivery	Does not demonstrate preparation and effective delivery skills Fails to facilitate discussion, provide opportunities for involvement.		Demonstrates limited preparation and effective delivery skills. Limited ability to facilitate discussion, provide opportunities for involvement.		Demonstrates some preparation and delivery skills along with some ability to facilitate discussion and provide opportunities for involvement.		Follows most instructions for presentation and effective delivery skills. Sound ability to facilitate discussion, provide opportunities for involvement.		Demonstrates excellent preparation and effective delivery skills. Excellent ability to facilitate discussion, provide opportunities for involvement.		/10
Creativity	Does not use various teaching and information sharing techniques. No interactive activities used to engage students.		Limited use of various teaching and information sharing techniques. Minimal use of interactive activities used to engage students.		Uses some teaching and information sharing techniques. Some interactive activities used to engage students.		Follows most instructions on use of various teaching and information sharing techniques. Successfully uses interactive activities to engage students.		Extensive use of various teaching and information sharing techniques. Makes extensive use of various interactive activities to engage students.		/30
Steps to Social Action and Current Social Action Initiatives	Does not present step-by-step outline for social action as it relates to social analysis. Provides no information or resources about current approaches to address social problem.		Provides limited step-by-step outline for social action as it relates to social analysis. Vaguely presents information or resources about current approaches to address social problem.		Provides a step-by-step outline for social action as it relates to social analysis but omits some necessary detail. Indicates some information and/or resources about current approaches to address social problem.		Provides most of a step-by-step outline for social action as it relates to social analysis and information and/or resources about current approaches to address social problem.		Provides detailed overview and step-by-step outline for social action as it relates to social analysis and extensive information and/or resources about current approaches to address social problem.		/20
Time Management	Does not make effective use of time and adhere to prescribed time limit for presentation.		Limited effort to make effective use of time and adhere to prescribed time limit for presentation.		Some effort to make effective use of time and adhere to prescribed time limit for presentation.		Follows most instructions to make effective use of time and adhere to prescribed time limit for presentation.		Follows all instructions to make effective use of time and adhere to prescribed time limit for presentation.		/10

Identity and Values Assignment

The purpose of the Identity and Values assignment is to closely examine and analyze your personal identity and values and the different components which shape each. There are three options to this assignment. Please check with your instructor to determine which option your are required to complete.

Grade Value of Assignment

The Identity and Values assignment is worth 15% of your final grade.

Option 1: I Am The Sum of All My Pieces

For this assignment you can use any one of the formats outlined below:
- Written
- Animoto & WIKI
- Paper/ On-line Collage
- Web-page
- Other format.

Creativity could involve the use of music, colour, pictures, images and the overall presentation format of the assignment. You are required to present a rationale for your particular selection of format, which must be thoughtful and relevant to the assignment. This rationale can be incorporated into the narratives on each of the puzzle pieces used.

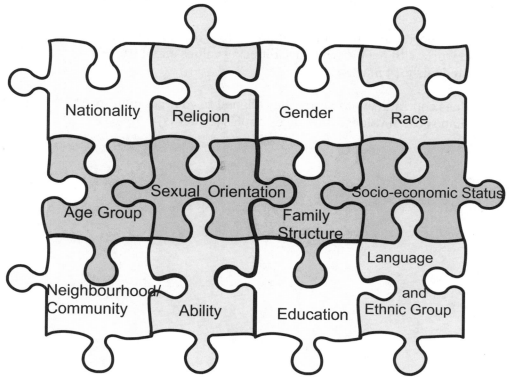

Identity and Values Assignment

Option 1: I Am The Sum of All My Pieces Continued

1. Using any 10 of the 12 puzzle pieces write a statement that honestly represents each aspect of you. That is, how do you see yourself and your life right now with regards to each aspect? You may choose to include pictures or other images, however these must be thoughtful and relevant. (10 Marks)

2. What aspects of yourself give you power, privilege and prestige, and which create a lack of power and prestige? Which pieces of your identity were fluid/ changeable, depending on situations/ circumstances/ events? (4 Marks)

3. Write a self-reflection on the process of doing this exercise. What was the process like for you? What did it make you think of? How did it make you feel? Are there any areas that helped you or hindered you in your relationships with others? As you learned about yourself and others (including your classmates) did it help you to gain and give respect to others? When you read over your finished "Sum of the Pieces" were there areas that you were proud of and/ or areas that you think you would like to change? (6 Marks)

4. Identify ways in which you have been identified by others based on your race, gender or ethnicity and, is this different from how you see yourself? (3 marks)

5. Can you give an example of a time when you judged someone in a manner that you found out later was not an accurate judgment of who they were as a person? Identify why or what was behind the judgment (upon what values and/ or norms were these based). (4 marks)

6. Our personal values and norms are sometimes different from that of other people. How do you suggest that we socialize and work with people who have differing values and norms from ourselves, to ensure that everyone is treated fairly?(4 marks)

7. Do your personal values contradict with or are they aligned to your community/the cultural group you identify with/ Canadian societal values? Provide examples (4 marks)

Identity and Values Assignment

Option 2: The Flower of Life's Values Award

Part 1: Imagine that you are over 70 years old. You have been nominated to receive a Life Time Achievement Award. In order to get the award you must write a 3-5 page paper about yourself, your identity, your norms, and your values to be presented to a panel.

The paper should include the following information:

Part A: Discuss at least 10 aspects of your identity. You can choose from the following or include other classifications:

- Socio-economic status
- Religion
- Gender
- Race
- Sexual-orientation
- Family structure
- Nationality
- Neighbourhood/ community
- Ability
- Age-group
- Education
- Language
- Ethnic group

Part B: Describe how your interaction with different groups of people helped to shape your identity.

- How did these interactions affect your behavior and your treatment of others? Provide some examples.
- What were some of the stereotypes and biases you held about particular groups?
- Evaluate the root of your thinking. Have these changed? What did you do to change them and why?
- Discuss some of your shared values and values that may have been contradictory or different from groups of people in Canadian society. Provide examples.
- Write about your norms – the rules of behaviour that you have applied to your life.
- Describe some Canadian societal norms that were different from ones you were used to. If you spent your entire life in Canada, can you recall norms that were different from ones used by other groups of people living in Canada? Provide examples.
- Discuss your understanding about the different groups discussed above with regards to the power and prestige they may or may not hold in society, and your recommendations for change on how they should be treated, by yourself and others. For example, the treatment of Canadian Aboriginals and First Nations peoples.
- How did you ensure the fair treatment of others in today's society?
- What were some of the steps you took to ensure that you and others were being treated fairly? Provide some examples.

Option 2: The Flower of Life's Values Award Continued

Part C: Referring to the above information, write a compelling argument as to why you should receive the award for the contributions you have made over the course of your lifetime

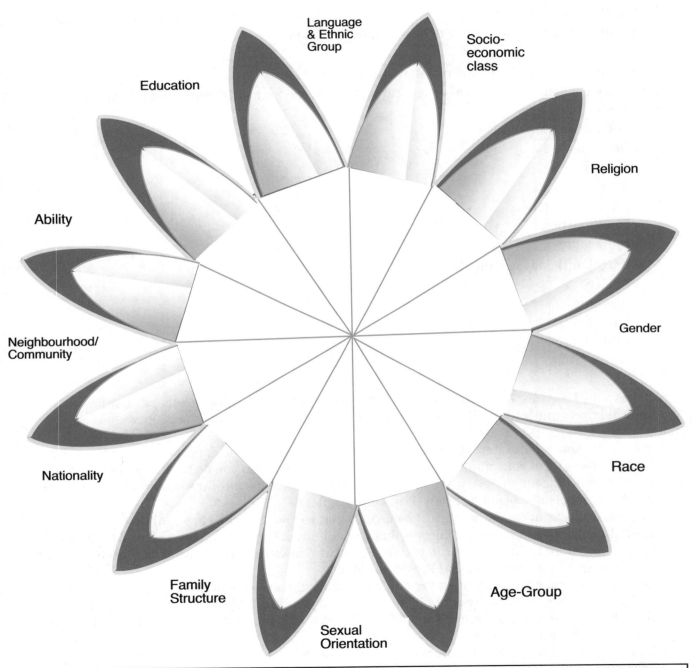

ADAPTED FROM EDUCATING FOR CHANGE, Between the Lines, Toronto (1991)

Option 2: The Flower of Life's Values Award Continued

Part 2: Complete the following tasks using the flower diagram.

- Shade in the areas/ aspects of your identity that in your view give you most power and prestige
- Write 2-3 lines providing an explanation for each of your selections
- Using a contrasting colour, shade in the areas/ aspects of your identity that in your view, **do not** give you power and prestige
- Write 2-3 lines providing an explanation for each of your selections
- Write a short reflection on the process of doing this assignment. What have you learned about yourself and others? How did doing this exercise make you feel? What are you most proud of? What would you like to change?

Option 3: Life Video/Documentary

Film a documentary about your life, exploring your identity. This video should be a reflection/ representation of a day in your life.

Describe yourself. Who are you? Include at least <u>10</u> of the following 12 elements about yourself:

1. Neighbourhood/ community
2. Living environment
3. Religion/ spirituality
4. Race
5. Family structure
6. Ability/ Educational Status
7. Languages spoken/ Ethnicity
8. Social Status (as it relates to transportation, neighbourhood, friends, community and/ or other relevant aspects of your life)
9. Nationality
10. Gender
11. Sexual Orientation
12. Age-group

- What are some of the struggles you have had to endure with regards to stereotypes and biases – your own and those that other people have or may have about you?

- What biases and stereotypes have you had to endure?

- Have you always treated others fairly? Why or why not? Provide examples, explanations, dramatic illustrations or stories reflecting this. These stereotypes and or/ biases may be related to the aspects of your identity listed above

Option 3: Life Video/Documentary Continued

- Based on the descriptors you have used for defining your identity, what is your position in society? Do you occupy a position of prestige? Why or why not? What aspects of you identity make you feel powerful? What aspects of your identity make you feel powerless? Explain.

- Additionally, please include comments and/ or other information that address questions such as, what's wrong with the world? What's wrong with society? What can you as a student do to impact changes about the stereotypes and biases that exist?

- What was the process of doing this videography/ documentary like for you? Reflect on the experience.

Upload your documentary into an animoto, video clip, webpage or website. Your completed production must be 7-12 minutes in length and reflect responses to the questions and issues raised above. Provide the on-line link to your creation.

PRIVACY & CONFIDENTIALITY

Please ensure that you maintain the privacy of the environment and persons in your film. Please also ensure that you have obtained the permission of family members, acquaintances, friends and others that you may want to include in your documentary. Use creative ways to obscure buildings, license plate numbers, home and street address information, and/or other identifying information.

Identity and Values Assignment Rubric

Outcome Assessed	Emerging Level I		Developing Level II			Competent Level III			Strong Level IV			Outstanding Level V		Mark
	1	2	3	4	5	6	7	8		9	10			
Content	Does not respond to the questions from the assignment No application of the concepts of identity, norms, prestige, stereotypes, biases, values and power to the assignment.		Inconsistently responds to the questions from the identity and values assignment – addresses only some questions from the assignment, without an explanation for their omission. Does not discuss power, biases, prestige, values, norms and stereotypes.		Responds to all questions from the assignment on identity, biases, prestige, values, norms, stereotypes and power; however, answers are vague/ ambiguous/ lacking in detail. Makes an effort to define the terms, but definitions are incomplete.		Demonstrates a clear understanding of identity, values, biases, norms, power, prestige and stereotypes – able to differentiate and define those terms and use appropriate examples/ based on lived experiences. Demonstrates how our internalized values are connected to power, which in-turn affect our identity and the identities we create for others. Provides explanations/responses not requested as part of the assignment.			Provides a thorough response to all questions from the assignment on identity, power, values, biases, norms and stereotypes, clearly distinguishing each term; discusses how values and identity are connected and can or may change, depending on personal growth experiences and life events, through the use of specific examples.		/40
Critical Analysis	Is unable to demonstrate how values and identity are linked. Nor is there any discussion of power, biases, prestige, norms, values and stereotypes.		Discusses own values and identity, but does not illustrate how they are linked to each other, nor their connection to power, biases, norms, prestige and stereotypes.		Demonstrates some understanding of how values and personal identity are connected. Makes an effort to connect or provide examples that show the linkages between identity, values, power, norms and prestige.		Is able to clearly describe how personal identity and values are connected and to use examples to explain how these form stereotypes and biases. Is able to connect this knowledge to explain the linkages to power, norms and prestige.			Applies an understanding of power, identity, values, norms and prestige by discussing the personal actions they would be willing to undertake, given their awareness of the connections between personal identity and values and one's tendency towards biases and stereotypes.		/30

Identity and Values Assignment Rubric Continued

Outcome Assessed	Emerging Level I		Developing Level II		Competent Level III		Strong Level IV		Outstanding Level V		Mark
	1	2	3	4	5	6	7	8	9	10	
Adherence to Assignment Expectations	Does not follow the assignment template. For example, there is no title/ cover page and structure to the assignment. Assignment responses are too short and/ or vague.		Follows the assignment template, but omitted many aspects of the assignment. For example, there is a cover page or assignment title. The assignment however, only includes text. There are no pictures, graphics, other images or stylistic fonts on the assignment. The assignment is also lacking in structure/ the presentation of the information is illogical.		Follows the assignment template but omitted some aspects of the assignment. For example, provides a cover/ title page and folder / other innovative presentation format, such as on-line and/ or audio. Includes stylistic fonts, pictures, photographs and or videos, but does not provide any explanation about their connection to the assignment.		Follows most of the instructions for completing the assignment. For example, provides a cover/ title page and folder / other innovative presentation format, such as on-line and audio. Embeds videos, pictures, photographs or other images or stylistic fonts, and provides some description about their connections to the assignment.		Follows all of the instructions for completing the assignment. For example, provides a cover/ title page and folder/ other innovative presentation format, such as on-line and audio. Embeds videos, pictures, photographs, innovative font types or other images and describes a clear connection to each element of the assignment.		/20
Language Conventions	There is little or no clarity. Meaning is distorted because the product/ project has many grammatical and formatting errors.		Topic is unclear and there are many grammatical and formatting errors, which affect meaning.		Product/ project lacks punctuation. Has frequent grammatical and formatting errors; however, these do not interfere with meaning.		Product/ project is clear with few spelling, grammatical and formatting errors. Information is clearly and meaningfully organized.		Project / product is clear, has no grammatical errors; is logically organized and well structured.		/10

Post Reflection

Post Reflection Journal:

Purpose:

- The goal of journal reflection assignments is to provide students with an opportunity to reflect on the materials covered in the unit and to aid in the development of a critical and individual perspective on the issues

Expectation:

- You will write a 500 word (double spaced, two page) journal at the end of the course. The journal reflection should be in your own words on your learning in this course. You do not require any additional resources or research.

Format:

- Retell – Describe your learning
- Relate - How does the learning in this course relate to you, as a person, or to your experiences?
- Reflect – Connect artifact(s) to key concepts of global citizenship

Instruction:

In your reflection, discuss and connect each of the following content areas covered in the course to the roles and responsibilities of a global citizen

- Social Analysis
- Media Literacy
- Identity and Values
- Equity and Equality
- Social Action

1. Discuss your personal growth and/or challenges you experienced in the course as they relate to your learning.

2. Provide examples of personal experiences as they relate to the concepts identified in the course.

3. What new knowledge have you learned or gained as a result of taking this course?

Post Reflection Rubric

Outcome Assessed	Emerging Level I		Developing Level II		Competent Level III		Strong Level IV		Outstanding Level V		Mark
	1	2	3	4	5	6	7	8	9	10	
Language Conventions	Contains too many grammatical, spelling and sentence structure errors. Readability is seriously affected and not clear.		Contains grammatical, spelling and sentence structure errors. Readability is somewhat affected.		Contains few grammatical, spelling, punctuation, errors, etc. The document is readable and expresses ideas well.		Contains almost no grammatical, spelling and sentence structure errors. The document is readable & expressive.		Contains no grammatical, spelling, and sentence structure errors. The document is well written and exceptional.		/10
Connection to Course Content and Critical Analysis	Does not identify or restate ideas or issues from course materials. Does not connect to the roles and responsibilities of a global citizen.		Identifies and restates some general ideas or issues from course materials. Does not connect to the roles and responsibilities of a global citizen.		Addresses the components of the course with some analysis. Connections are made between course material and the roles and responsibilities of a global citizen. Connections may be made with only some of the course materials.		Addresses the components of the course with good analysis. Connections are made between course materials and the roles and responsibilities of a global citizen.		Shows excellent insight and understanding of the materials covered in the course: - Social Analysis - Media Literacy - Identity and Values - Equity and Equality - Social Action Clear connections are made between all course materials and the roles and responsibilities of a global citizen. Course concepts/ideas are discussed and evaluated.		/40

Post Reflection Rubric Continued

Outcome Assessed	Emerging Level I		Developing Level II		Competent Level III		Strong Level IV		Outstanding Level V		Mark
	1	2	3	4	5	6	7	8	9	10	
Self-Reflection and Personal Position	There is no self-reflection and no risk is taken to connect concepts/ideas from class to personal experiences. Self-evaluation is has no meaning without self-reflection. Does not have any evidence of a personal response.		There is little self-reflection and little risk is taken to connect concepts/ideas from class to personal experiences. Self-evaluation has little meaning without self-reflection. Has little or no evidence of a personal response.		There is some self-reflection but lacks depth. Reflects on self from a single view and sometimes defensively. Some reflection but lacks depth. Asks some probing questions but does not seek to answer them. Examines own past experiences somewhat as they relate to the concepts/ideas of the course. Has a personal response that is somewhat neutral.		There is self-reflection from a single view very rarely defensively. Some in-depth reflection. Asks some probing question. Examines own past experiences as they relate to the concepts/ideas of the course. Has a personal response that is relevant and strong.		There is self-reflection from many views (self and others) in an open and non-defensive way. Discussed both growth and frustrations as they relate to the learning in the class Takes risks by asking probing questions about self and seeks to answer these. Examines own past experiences openly as they relate to the concepts/ideas of the course. Expresses a personal response that is thoughtful demonstrates impact on future directions.		/40
Assignment Expectations	No evidence of development; 1 page or less. Not word processed		Not very developed; 1 page or less. Not word processed		Less than 2 pages (500 words). Word processed according to guidelines – double spaced, 12 point font		Well developed – minimum 2 pages (500 words) Word processed meeting guidelines and with formatting that makes the document easy to read and professional – headings, paragraph structure etc.		Very well developed – minimum 2 pages (500 words) Word processed is more than the guidelines and with formatting that makes the document easy to read and professional – headings, paragraph structure, etc.		/10

Glossary of Terms

Activist: An individual who devotes their time, either paid or unpaid, to social change work.

Artifact: An item that is included in the portfolio that demonstrates a particular area of learning, discovery, skill or accomplishment. Artifacts can be course work or assignments but can also come from activities in your personal life or community.

Assimilate: To fully become a part of the dominant culture; taking on the culture, language, and customs of the dominant group, to a greater or lesser extent.

Bias: When one particular opinion or perspective takes one side over another. In media, bias refers to the selection of which events and stories are reported and how they are covered (Wikipedia).

Charity: Generosity and helpfulness especially towards the needy or suffering; aid given to those in need. Also, an institution engaged in relief of the poor (Merriam-Websters Dictionary).

Citizenship: A concept that implies membership or identity in a wider community along with a set of rights and responsibilities (Reynolds & Evans, 2004).

Construction: The way in which something is created or formed. *Social construction* of identity refers to the ways in which society contributes to and shapes the formation of your identity.

Critical Media Literacy: Media literacy is the ability to sift through and analyze the messages that inform, entertain and sell to us every day. It's the ability to bring critical thinking skills to bear on all media— from music videos and Web environments to product placement in films and virtual displays on NHL hockey boards. It's about asking pertinent questions about what's there, and noticing what's not there. And it's the instinct to question what lies behind media productions— the motives, the money, the values and the ownership— and to be aware of how these factors influence content (Jane Tallim in Media Awareness Network; www.media-awareness.ca)

Critical Thinking: A process of reflective thinking that questions and examines the assumptions and values that underlie what we do, believe, feel, read, see and hear with the goal of making a judgment, decision or solving a problem. Critical thinking is essential in bringing about social change and justice.

Diversity: A concept based upon the idea that each individual is unique. It encompasses respect for our individual differences. These can be along the dimensions of race, ethnicity, gender, sexual orientation, religious beliefs, socio-economic status, age, physical abilities, political beliefs, or other ideologies.

Dominant Group: Those who are disproportionately at the top of the hierarchy of class.

Equity: A concept based on fairness and the equality of outcomes. It recognizes that particular groups in society do not have the same opportunities and thus, aspects of the system should be changed to achieve equality.

Fair Trade: An alternative approach to conventional international trade. It is a trading partnership which aims at sustainable development for excluded and disadvantaged producers. It seeks to do this by providing better trading conditions, by awareness raising and by campaigning (Oxfam).

Globalization: Refers to an economic process of political, social, and cultural integrations across the entire planet.

Grassroots: A term used to describe social activism at a local or community level.

Hyphenate: To merge together the cultures of more than one cultural, ethic, and or linguistic group.

I

Identity: The distinguishing character or personality of an individual (Merriam-Webster Dictionary).

Ideology: A set of beliefs, or way of thinking that shapes how a person sees the world.

Inclusion: A concept based on the belief that all people in society are valued and able to fully participate in economic, social and cultural aspects of society.

Internalization: Refers to a process whereby people incorporate external ideas, thoughts, or beliefs into their own sense of self or their beliefs about the world. Internalization can create risks when those external influences are negative, and are repeatedly stated and circulated by those in power. In other words, if you constantly heard someone tell you as a child that you were bad, then chances are you would grow up believing this. A consequence might be that you would act it out your belief in your own "bad" self, and this might lead to aggressive behavior and even criminal activity.

Intersectionality: Occurs when different facets of our identities merge or connect.

Inequality: Refers to any difference in the treatment of people on the basis of class, gender, age, ability, race, ethnicity, sexuality, or citizenship.

L

Location: The term refers to how we identify ourselves in terms of socio-economic class, culture, gender, sexuality, religion, and so forth.

M

Matrix: A grid, or graph, with X and Y axes, upon which you can plot things visually.

Media: Refers to television, internet, radio, advertising, newspapers, books, magazines, and any form of mediated communication.

Medium: Is the means by which a message is sent. It is what enables a message to travel from a sender to a receiver.

Message: The encoded information that is sent over a communications channel (e.g. a letter, an e-mail, a television transmission) and is then interpreted by a receiver.

Micro: Basic or small scale (Free Dictionary Online by Farlex, thefreedictionary.com).

Mid: Medium or middle scale

Macro: Large scale (Free Dictionary Online by Farlex).

N

Norms: Socially acceptable or established rules of behavior of individuals, groups and society.

Non-dominant Groups: Those whose members are not in positions of power with limited access to power.

Personal Identity: Refers to how individuals see, understand, and shape their own identities.

Portfolio: A purposeful collection of student work that exhibits the student's efforts, progress, and achievements in one or more areas (Paulson, Paulson & Meyer, 1991).

Portfolio Learning: An ongoing process of personal and professional growth that demands continuous self-reflection and critical thinking through a system of collecting and reflecting upon items that represent student work, efforts, progress and achievements.

Power: Refers to the control people may have over individuals, groups of people, resources, territories, wealth, institutions, to name a few.

Power: The capacity to control resources, which allows structures of dominance and subordination to be created and maintained among social groups (McMullin, 2004 p. 29)

Privilege: Refers to a benefit that people can accumulate, be born into, or be given based on their place of origin, class status, community or professional affiliations. Often people are not aware of the privileges that they have access to.

Privilege: "Is gained through unearned power that gives dominant group members economic, social, and political advantage" (Lopes & Thomas, 2006, p.266).

R

Reflective Practice: The process of thinking about your experiences in a way that asks you to examine your own knowledge so that you might improve improve upon your practices and behaviors. Reflective practice demands that we question own knowledge, behaviors and practices. Reflective practice is the basis for individual growth and a necessary component of professional and personal development.

Regulation: The rules and guidelines that set limits and determine policies relevant to the organization of media and communications.

Representation: (In Media) Refers to how people, events, places, and stories, are portrayed on television, the internet, on the radio, or in newspapers.

Separate/Isolate: To be completely apart from or feel unassociated with a cultural, ethnic, and or linguistic group.

Social Action: Individual or group behavior that involves interaction with other individuals or groups, especially organized action towards social reform (Dictionary.com).

Social Identity: How we see ourselves as individuals who are members of *groups*, and how we are perceived by *others* both inside and outside the group.

Social Justice: A concept based upon the belief that each individual and group within a given society has a right to civil liberties, equal opportunity, fairness, and participation in the educational, economic, institutional, social and moral freedoms and responsibilities valued by the community (Degan & Disman, University of Toronto).

Social Movement: A group of people with a common ideology who try together to achieve common goals (Free Online Dictionary).

Social Problem: A social condition (such as poverty) or a pattern of behavior (such as violence against women) that people believe [requires] public concern and collective action to bring about change (Centennial College, 2009, p.7).

Social Stratification: Refers to "...the hierarchical arrangement of large social groups on the basis of their control over basic resources" (Kendall, 2010, p.214).

Social Structure: Refers to how society is organized, including relationships between various social institutions an d socio-economic classes.

Stereotype: Commonly held beliefs or notions that include generalizations and assumptions about individuals or groups of people based on their social identity, appearance, and behavior.

Values: Deeply held personal beliefs and ideas that we feel very strongly about, and they help us to define what we think is good, bad, right, wrong, desirable, undesirable, appropriate or not appropriate.

Vertical Integration: Refers to corporate control over the production of media content through the acquisition of smaller media companies into the large corporations.

Xenophobia: A very strong fear or dislike of individuals who are different from the self or foreign.